The New Industrial Order
Concentration, Regulation,
and Public Policy

Also by the Same Author

Mergers, Managers, and the Economy
McGraw-Hill Book Company
McKinsey Foundation Book Award, 1968

The New Industrial Order
Concentration, Regulation, and Public Policy

Samuel Richardson Reid

Professor of Economics and Business
Whittemore School
University of New Hampshire

McGraw-Hill Book Company

New York   St. Louis   San Francisco   Auckland   Düsseldorf   Johannesburg
Kuala Lumpur   London   Mexico   Montreal   New Delhi   Panama
Paris   São Paulo   Singapore   Sydney   Tokyo   Toronto

The New Industrial Order:
Concentration, Regulation, and Public Policy

234567890 DODO 79876

This book was set in Times Roman by University Graphics, Inc.
The editors were J. S. Dietrich and Annette Hall;
the cover was designed by Rafael Hernandez;
the production supervisor was Charles Hess.
The drawings were done by J & R Services, Inc.
R. R. Donnelley & Sons Company was printer and binder.

Library of Congress Cataloging in Publication Data

Reid, Samuel Richardson.
    The new industrial order.

    1. Big business—United States.   2. Industrial
concentration.   3. Consolidation and merger of
corporations—United States.   4. Trusts, Industrial
—United States.   I. Title.
HD2795.R33   338.8'0973   75-29284
ISBN 0-07-051779-7
ISBN 0-07-051780-0 pbk.

To my mother, Margaret Anheuser Reid,
and in memory of my father,
Samuel Richardson Reid

Contents

Tables

Charts

Preface

A former business executive and the author of a best-selling book, Robert C. Townsend, has sounded the following alarm to his fellow Americans: "It's getting late. The time to start is now. In the Consciousness Zero land of the corporate giants, competition where it counts is a myth, and what's left of a free America is being eaten alive by a few hundred monster corporations while government agencies serve as chefs, waiters, and busboys."

America has indeed developed a distinctly lopsided economy over the years and particularly in the past couple of decades. The largest industrial firms have continued increasing their relative share of the nation's productive capacity. In the regulated sectors of the economy, holding companies have caused radical changes in recent years. For example, since 1947 nearly all sizable independent telephone companies—more than 4,200 of them—have consolidated and been acquired by holding companies. In the commercial banking field, the percentage of deposits controlled by bank holding companies has increased from 6 percent to over 70 percent in the past two decades. Similar patterns have been repeated in section after section of the American economy to the point where the United States has a comprehensive concentration of economic power that is a threat to both private and public interests.

This book represents an attempt to examine some of the dimensions and causes of the economic power pattern that has developed over the years. The first part of the book is concerned with these developments. Some traditional concepts and observations are challenged in this part, including the American preoccupation with bigness and the assumed accompanying economies of scale and propensity for invention and innovation. The recent so-called conglomerate merger wave is also examined and reappraised in a new and different light.

The second and third parts of the book concentrate on the banking and transportation mess and the role of the public interest in these regulated sectors of the economy. Significant developments of a microeconomic nature have transpired in these areas in recent years and have generally been overlooked in the process.

The final part of the book is concerned with the effects of the imbalanced nature of the economy and related developments upon people, places, and the quality of life in America. The last chapter presents a series of alternative public policy proposals designed to stimulate thought and action toward the development of a new economic America which is more balanced in power and responsive to public and private interests.

A growing number of economists are beginning to focus attention on industrial, financial, and governmental *structure* and *behavior*. This development has received its impetus largely from the failure of monetary policy, fiscal policy, and governmental controls designed to curtail inflation in the economy. In his presidential address to the American Economic Association, John K. Galbraith warned that by neglecting the market and political power of large corporations, unions, and government, "economics leads to the wrong solution of the microeconomic problem and to no solution of the macroeconomic problem." Galbraith further stated that if economists can only learn to figure economic and political power into their calculations, they will find that their work "is not yet done; on the contrary it is just the beginning." This should serve as a challenge to the growing numbers of young people and others who have become interested in economics.

This book represents the work of a number of years and was written from a vantage point on a farm and campus in New Hampshire, a few short miles north of the expanding eastern Boston-Washington megapolis. My observance of the northern New England life-style in the past few years has no doubt strengthened some of my observations and convictions as they relate to many of the basic issues and problems treated in this book.

Among those who have helped to make this present work possible and who deserve special mention are Dean Jan E. Clee and Assistant Dean Lawrence P. Cole of the Whittemore School of Business and Economics of the University of New Hampshire. Both of these men have displayed an element of understanding over the last few years as this work progressed. My long-time friend and colleague, Professor James O. Horrigan, has provided encouragement and insights, both of which have been valuable and sustaining.

I would also like to express my appreciation to numerous students and friends who challenged me continually to complete this work. Also, special mention is due to the staffs of the library and computer center at the University of New Hampshire, where much of the research and writing was conducted, and to Ms. Leslie Perna of Steamboat Springs, Colorado, and Mrs. Elaine Vachon, Mrs. Linda Fitzgerald, and Mrs. Jennifer McKinnon of Durham, New Hampshire, for typing the manuscript. The final word of gratitude is reserved for my wife and children, Rich, Peter, Meg, Lucy, and Joe, who have given up numerous potential trips to the mountains and the seashore in this beautiful region so that this work could be completed.

Finally, this book is being published in the midst of our year at the Yale Law School where I am in the Master of Studies in Law program. The Yale Law School has been a leader in making use of the findings, concepts, and suggestions of the social sciences in the study of law. My personal interest in the study of the legal aspects of economics and the economic dimensions in law is one of long standing and is evident in various places in this book.

Samuel Richardson Reid

The New Industrial Order
Concentration, Regulation,
and Public Policy

Chapter 1

Introduction: A Perspective

Industrial organization is the name given to a specific field of microeconomics that is devoted to the study of the structure, behavior, and performance of various components in the economy. This is a relatively new area of economics which should receive increasing attention in the years ahead as students, participants, and policymakers attempt to search out alternative solutions to the economic problem. The repeated failures of monetary and fiscal policies in recent years have prompted a need to examine more closely the various microeconomic facets in the economic mosaic in order to develop a more comprehensive view of performance and policy. The purpose of this book is to examine a collage of microeconomic developments and to focus on particular aspects that tend to be overlooked in the search for various solutions to the economic problem.

The celebration of a national bicentennial provides an opportunity to reexamine the basic tenents upon which the new nation was founded by those assembled in Philadelphia a couple of centuries ago. In that spirit, it is worth studying and reflecting upon basic changes in the economic and

1

political system which have evolved over the years. The founding fathers carefully constructed the Declaration of Independence and later the Constitution in an attempt to create and preserve individual rights and to gingerly balance rights and responsibilities between the branches of government in order to avoid the pitfalls of concentrated power. While the government has survived numerous crucial crises, the growth and development of concentrated economic power have been the hallmark of the nation since the turn of the century. The continued examination of this dimension of the political economy is a modern obligation rather than an exercise of academic or personal prerogative. In that spirit, a special focus will be directed to the state of the union as it pertains to the dimensions of economic power and concentration.

It is important to recognize that various centrifugal and centripetal forces are continually at work in any economic system pulling toward and away from concentrations of power.[1] Since economic concentration has been, on balance, increasing in the United States for the past couple of decades, it appears that the centripetal forces (those leading to concentration) have been especially potent. These forces consist of a variety of factors, among the more important are barriers to entry,[2] nonprice competition (product or service differentiation), government policies and activities (i.e., procurement, leases, patents, tariffs and quotas, and regulatory actions), and merger activity.[3] The relative potency of each of these forces will vary over time, with mergers and acquisitions playing a dominant role during periods of intense activity as evident in the United States at various points in the continuum. Thus, the recent merger wave is given special focus in this book along with some specific examples of regulatory behavior which have contributed to the new industrial order.

THE MERGER PATTERN

One of the more important facets of the microeconomic collage both in the United States and internationally has been the recent major merger wave which swarmed over all the industrialized nations of the noncommunist world. In the United States, this was the third great major wave since the late nineteenth century and, by all measures, the most prolonged and severe in economic history. A glance at Chart 1.1 should provide a clear visual illustration of this important economic phenomenon.

Two other related facets of the merger pattern are also clearly evident in the chart. The first relates to the legal environment at the time of each major merger wave. Important antitrust legislation has been passed *prior* to the development of each wave of activity. The Sherman Act was passed in 1890, prior to the turn-of-the-century consolidation movement. The Clay-

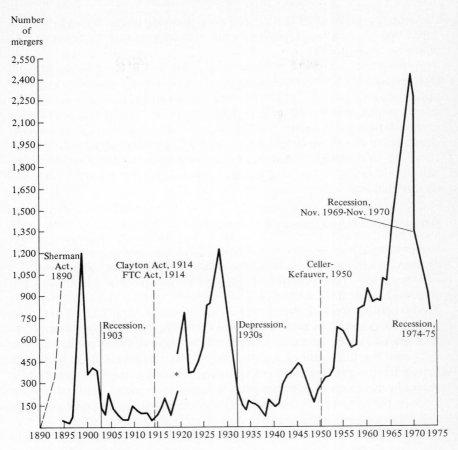

Number of mergers

*The two series are not directly comparable.

Chart 1.1 Major merger waves, antitrust laws, and business conditions. [*Sources:* National Bureau of Economic Research (Nelson), 1895–1920; Federal Trade Commission (and T.N.E.C.), 1919–1974.]

ton Act (1914) and the Federal Trade Commission Act (1914) were passed *prior* to the late-1920s merger wave. The Celler-Kefauver antimerger amendment became law in 1950, *prior* to the massive recent combination movement.

Perhaps the most significant facet evident in the chart is that each major merger wave has been *followed* by a recession/depression. The panic of 1903 *followed* within a few years the peak of the turn-of-the-century merger wave. The deep and prolonged depression of the 1930s *followed* the late-1920s merger wave. More recently, the recession of late 1969–1970 and the deep recession of 1974–1975 *followed* the peak of the massive wave in 1968. This is a significant microeconomic development which needs special attention and recognition.

History has provided the pattern and the lesson to be garnered from this periodic economic phenomenon. Since only fools ignore history, the opportunity to provide for the future beckons to those interested in economic power and public policy. Unfortunately, the record indicates a general tendency to ignore the merger wave problem in its wake, and to concentrate on other economic problems and policies. Due to the significance of this special situation, this book examines the comprehensive nature of this important facet of the economic problem which is currently an international development.

THE INTERNATIONAL MERGER PATTERN

The pattern of merger activity in Great Britain has been quite similar to that of the United States over the years, although on a smaller absolute scale. For example, Great Britain had a major merger wave at the turn of the century, one during the late 1920s, and a major recent wave.[4] The Board of Trade reported over 10,600 mergers with a value of about £8 billion for the 1954–1970 period. The main thrust of the activity was during the late 1960s, with a peak in 1968. Mergers reduced the numbers of listed firms in Britain by almost one-third, from 1,312 firms in 1961 to 908 firms in 1968. Studies in Britain have confirmed the fact that mergers have played an important role in increasing levels of concentration in many industries.[5] Sixty percent or more of the concentration change in the food, drink, metal manufacturing, and paper and printing industries was brought about by mergers.

The Canadian experience with merger activity is also closely related to the pattern observed in the United States and Great Britain. There was a major wave at the beginning of the century, especially in the food, steel, cement, and asbestos industries.[6] A major upsurge took place during the 1960s, with a reported 1,025 domestic and 580 foreign mergers, with a peak reached in 1968. A study of the performance of 369 merging firms in Canada for the 1960–1970 period indicates these firms tended to increase in size and did not show a corresponding growth in profit margins.[7]

Each of the Scandinavian countries experienced a sharp and significant increase in mergers during the 1960s. Most of the activity took place in Sweden, where a total of 2,459 mergers were reported between 1946 and 1970, with nearly half consummated in the 1966–1970 period. The major industries affected were food, fabricated metals, machinery, and chemicals. A study of the performance of Swedish mergers indicated that they expanded their sales more rapidly and there was no such association between profitability to stockholders and merger activity.[8]

In the European Economic Community, there were over 3,000 mergers and 5,000 poolings from 1961 to mid-1969. Each of the countries appears to have participated in the movement. In Germany, a major wave of mergers developed in the mid-1960s and reached an all-time high in 1972. There were 269 mergers of such sufficient size that they had to be reported to the Federal Cartel Office, since they led to a market share of 20 percent or greater, or had combined sales exceeding DM500 million. The Netherlands also experienced a sharp rise in activity during the 1960s; for the 1958–1968 period, there were 689 mergers in five important industries: chemicals, fabricated metals, machinery, paper, and textiles. In France, the government has actively promoted mergers, and the tempo increased in the late 1960s. The industries which were most active were fabricated metals, food, chemicals, machinery, and motor vehicles. The French have no controls over mergers and offer a contrasting example to the legal approach in the United States.

Australia has also experienced a sharp rise in merger activity since World War II which reached major proportions during the peaks of 1959–1961 and 1968–1972.[9] There were over 700 mergers in the 1958–1972 period, with a peak in 1972. The trend toward increasing concentration is apparent in Australia, where more than half the 103 largest (in 1956) firms either had been taken over or had significantly changed due to mergers by 1972.[10] The first comprehensive study of the performance patterns of merging and nonmerging firms in Australia concludes that mergers have a significant effect in reducing shareholder utility and that internal growth was far superior to any of the three merger strategies (horizontal, vertical, and diversified).[11]

This international profile of merger activity in recent years indicates a movement of substantial proportions among the industrialized nations in the noncommunist world. Further, virtually all these nations have followed a different path as related to the regulation of this economic activity, ranging from legal constraints (United States), to criminal sanctions requiring proof beyond a reasonable doubt (Canada), to government promotion (France).

Structural developments and the growing realization that mergers frequently have not yielded the benefits originally proposed have caused a changing public policy response. In Great Britain, a new Fair Trading law providing stronger merger controls was passed in 1973, and in the same year the German Parliament approved a new competition policy introducing, among other things, a merger control mechanism.[12]

A MICROECONOMIC BENCHMARK

The arsenal of antitrust laws which has developed in the United States over the years is based upon a belief that competitive markets provide the most economically desirable results. The competition referred to is something quite different from rivalry or other forms of nonprice competition. A brief look at the conditions which exist and the results obtained in competitive markets should serve as a benchmark in examining microeconomic areas of the economy.

Structure: Many buyers and sellers, none of which is powerful enough to influence prices; undifferentiated product; ease of entry and exit; and market knowledge.

Behavior: Price is determined by market supply and demand conditions, while output and product development decisions are determined by the individual firm.

Performance: Long-run price-cost differentials approach zero, long-run excess capacity is nonexistent, and the scale of plant and the firm approaches the optimum size.

This particular benchmark would clearly seem to provide the most economically efficient organization of industry and significant departure should be examined in light of public policy. It appears that an inordinate amount of resources is spent on continuing attempts to disrupt these basic conditions outlined above which influence behavior and performance. For example, in concentrated markets some firms become price *makers* rather than price *takers*. Prices tend to become administered, rather than determined by the unconstrained forces of supply and demand. Observation alone tells us that there can be a variety of barriers to entry and exit in various markets, ranging from basic discrimination to financial and/or legal and other barriers. Advertising, location, design, and other factors contribute to an extensive array of expenditures designed to differentiate goods and services. The benchmark can serve as a measuring device and a policy guide in industrial organization microeconomics and should be kept in mind when examining economic power and public policy.

THE BENCHMARK AND THE NEW INDUSTRIAL ORDER

The microeconomic philosophy which has been handed down since the days of Adam Smith is particularly germane when examining the new industrial order. The emergence of high and growing levels of concentration in a variety of industries beyond the basic manufacturing sector is one facet of the new industrial order. The hypertonic growth of individual business firms to size dimensions that appear to relate more to economic power than to economic efficiency is another paragon of the new industrial order. The growing role of government in disrupting markets and preserving inefficient units, both private and governmental, is likewise a hallmark of the new order.

Each of these developments emphasizes the need to examine the fundamentals underlying the political economy. Benchmarks, long accepted and often neglected, need renewed attention when examining the impact of the new industrial order. Traditional economic concepts, such as price competition, scale economies and diseconomies, efficiency, productivity, and consumer sovereignty, deserve renewed attention when private and public policy alternatives are considered in the quest to treat the economic problem.

This book is divided into four parts and examines various aspects of structure, behavior, and performance. In addition, a variety of public policy alternatives is presented with the intention of stimulating a thoughtful response to the economic problem from a *micro*economic perspective. At a time when there is a rising swell of voices calling for increased national economic planning, a renewed examination of fundamentals and a critical evaluation of failures of public policy are appropriate. The failure of government in the areas of traditional macroeconomic solutions and microeconomic regulation of the economic problem need not necessarily justify more of the same, but rather a fresh new approach based upon the fundamentals so evident in Philadelphia a couple of centuries ago.

NOTES

1 For a detailed examination of each of these forces, see John M. Blair, *Economic Concentration: Structure, Behavior and Public Policy,* New York: Harcourt Brace Jovanovich, 1972.

2 See Joe S. Bain, *Barriers to New Competition,* Cambridge: Harvard University Press, 1956.

3 A detailed treatment of the various merger waves is available in Ralph L. Nelson, *Merger Movements in American Industry, 1895–1956,* Princeton, N.J.: Princeton University Press, 1959 and Samuel R. Reid, *Mergers, Managers, and the Economy,* New York: McGraw-Hill, 1968. The best study available of the late-1920s merger wave is contained in a journal article, see Carl Eis, "The 1919–1930 Merger Movement in American Industry," *The Journal of Law and Economics,* vol. 12, no. 2, pp. 267–296, October 1969.

4 Martin Harve, "Rethinking British Merger Policy," *The Antitrust Bulletin,* vol. 17, no. 1, pp. 283–310, Spring 1972.

5   See M. A. Utton, "The Effects of Mergers on Concentration: U. K. Manufacturing Industry, 1954–65," *The Journal of Industrial Economics,* vol. 20, no. 1, pp. 42–58, November 1971 and G. Whittington, "Changes in the Top 100 Quoted Manufacturing Companies in the United Kingdom 1948 to 1968," *The Journal of Industrial Economics,* vol. 21, no. 1, pp. 17–34, November 1972.

6   See L. A. Skeoch, "Merger Issues in Canada," *The Antitrust Bulletin,* vol. 16, no. 1, pp. 131–145, Spring 1971.

7   S. N. Laiken, "Financial Performance of Merging Firms in a Virtually Unconstrained Legal Environment," *The Antitrust Bulletin,* vol. 18, no. 4, pp. 827–851, Winter 1973.

8   Bengt Rydén, *Mergers in Swedish Industry,* Stockholm: Almquist & Wiksell, 1972.

9   See J. A. Bushnell, *Australian Company Mergers 1946–1959,* Melbourne: Melbourne University Press, 1961 and Douglas L. Henderson, "Analysis of Company Mergers in Australia," unpublished dissertation, University of New South Wales, 1974.

10 Henderson, ibid.

11 Ibid.

12 See F. M. Scherer, "Secrecy, the Rule of Reason, and European Merger Control Policy," *The Antitrust Bulletin,* vol. 19, no. 1, pp. 181–197, Spring 1974.

Part One

The Economic Power Pattern

An important component in industrial organization economics is the structure of an economy and all the various dimensions associated with the structure. This introductory part is concerned with structure and related components of the economic power question.

Chapter 2 presents a variety of material drawn from the balance of the book and is titled "A Microeconomic Collage." The reader is presented a glimpse of a number of related and quasi-related business, economic, and governmental developments, and movements of a contemporary or recent vintage that have a direct bearing upon the American economic problem.

Chapter 3 explores the various dimensions of economic concentration as they relate to the national, industrial, financial, regional, and local sectors. A related question is that of the relative size of firms and their distribution. In addition to the traditional presentation of data related to industrial concentration, a variety of other sectors and markets is briefly examined, i.e., banking, agriculture, the stock market, and communications media.

The title of Chapter 4 asks the pertinent question, "Bigness and Concentration for Whom?" The various dimensions of this question are explored, i.e., profitability, economies of scale, innovation, invention, success, and failure. This first part introduces the reader to the theme of the book and provides a perspective for involvement.

A Microeconomic Collage

There have been numerous significant developments in the American economy in recent years. The purpose of this chapter is to present some of these events and movements in the form of a microeconomic collage. The aim is to provide an overview for understanding the nature of the economic problem and to illustrate the diversity of these developments and the need for a comprehensive comprehension of the microeconomic aspects in formulating economic policy and understanding. Each aspect will be examined more thoroughly in the chapters that follow, culminating in an array of public policy prescriptions.

THE INDUSTRIAL STRUCTURE

Less than 1 percent of American manufacturers control 88 percent of the industrial assets and receive over 90 percent of the net profits of industrial firms in the American economy. About 100 firms receive a greater share of net profits than the remaining 370,000 corporations, proprietorships, and partnerships engaged in manufacturing. The sales of *Fortune*'s 500 Largest Industrials are almost ten times greater than the "second" 500 largest firms (those ranked 501–1,000). The assets of this second group are also less than one-tenth of the 500 largest industrials. Combined, the 1,000 largest industrials, a fraction of a percent of American business firms, employ about 80 percent of the workers in manufacturing and mining.

The familiar measures of aggregate concentration in the economy, the assets and value added of the 200 largest firms, have increased significantly since the end of World War II. In the period from 1947 to 1968, the assets controlled by the 200 largest industrials increased from 45 percent to 60 percent, and are pushing toward the two-thirds mark in the 1970s. Value added by the 200 largest firms increased from 30 percent in 1947 to 42 percent in 1967, a change of 40 percent in the postwar years. Everywhere one looks, the lopsided economy becomes more apparent. For example, *Forbes* lists 395 American corporations with assets of more than $1 billion in 1973. In summary, big business, composed of a relatively few supergiant firms, consistently dominates and controls vast segments of the economy and has amassed substantial economic and political power in the process.

BANKING STRUCTURE AND REGULATION

Commercial banking occupies a special place in the American economy, since these institutions are endowed with unique qualities and benefits not to be found in any other business—namely, the sole right to accept and create *demand* deposits—the major component of the nation's money supply. In return for this significant privilege, a regulatory superstructure has been imposed on the operations of these firms with the purpose of protecting them and the public.

There are three distinct agencies concerned with banking at the national level, and, in addition, each state has its own regulatory operation. While all these agencies are concerned with the traditional element of deposit safety, other important decision-making powers have been entrusted to them related to structural characteristics of the various banking markets, especially control over bank mergers and branching activities.

Despite repeated congressional interest, which has manifested itself in numerous hearings and legislation over the years, commercial banking exhibits the same imbalanced structure apparent in other segments of the economy. While some of this can be traced to population shifts and the growth of urban centers, important changes in the structure can be directly attributed to *regulatory permissiveness* and the commercial bankers' quest for spatial and business *diversification*.

The banking structure, in brief, is dominated by a powerful few. A fraction of 1 percent of the banking institutions (100 of about 14,000 banks) has 70 percent of all deposits. In the important area of bank trust business, which accounts for the largest single pool of financial resources in the world, $300 billion of assets, a mere 19 banks (mainly in New York) control most of this pool.

In addition, a handful of registered and regulated multiple-bank holding companies have increased their deposits tenfold in the past decade, and they dominate the activity in most states despite a statutory mandate designed to truncate such activity. For example, the average change in the percentage of deposits controlled by bank holding companies in the 10 states with the most activity was 577 percent from 1957 to 1970. Contrast this fantastic growth with the average decline of minus 17 percent in the states where there was *no* approved activity. These results are statistically significant and indicate that important changes in the banking structure can be directly linked to regulatory behavior.

Bank regulators have also permissively rubber-stamped the overwhelming majority of bank mergers reviewed by them; 97 percent of the applications were approved despite the fact that the Department of Justice noted "adverse competitive" consequences in more than half the cases. The states with the most *approved* mergers experienced a decline in the number of independent banking firms and an increase in concentration. The reverse pattern was evident in the remaining states and the differences are highly significant statistically. In summary, commercial banking is dominated in the national market by a handful of powerful individuals and institutions, while regional and local markets are being swamped by "regulated" bank holding companies.

BIG GOVERNMENT

The role of big government may appear ambivalent, since government has traditionally been charged with the responsibility of preserving and promoting a competitive, free enterprise system. However, big government has been a substantial contributor in the shaping of the imbalanced economy. John M. Blair, a leading scholar of economic concentration, has observed this phenomenon. Blair says:

> . . . government is a powerful contributor to higher concentration and the suppression of competition. It contributes directly to concentration by the manner in which it procures what it needs, disposes of what it no longer needs, and leases to others what it owns. It directly suppresses competition through quotas, patents, tariffs, and a wide variety of other restraints imposed by different agencies.[1]

Government activity has contributed to the development of an imbalanced economy through its legislative, executive, and regulatory actions. As noted by Walter Adams, "Some [corporations] are big because Government itself has frequently promoted the very concentration which the antitrust laws are designed to prevent."[2] Thus, big government, through its procurement policies, tax laws and loopholes, minimal antitrust enforcement, tariff and quota systems, and regulatory policies has done much to deposit economic power in the hands of a few.

Two-thirds of the 50 largest American business firms come under the direct influence of public regulators. These giant firms, largely protected from competition, control over $600 billion of resources and represent significant economic power. These firms appear to be beyond the reach of the public regulators who, for the most part, appear to have difficulty in distinguishing between the public interest and special interests.

THE LABOR MOVEMENT

There have been periods in the United States when the labor movement has dominated the economic scene. Historic clashes have developed over organizing and bargaining methods, and major strikes have affected firms, industries, and communities in varying degrees. Powerful individuals emerged on the national scene in the aftermath of these developments. The trend toward concentration of power in national and international unions appears to have followed the development of concentrated industries and dominant large firms, in the name of countervailing power.

While the labor component is important in the national economic scene, it has been generally overshadowed by other developments in the microeconomic area in recent years. Less than 25 percent of the labor force belongs to unions, and membership grew only 12 percent in the 1960–1970 period, while employment in nonagricultural establishments grew 23 percent during the same period. In addition, the number of unions affiliated with the AFL-CIO declined from 134 to 120 during the 1960–1970 period, for a minus 12 percent change. This does not imply that union power is not a significant factor, but only that it has been less spectacular than other aspects of the economic and political power complex.

Worker dissatisfaction appears to be increasing, since unauthorized work stoppages have increased considerably and have contributed to productivity declines. The number of workers involved more than doubled between 1960 and 1970, and the worker days idle during the year increased from 19.1 million to 66.4 million during this period. This is almost a month lost per year per worker involved. Thus, some developments on the labor front are an important element in the economic collage.

THE MERGER GAME

In nearly every year since 1948, the 200 largest industrial firms were responsible for over two-thirds of the assets of large firms acquired in the merger game. Most of the increase in concentration during the 1947–1968 period was due to merger activity by these *large* firms. Mergers have been almost exclusively responsible for the increase in the relative power of the large firms since 1960.

The magnitude and persistence of the merger game during the latter half of the 1950s and the relatively prosperous 1960s were significant. The Federal Trade Commission reported over 17,000 mergers involving manufacturing and mining firms from 1955 through 1970, and more than half were consummated in the 1965–1970 period, with a peak of 2,407 reported mergers reached in 1968. Close to 1,500 firms with assets of $10 million and over disappeared as independent entities in the third giant merger wave in American economic history.

A closer look at the data reveals that the 25 most active merging firms (among the 200 largest) were involved in about 700 mergers, involving more than $20 billion in assets, or about 59 percent (a majority) of the activity. Among the 25 most *active* firms, the "new" conglomerates dominated the action by acquiring close to $11 billion of assets. Thus, a relatively small fraction of the giant firms dominated the merger game, and the activity of these firms looms large in the economic collage.

The Economic Consequences of the Merger Game

A substantial, consistent, and growing body of major empirical research studies concerning the relative performance of merging firms reveals a significant body of evidence which strongly suggests that the merger game is a suboptimal method of allocating economic resources.

The only groups which appear to win with any regularity in the merger game are the brokers and the top managers of the firms involved, who promote much of the activity. The average and median remuneration of top management (excluding deferred compensation and stock options) of both the most active merging firms and the "new" conglomerates was considerably above the median salary of more than 700 chief executives of the largest United States corporations in 1970. As a matter of fact, the excess compensation exceeded $100,000 for the year per chief executive. This development occurred despite the recession and the substantial decline in the market value of the stock of these firms.

By contrast, the merger game contributes little or nothing to the accomplishment of national economic goals and the quality of life. These economic events also have a *negative* effect on the economic fiber of the nation and aid in the imbalanced development of the economy, since the most significant factor contributing to growing concentration has been the record merger activity in the recent wave of combinations.

Merger Charades

Due to a classification error made by the Bureau of Economics of the Federal Trade Commission some years ago, the true nature of the recent major merger wave in the United States has been grossly distorted. The mistake was not intentional; however, the consequences have been noteworthy.

The faux pas was the result of a definition error based upon a "residual" approach concerning the classification of mergers by the Federal Trade Commission. Using their fallacious approach, any merger which is not clearly a pure horizontal or pure vertical type becomes a *conglomerate* merger.

Utilizing the Federal Trade Commission definitions, the relative distribution of merger types (based upon firms acquired with $10 million or more of assets) during the 1948 to 1971 period is as follows: horizontal mergers, 15.2 percent; vertical mergers, 11.9 percent; and conglomerate mergers, 72.8 percent of the activity. Clearly, the *conglomerate* category dominates the action in this the largest merger wave in American economic history.

When alternative definitions are utilized, the relative distribution during the same time period is as follows: horizontal mergers, 19.4 percent; vertical mergers, 11.9 percent; *circular* mergers, 47.2 percent; and conglomerate mergers, 21.4 percent of the action.

Obviously, this latter pattern is quite different from that sketched by the Federal Trade Commission. Focusing on the peak year of merger activity, 1968, for example, the Federal Trade Commission reported that 89 percent of the mergers were conglomerate, while an analysis of a different sample revealed that 28 percent were of this type; which is close to the findings of W. T. Grimm & Company, a Chicago-based consulting firm, that only 16 percent of the merger announcements were conglomerate merger types.

This finding is not intended to be iconoclastic, but rather to indicate that a regulatory mistake can have important ramifications. During the recent major merger wave in the United States, the agencies responsible for enforcement of the *existing* antitrust statutes could have successfully enforced the laws and brought order to the economic scene. Instead, they neglected the dominant merger type and mistakenly believed and announced that most mergers were *conglomerate* and waited either for *new* legislation or for a Supreme Court decision on the legality of these mergers. The wait has proved to be in vain, mainly due to some dubious consent decrees entered into by the Department of Justice.

THE CONGLOMERATE SPECTACULAR

While the main thrust of the recent major merger wave has been *circular,* that is, emphasis being placed on *product extension* rather than conglomeration, the emergence of a special breed of firms termed "conglomerates" was a distinguishing characteristic of the movement. Few developments in the business world can rival this phenomenon in terms of the interest and controversy aroused by this small (but active) group of firms in a relatively brief period of time.

The flamboyant behavior of these unique firms, in terms of financial manipulations, stock price movements, rapid size growth, and management philosophy, caught the fancy of important segments of the business and economic community. Proponents placed these firms in exalted positions, singling them out as the "firms of the future." One executive, in a heady manifestation of overt enthusiasm, stated that within a few years there would be only 200 firms—all conglomerates.[3] Some observers erroneously believed that a new, advanced type of entrepreneurship had been discovered and welcomed the development as an alternative to the existing large, bureaucratic business establishment. Concepts such as "free form" management and "synergy" were bantered around as if some new mysterious breakthrough had suddenly emerged on the business and economic scene.

Outspoken critics were less enthusiastic and agreed with the definition that conglomerates were "firms that serviced industry the way Bonnie and Clyde serviced banks."[4] Research results published prior to the peak of activity indicated that while these firms grew significantly faster than other firms, their profitability performance was serendipitous, indicating a considerably higher degree of risk than generally recognized.[5] The ultimate test of this finding was rapid in coming, since the recession in 1969–70 and the accompanying stock market collapse provided rapid feedback. Billions of dollars of value literally vanished as numerous investors, large and small, were taken to the cleaners. Whether or not the cleaners were owned by the conglomerates is a matter of speculation.

Numerous basic and fundamental economic and mathematical principles were overlooked by the proponents of conglomeration. The result was an exercise in economic nonsense of substantial magnitude. The microeconomic effects (at the level of the firm) should have been recognized by observers of the financial scene. The macroeconomic effects are just as serious, perhaps more so since the adverse impact is more widely distributed. The generally negative contribution of mergers (of all types) toward the accomplishment of national economic goals is one aspect of the economic collage which should receive more congressional and regulatory attention and will be examined in more detail in the chapters that follow.

The Well-Heeled Conglomerate Managers and the Battered Stockholders

The officers and directors of *one* American conglomerate business firm (IT&T) had more compensation paid them during 1970 than the combined salaries of the President of the United States of America; the Vice President of the United States of America; the 100 Senators in the United States Senate; the 50 State Governors in the United States; the 12 Cabinet members; the 9 Justices of the United States Supreme Court; and the 50 major regulators of American business.

Meanwhile, the stockholders (owners) of IT&T took a financial blood-bath with the value of a share of IT&T common stock declining over 75 percent during the 1970–1974 period. This is three times the decline of the Dow Jones industrials in the same period. In addition, the total market value of IT&T dropped from $3.69 billion at the end of 1968 to $1.38 billion at the end of 1974, a loss of more than $2.3 billion in the post-merger-active period.

THE IMBALANCED SUPERSTRUCTURE—BIGNESS FOR WHOM?

There are obviously some advantages to bigness in business; however, it appears they have been grossly overplayed. Certainly, bigness does not guarantee profitability. As a matter of fact, in many industries, the most efficient and profitable firms are those in the medium or even smaller size classes. Bigness is, of course, a relative concept. The data suggest that many of the giant firms in the economy have reached a point where diseconomies of scale are affecting their operations, yet they continue to seek increments of size. The business-oriented magazine, *Fortune,* has recognized the potential problems of bigness in the following statement:

> Big business also has a problem, somewhat less publicized, about its prof-
> its. . . . One possibility is that all the conglomerating, merging, and diversify-
> ing that companies engaged in during the past decade or so simply failed to pay
> off. It also seems possible that a good many of the largest companies have
> exceeded the size at which their operations would yield optimum profits—i.e.,
> that size increasingly involves *dis*economies of scale. It is possible that foreign
> operations—now significant for many of the companies on the 500—have
> become less remunerative. [6]

Bigness is also no guarantee that inventions and innovations will be forthcoming and implemented. Actually, it is the largest firms that have the most to lose in the process. For example, in steel, the industry's dominant firms have continually lagged behind their smaller rivals in introducing new products and processes. The history of invention and innovation is rich with examples of the key role played by the small organization or the outsider in stimulating economic and technological progress. It appears as if invention and innovation have the best opportunity in an unbureaucratic environment, since many inventions are of a low-budget type, developed by individuals.

MEANWHILE, DOWN ON THE FARM

The agriculture sector of the American economy has also been involved in the changing structural patterns evident in other areas of the economy. Between 1960 and 1972, the farm population declined from 15.6 million people to 9.6 million; a decline of almost 40 percent; the decline in the number of farms was 28 percent, as more than a million farms disappeared as independent decision-making units; in addition, the amount of land devoted to farming declined by 7 percent.

Meanwhile, the average farm increased in size from 297 acres to 381, for a gain of 32 percent during the 1960 to 1972 period. Rising levels of concentration also became apparent, as the larger farms, those with sales of $40,000 and more, comprised only about 13 percent of the farms and sold 57 percent of the total sales value. In 1969, the largest farms in acreage, those with 2,000 acres and more, were only 2 percent of the farms, yet held 43 percent of the farmland, and harvested only 14 percent of the total cropland.

The role of government in agricultural markets has been substantial in the area of price supports and soil banking, which have not been particularly effective in preserving the family farm. Direct government payments to farms have increased from $870 million in 1960 to about $4 billion in 1972, a gain of 464 percent in government spending. The bulk of this support has gone to special interests such as feed grain, wheat, cotton, wool, and sugar. These are the same commodities that have increased so rapidly in price since 1972.

Actually, the farmer is caught in the middle of comprehensive concentration in the food industry where each phase—production inputs, production, processing, packaging, shipping, wholesaling, and retailing—is coming under more concentrated control of large and powerful firms. On the one hand, the farm machinery and equipment industry is highly concentrated, as are many of the farm supply industries. At the processing level, there are a number of highly concentrated sectors including breakfast cereals, bread and prepared flour, baking, fluid milk and dairy products, processed meats, sugar, canned goods, and soups, to name a few. The pattern follows down to the checkout counter.

THE DIVERSIFICATION MOVEMENT

Another of the major aspects of the economy is the apparent rush of big business and big banking to join in the *diversification* game. This is an old game which is continually revived and may take various directions. Product, service, and spatial (geographical) diversification are the major components.

In the quest for risk aversion or minimization, firms move into new fields or markets with about as much knowledge as the contestant in a classic "shell" game, and the performance results demonstrate this situation. At the extreme are the large multinational conglomerates which have utilized each type of diversification in a substantial manner. In between are firms that have exported facilities in a more narrow industry context and become multinational firms, as well as the domestically-oriented conglomerate firms engaging in a potpourri of activities. These special firms have produced some of the poorest performance records in the business world in recent years.

Lagging behind in timing, the big bankers have also moved into each area of diversification. The bank holding company movement, particularly since the amendment to the 1956 act was passed in late 1970, has caused a spurt into "related" but different types of services. The implications of this movement are profound and have not been sufficiently recognized or analyzed.

THE MULTINATIONAL MOVEMENT

Few business developments have sparked as much interest as the multinational business and banking movement. This is an economic and political power movement of considerable dimension, and involves a substantial number of big business and banking firms. Among the 15 largest multinational firms in the world are 11 United States giants (see Table 2.1). Five of the United States firms are petroleum multinationals which have made substantial foreign investments, since about one-third of total United States investment in foreign plant and equipment originates in this single industry.

Arguments against and in defense of these firms are legion. Opponents of the movement, such as organized labor, claim that multinational operations are responsible for "the dimming of America" and claim they have contributed to a loss of domestic employment and resources and a give-away of United States technology. The AFL-CIO believes these firms are rapidly turning the greatest industrial power into "a nation of hamburger stands." The proponents make many arguments revolving around the

Table 2.1   The Top 15 Multinational Companies

Company	Total 1971 sales ($ billions)	Foreign sales as a percentage of total	Number of countries in which subsidiaries are located
General Motors	28.3	19	21
Exxon	18.7	50	25
Ford	16.4	26	30
Royal Dutch/Shell	12.7	79	43
General Electric	9.4	16	32
IBM	8.3	39	80
Mobil Oil	8.2	45	62
Chrysler	8.0	24	26
Texaco	7.5	40	30
Unilever	7.5	80	31
IT&T	7.3	42	40
Gulf Oil	5.9	45	61
British Petroleum	5.2	88	52
Philips Gloulampenfabrieken	5.2	N.A.	29
Standard Oil (California)	5.1	45	26

Source: "The U.N. Sizes Up the Global Giants," *Business Week,* p. 26, August 18, 1973.

theme that there is a better allocation of world resources, leading to an increase in the total level of material well-being for all.

An analysis of the costs and benefits of this development indicates that while there may be some benefits in these operations, they are generally costlier than supposed. From the viewpoint of the United States, direct foreign investment means the exportation of capital and jobs rather than goods and services. Domestic employment opportunities are diminished by this type of expansion. Balance of payments problems are also affected in two major ways. Dollars are spent in foreign areas, which gives rise to a claim; balanced against this claim is the return of profits on these investments. Posed against this situation is the export effect; that is, a part of the potential export market is eliminated by the construction of the foreign facilities. An example is the gasoline market, where the United States was a sizable exporter of this product until 1961 and has become a net importer since. Certainly, there are other reasons; however, the construction of numerous foreign refineries by the United States petroleum multinationals has had a significant effect.[7] In 1961, the United States had 47 percent of the world's refining capacity. By 1972, the United States share had declined to 27 percent.

Probably the most interesting aspect of the whole multinational movement is the lack of any pattern of real success. Some firms do well while others do not, and it appears to be more an industry effect, or a size effect, than a multinational spatial effect. For example, as noted in Chapter 8, the five United States multinational petroleum firms have not performed as well for their shareholders as the other smaller firms in the industry even during the so-called energy crisis. The more general problems relating to *dis*economies of scale are apparent in multinational operations as well as domestic. This finding is substantiated by two experts in this field, Robert B. Stobaugh, of Harvard, and Sidney M. Robbins, of Columbia University. Over the past 7 years they have studied the finances of 187 multinational firms that account for about three-quarters of United States direct investment abroad.[8] In discussing the level of financial management of these firms, Stobaugh observes:

> Of the 187 industrial companies we studied, only about sixty could be described as financially aggressive. In general these are the middle-sized companies—those with foreign sales of between $100 million and $500 million. The rest of the companies do not manage their money very effectively . . . the surprising fact is that the largest and best-known companies—the G.M.'s, the I.B.M.'s, the I.T.T.'s—are missing so many opportunities for extra profits through better financial management.[9]

Thus *bigness* appears to have its cost in foreign operations, as well as in domestic operations. Inventory costs and management may also be a substantial problem, as noted by Stobaugh and Robbins, who estimate that almost half ($15 billion of $32 billion) of foreign inventories were in excess of what would be needed for a similar volume of operations in the United States.[10] The risks of foreign spatial diversification are substantial, and some of the former advantages to the firm, such as lower labor costs, are vanishing in many areas. In short, the problems with multinational spatial diversification may well turn these large firms into the conglomerate-type failures of the future. Since the larger they are, the harder they fall, big government will again be called to the rescue as it was in the Penn Central case and with the Lockheed problem.

The international economic and political power of these supergiants is a legitimate source of concern to the world and national communities and should receive more attention in the upcoming years. IT&T, for example, has more overseas employees than the State Department, and Exxon's tanker fleet is half again as large as that of the Soviet Union. In a combined list of 100 countries and corporations ranked according to gross national product and annual sales, close to half are *multinational firms*. Since economic and political power go hand in hand, we can expect these large firms to engage in bribery, lobbying, and attempts to influence policy in the areas where they operate.

THE TRANSPORTATION MESS

After years of combination activity and various kinds of diversification, the rail system in the United States has degenerated into a mess. The government- and regulatory agency–*approved* merger creating the Penn Central system has resulted in the largest economic and financial failure in the history of commercial affairs. The government has been forced to make a public corporation out of the formerly privately owned rail passenger business. In addition, government loans, grants, and subsidies continue to pour taxpayer money into this all-but-abandoned system. Meanwhile, it becomes more difficult and costlier for a shipper to find a freight car and a commuter or traveler to get a rail passenger car at a time when energy should be conserved and the rails, while energy users, are also major savers of energy.

In addition to the inefficient and inept management, regulation, and labor practices in the rail area, gasoline tax dollars have poured into the highway trust funds, and then into the building of superhighways that have contributed to various types of problems. It appears to be a national paradox to build a massive network of highways for automobiles when alternatives are needed to conserve resources.

Even the newer and more glamorous airlines appear to be following the road (or rail) to ruin. Neglecting the lessons of history and the wisdom of experience, many of these firms and the regulators who govern them are generally ignoring sensible economic solutions to their problems. As noted in Chapter 9, the major airlines seek higher prices when demand falls in order to achieve target rates of return, instead of lowering prices to increase load factors and profitability. These policies have been followed with full knowledge and compliance of the Civil Aeronautics Board, a regulatory agency. The transportation mess is a national tragedy resulting from years of inept management and poor government regulation.

CONGRESSIONAL HEARINGS

By 1970, there were no less than eight agencies and congressional committees studying the conglomerate phenomenon in the United States after it had peaked. In the early 1970s the operations of the multinational firms were also under investigation. Conducting hearings is something that congressional subcommittees do well. For example, the Senate Subcommittee on Antitrust and Monopoly produced a multivolume work, *Economic Concentration,* which is a uniquely valuable collection of varied testimony on the problem. Senator Philip Hart utilized these hearings in framing the Industrial Reorganization Act which he introduced in the summer of 1972 (discussed in Chapter 15), yet there has been virtually no congressional interest in this important legislation.

The present makeup of the Senate Antitrust Subcommittee makes it extremely difficult to count on new legislation in the antitrust area since it appears to be a den of *anti*-antitrusters. This appears to be work of Senator James Eastland, as noted by Mark Green, who says:

> Most observers agree that Senator Eastland, Chairman of the full Judiciary Committee, stacked the Subcommittee with antitrust opponents after the death in 1963 of Senator Estes Kefauver, former head of the Subcommittee and an independent Senatorial power. Now, with rare exceptions, only legislation which erodes antitrust can get by the Subcommittee. And for the Congress as a whole in the 20 years since the Celler-Kefauver Act, the record is identical: there has been *no* legislation broadening the substantive scope of the antitrust laws.[11]

The lesson is clear, and the hearings drone on and produce volumes of testimony which seldom develop into legislation. The only exception is when powerful special interest groups flex their muscles and influence elected officials in various ways.[12]

This microeconomic collage has presented a preview of the more extensive material in the chapters that follow. Hopefully, the reader will wish to explore these various aspects in a more detailed manner and to examine some public policy suggestions provided to stimulate the quality of life and restructure the system in the future.

NOTES

1   John M. Blair, *Economic Concentration: Structure, Behavior and Public Policy,* New York: Harcourt Brace Jovanovich, 1972, p. 372.
2   *Hearings on Administered Pricing,* Part 9, p. 4785.
3   See Gilbert Burck, "The Merger Movement Rides High," *Fortune,* p. 80, February 1969.
4   See "Conglomerates," *Business Week,* p. 74, November 30, 1969.
5   Samuel Richardson Reid, *Mergers, Managers, and the Economy,* New York: McGraw-Hill, 1968, pp. 177-205.
6   See "A Large Question about Large Corporations," *Fortune,* p. 185, May 1972.
7   Construction in foreign areas creates claims against the dollar; if the balance is unfavorable over time, a devaluation takes place. Following devaluation, the costs of foreign operations and expansion will increase, and more dollars are needed for foreign operations, which contributes to the problem.
8   See Robert B. Stobaugh and Sidney M. Robbins, *Money in the Multinational Enterprise: A Study of Financial Policy,* New York: Basic Books, 1973.

9 "How the Multinationals Play the Money Game," *Fortune,* p. 60, August 1973.

10 Ibid.

11 Mark Green et al., *The Closed Enterprise System,* New York: Grossman Publishers, 1972, p. 56.

12 Two developments in the spring of 1975 may change this situation in the Senate. The number of members on the Subcommittee on Antitrust and Monopoly has been expanded, and a vigorous anti-antitruster, Senator Roman Hruska of Nebraska, has announced his planned retirement from the Senate.

Chapter 3

Bigness and Comprehensive Concentration

A profile of the American economy as it relates to the structural characteristics of both concentration levels and the size dimensions of firms reveals
an interesting pattern. Industrial organization economists measure concentration in a variety of ways, including aggregate, industry, market, regional,
state, and local measures. The size of firms may also be measured in a
variety of ways, such as sales, assets, profits, total market value, and
employees. The choice of measure in any case depends upon the purpose of
the study. In order to gain a perspective on the extent of economic
concentration and relative firm size, it is necessary to examine a variety of
the available data. The purpose of this chapter is to present a mixture of
data related to concentration and firm size to develop a contemporary
profile of the existing economic structure.

CONCENTRATION—RELATIVELY FEW HANDS

The late Senator Estes Kefauver warned his fellow Americans more than a
decade ago about the inherent dangers of concentrating economic and
political power into the "hands of a few."[1] The same concerns of the

Senator have been shared by many others since the founding of the republic, yet the imbalanced economy observed by Kefauver in the early 1960s has become even more so since his untimely death.

The 750 largest firms, as identified by *Fortune* (including the 500 largest industrials and the 50 largest banks, life insurance companies, utilities, and retailing and transportation companies) have assets of about $1.5 trillion which is a substantial portion of the national wealth. In addition, these relatively few firms employ about one of every four members of the nation's labor force (see Table 3.1). This is a substantial amount of power for a minor fraction of 1 percent of the business firms in this country. It appears as if the American situation is not very different than Japan, which is usually thought of as a nation dominated by combines or *zaibatsus* rather than having a competitive, free enterprise system. Fewer than 1 percent of Japan's manufacturers employ a third of the labor force and account for half of all production. Thus, both these industrial nations, which were bitter enemies during World War II, are dominated by a relatively small number of big power centers.

The total sales of *Fortune's* 500 largest industrials during 1973 was a new record of $667 billion compared with the much smaller volume of sales for the second 500 largest (501–1,000) which was $69 billion for the year. The assets of the second 500 largest were about $53 billion at year-end 1973—less than one-tenth the assets of the 500 largest firms. Combined, the 1,000 largest industrial firms employed eight out of every ten people working in American manufacturing and mining. In the United States, a fraction of 1 percent of the manufacturers employ more than 80 percent of the industrial workers.

Table 3.1 The Assets, Sales, Income, and Employees of the 750 Largest Industrials, Banks, Insurance Companies, Retailing Companies, Transportation Companies, and Utilities

	Assets ($000)	Sales ($000)	Income ($000)	Employees
500 largest industrials	555,462,284	667,105,712	38,680,461	15,531,683
50 largest commercial banks	459,027,367	364,704,942*	2,401,867	427,412
50 largest life insurance	204,848,629	31,860,578†	1,075,471	410,918
50 largest retailing	44,318,645	100,493,724	2,113,727	2,683,337
50 largest transportation	48,153,394	30,602,389	856,368	924,314
50 largest utilities	181,203,583	55,795,040	7,248,364	1,275,943
Total	1,493,013,902	1,250,562,385	52,376,258	21,253,607

*Deposits.
†Premium and annuity income.
Source: Fortune, May 1974.

Table 3.2 Absolute Value Added by Manufacture by the 50, 100, and 200 Largest Firms and by All Manufacturing Companies, 1947–1967

Period and percentage change in value added by manufacture	50 largest manufacturing firms			100 largest manufacturing firms			200 largest manufacturing firms		All manufacturing firms
	In each year	In 1947	In 1967	In each year	In 1947	In 1967	In each year	In each year	In each year
1947	$12,629	$12,629	$11,144	$17,087	$17,087	$14,850	$ 22,287	$ 74,290
1967	65,533	52,426	65,533	86,503	70,755	86,503	110,095	262,131
Percentage change	419	315	488	406	314	482	394	253

Sources: 1967 *Census of Manufactures,* "Concentration Ratios in Manufacturing," Special Report Series, Part I, MC67(s) 2.1, U.S. Bureau of the Census, Washington, D.C., 1970; 1967 *Census of Manufactures, Summary Series, Preliminary Report,* February 1970, p. 2; and 1963 *Census of Manufactures,* General Summary, Table 1.

The 2,710 American manufacturing corporations with assets of $10 million or more represented less than 1 percent of all manufacturing businesses, yet they controlled 88 percent of the assets and received over 90 percent of the net profits of corporations in the industrial sector. By the first quarter of 1970, the 102 largest firms received a greater share of net profits than the remaining approximately 195,000 manufacturing corporations and the 175,000 proprietorships and partnerships engaged in manufacturing businesses.

Another measure of concentration, in addition to assets, is the value added by manufacture. Data on this variable are available in a report, "Concentration Ratios in Manufacturing," published by the Bureau of the Census. The data in Table 3.2 include the absolute value added by manufacture by the 50, 100, and 200 largest firms and by all manufacturing companies viewed at different dates from 1947–1967. It is apparent that over the 20-year period value added for all manufacturing firms increased by 253 percent; while for the 50 largest in 1967, it increased 488 percent, or nearly double that for all manufacturing. For the 100 largest in 1967, the increase was 482 percent and for the 200 largest, the increase was 394 percent. Each increase by the various groups of large firms was consider-

Table 3.3   Absolute Value Added by the 200 Largest Firms and All Manufacturing Companies, Viewed at Different Dates, 1947–1967

Period and percentage change in value added by manufacture	200 largest manufacturing firms, in each year	All manufacturing companies, in each year	Value added of 200 largest as percentage of all manufacturing
1947	$ 22,287	$ 74,290	30
1967	110,095	262,131	42
Percentage change	394	253	
1947	22,287	74,290	30
1954	43,302	117,032	37
Percentage change	94	58	
1954	43,302	117,032	37
1958	53,786	141,541	38
Percentage change	24	21	
1958	53,786	141,541	38
1963	78,762	192,103	40
Percentage change	46	36	
1963	78,762	192,103	40
1967	110,095	262,131	42
Percentage change	41	36	

Source: See Table 2.2.

ably larger than for all manufacturing firms. This pattern is also true whether one examines the largest firms in each intervening year, or in 1947, as well as 1967.

The data in Table 3.3 present the value added by the 200 largest firms and for all manufacturing companies in each census year. The large firms *consistently* increased their percentage change in value added at a higher level than the change for all manufacturing firms. The average annual percent change in value added during the postwar period 1947–1967 for all manufacturing firms was 13 percent, compared to 24 percent for the 50 and 100 largest in 1967 and 20 percent for the 200 largest firms.

In 1967, the 50 largest firms had increased their share of value added by manufacture to 23 percent of the total value added, up from 17 percent in 1947. The share of the 200 largest firms increased from 30 percent in 1947 to 42 percent in 1967, a gain of 12 percentage points (or 40 percent). The pattern reveals that the big get bigger and that they do so at a faster rate than the balance of industry.[2]

CHANGES IN CONCENTRATION DURING THE 1960–1970 PERIOD

At the beginning of the 1970s, 102 corporations, each with assets of $1 billion or more, accounted for nearly half of all corporate manufacturing assets (see Table 3.4). Although the number of industrial corporations of every size expanded during the 1960s, only those in the rapidly growing $1 billion and over class enlarged their share of total assets—from 28 to 48 percent. Despite an increase of close to 40,000 in the number of corporations with assets less than $10 million during the period, these smaller firms' share of the total assets fell from 18 to 13 percent.

In addition to the smaller manufacturing corporations, there are about 175,000 proprietorships and partnerships classified as manufacturing businesses. The combined assets of these firms equal about 1 percent of the total, or less than one-third of the assets of Exxon Corporation.

The distribution of wealth in manufacturing is significant, with close to 370,000 firms holding *only* 12 percent of the assets and 13 percent of the profits in 1973. Contrast this with the 3,394 firms with $10 million and over of assets, which hold 88 percent of the assets and 87 percent of the profits. In the imbalanced American economy, less than 1 percent of the firms hold the vast majority of the economic power.

The Federal Trade Commission has noted the trend toward increasing concentration among the 1,000 largest manufacturers, a proportion which

Table 3.4 Distribution of Assets and Profits by Size of Firm, First Quarter of 1960 and of 1970

Size of firm	Percentage of assets (in italic)			Percentage of profits		
	1960	1970	1973	1960	1970	1973
$1 billion and over	28 companies *28*	102 companies *48*	136 companies *53*	40	53	54
$250 million–$1 billion	112 companies *23*	218 companies *19*	260 companies *17*	22	21	17
$100–$250 million	176 companies *11*	289 companies *8*	338 companies *7*	12	8	6
$50–$100 million	265 companies *8*	366 companies *5*	425 companies *4*	7	4	4
$25–$50 million	380 companies *5*	533 companies *3*	667 companies *3*	5	3	3
$10–$25 million	948 companies *6*	1,202 companies *4*	1,568 companies *4*	5	3	3
Under $10 million*	155,970 companies† *18*	193,000 companies† *13*	202,710 companies† *12*	10	9	13

*There are close to 175,000 additional manufacturing businesses that are classified as proprietorships and partnerships; their combined assets total only about 1 percent of the whole, or less than one-third of the assets of Exxon Corporation, the largest industrial firm in terms of assets.

†Estimated.

Source: *Quarterly Financial Report for Manufacturing Corporations*, Federal Trade Commission and Securities and Exchange Commission, 1960, 1970, and 1973.

has grown from 61.6 percent in 1941, to 76.6 percent in 1964, to over 81 percent in 1970. The 200 largest industrial corporations controlled over 60 percent of the total assets by 1970, a share of assets equal to that held by the 1,000 largest in 1941, when the Temporary National Economic Committee submitted its final report and recommendations in a report, *Investigation of Concentration of Economic Power,* to Congress.

INDUSTRIAL MARKET STRUCTURE

Market concentration refers to the share of a particular industry's business held by the largest firms in that industry. It is another dimension of the measurement of power in the economy and supplements the measures of *overall* or *aggregate* concentration presented above. Instead of measuring concentration of total industrial assets, sales, value added, or other measures, attention is focused on concentration in the manufacture of a particular product.

Although published concentration ratios on balance contain a decided downward bias (since the Bureau of the Census does not provide estimates of ratios in some industries to avoid disclosure), it is significant that a substantial share of industries are in the high concentration ranges. In 1963, there were 112 industries in which four firms accounted for more than half the production, and in 29 of these the big four accounted for more than 75 percent of production. Thus, close to a third of United States manufacturing production originates in *highly* concentrated national markets with even higher levels in the consumer goods markets.

Since concentration is not a static concept, it is reasonable to expect changes over time, with some increases and decreases. In the period 1947–1963, concentration in consumer goods industries increased in almost half the industries, and declined in about one-third. Between 1958 and 1963 concentration increased in 47 percent of the industries, but declined in only 12 percent of the consumer goods industries. The pattern was different in the producer goods industries, where about one-fourth of the industries increased and one-third decreased during the same period. Perhaps the most striking aspect of industry concentration data is the persistent existence of high levels of concentration in such a broad spectrum of products considering the supposed mobility of firms.[3]

In the important area of industrial market concentration, William G. Shepherd estimates that in 1966 close to half (199) of the industries had a four-firm concentration ratio of 50 percent or more, accounting for 64 percent of all industrial goods produced in the nation.[4] In the still higher range of industrial market concentration—four-firm ratios of 70 percent or

Table 3.5   Average (Unweighted) Four-Firm Ratios for 166 and 292 Manufacturing Industries, 1947–1970

Year	Average value added for 166 industries (four-firm)		Average value added for 292 industries (four-firm)
1970	42.7		41.2
1967	41.4		40.3
1963	41.3		39.9
1958	40.3		39.2
1954	40.6		N.A.
1947	40.9		N.A.
Change, 1947–1970	+1.8	Change, 1958–1970	+2.0

Source: Adapted from William F. Mueller and Larry G. Hamm, "Trends in Industrial Market Concentration, 1947–1970," *The Review of Economics and Statistics,* vol. 56, no. 4, p. 512, November 1974.

more—about a third of the manufacturing output (34 percent) was produced in 1966. A roughly similar pattern exists in the nonmanufacturing sectors of the economy, according to Shepherd, who concludes that " . . . at least 35 to 45 percent of market activity in the United States appears to take place under conditions of substantial market [monopoly] power."[5]

Further evidence, utilizing the 1970 data, confirms the trend and magnitude discussed above. Willard F. Mueller and Larry G. Hamm studied 166 industries (which had essentially the same definitions) for the 1947–1970 period, and a larger sample of 292 manufacturing industries.[6] Mueller and Hamm confirmed the upward movement of the average concentration ratio using value-added data for the most recent period (see Table 3.5). Concentration increased the most in consumer goods industries in the 1958–1970 period, with 69 increases and only 29 decreases. The producer goods industries also had more increases (95) than decreases (83) in this period. Mueller and Hamm found product differentiation to be a potent explanatory variable in the consumer goods industries, indicating the importance of the role of advertising in concentration analyses. Mueller and Hamm conclude:

> The public policy conclusion of our findings seem inescapable. High market concentration pervades much of American manufacturing. Some may quibble over the precise level and trend of concentration. But the indisputable fact of life is that in many industries production is concentrated in a few hands, has been concentrated in a few hands for decades, and will in all probability remain so unless some explicit public policy initiatives are taken to change things.[7]

REGIONAL AND LOCAL INDUSTRIAL CONCENTRATION

Spatial industrial concentration can also be measured on the regional and local level, in addition to the national scene. A study by David Schwartzman and Joan Bodoff revealed that "the average regional concentration ratio for every regional industry exceeds the corresponding national ratio . . . the average local concentration ratio in every industry exceeds the national concentration ratio."[8] These researchers found that the weighted-average national concentration for the industries studied was 19 percent, while the weighted average *local* concentration ratio was considerably higher at 61 percent. At the local level, they concluded that ". . . on the basis of the 50 percent criterion and local concentration ratios, most of these industries are concentrated."[9]

The lopsided pattern here is clear and reveals that industrial market concentration is unnecessarily high at the national level and appears to be even higher at the regional and local level. Thus, many large industrial firms dominate products markets in all spatial areas.

A BROADER LOOK AT SIZE

Looking beyond the largest industrials as identified in the annual *Fortune* reports, to a broader list of the 500 biggest corporations as identified by *Forbes,* reveals that there were 395 firms with assets of over $1 billion, and 248 firms with sales exceeding $1 billion at the end of 1973. Thus, whether one examines the *Fortune* data or the newer and more interesting *Forbes* material (contained in the Forbes annual directory), the dimension of American business stands out as big and getting bigger.

It should be apparent that no matter how one approaches the economic power and concentration question, the data continue to disclose a structure quite different than that envisioned by the early economists, as well as the founding fathers of America. In an economy where 50 business firms control more expenditures than all the state and local governments and the federal government combined, and where a small fraction of firms dominate whole sectors of importance in the economy, only a shadow of a broad-based competitive free enterprise system remains.

A CLOSER LOOK AT COMMERCIAL BANKING SIZE AND CONCENTRATION

The commercial banking structure in the United States is a prime example of the imbalance so prevalent in the economy. The relative size distribution is presented in Table 3.6 and indicates that the very largest banks had the

Table 3.6 Size of Banking Organizations: June 1957, 1961, and 1968

Size class ($, millions)	1957 Number	%	1961 Number	%	1968 Number	%
More than $500	45	0.3	56	0.4	106	0.8
$100–500	177	1.4	221	1.7	348	2.7
50–100	209	1.6	209	1.6	380	2.9
20–50	613	4.8	681	5.3	1,283	9.8
10–20	1,023	8.0	1,236	9.7	2,107	16.2
1–10	9,027	70.1	9,053	70.9	8,426	64.7
$1 or less	1,779	13.8	1,325	10.4	382	2.9

Source: Select Committee on Small Business, United States Senate, *Recent Changes in Banking Structure in the United States,* Washington, D.C., March 30, 1970, p. 7.

biggest increases in size while the number of smaller banks declined during the 1960s. A major reason for the shrinkage has been the regulatory-approved bank mergers, as well as limited entry, and both these factors will be treated in more detail later. It is worth noting that in commercial banking, the 100 largest firms in 1974 comprise less than 1 percent of the organizations and yet control 70 percent of all the deposits (see Table 3.7).

Since commercial banking is basically a locally oriented type of business, the relative concentration of deposits at this level assumes importance. The data in Table 3.8 list the standard metropolitan statistical areas by size groups and the percentage of deposits controlled by the largest and two largest banking organizations. It is apparent that the ratio is quite high in all areas, particularly in communities and cities which permit statewide branching activities.

Table 3.7 Commercial Bank Deposits Held by the 200 Largest Firms and Subgroups, 1974

Group	Total deposits ($, millions)	Percentage of all bank deposits
Top 50	406,011	60.0
51–100	70,468	10.0
101–150	43,830	6.5
151–200	30,006	4.4
Total, 200 largest	550,315	81.0
Remaining 14,138 banks	128,785	19.0
Total, all banks	679,000	100.0

Source: Annual Survey of Bank Performance, *Business Week,* pp. 60–63, September 21, 1974. Figures may not add due to rounding.

Table 3-8   Percentage of Total Deposits Held by Largest Banking Organizations in Metropolitan Areas in Mid-1968

Population of standard metropolitan statistical area SMSA	Largest organization			Two largest organizations		
	Statewide branching states	Limited branching states	Unit banking states	Statewide branching states	Limited branching states	Unit banking states
50–100,000	43.8%	38.9%	39.8%	69.5%	65.4%	68.5%
100,000–500,000	42.7	39.0	31.1	68.5	64.4	53.5
500,000–1,000,000	40.8	34.9	25.9	69.1	57.7	47.8
1,000,000 and over	32.7	31.1	23.9	55.0	51.5	42.7
All SMSA	41.1%	37.3%	31.5%	66.9%	61.7%	54.6%

Source: Recent Changes in the Structure of Commercial Banking," *Federal Reserve Bulletin*, vol. 56, no. 3, p. 207, March 1970.

Another method of examining spatial concentration in banking is to determine the ratio of deposits held by the five largest banking organizations in the individual states. This type of data is presented in Table 3.9 and indicates the dominant position of a few banking organizations in some states, again those firms located in states permitting statewide branching. An inverse pattern exists between the statewide group on the one hand and the unit banking and limited branching states on the other. A substantial 85 percent of the statewide branching states had concentration ratios of over 50 percent, compared with 25 percent for the limited branching states, and only 13 percent for the unit banking states.

The concentration pattern in commercial banking indicates that state laws, as well as federal regulations, can have a serious effect upon the banking structure operating in any given area. The particular problems related to this development will be thoroughly examined in Chapters 11, 12, and 13.

BIG BUSINESS AND BANKING INTERLOCKS

As business firms become larger and more diversified, they tend to increase their formal and informal ties with other large firms (both business and banking) through common board members or officers. While the law (section 8 of the Clayton Act) prohibits firms in direct competition with one another to have common directorates, large firms are still often interlocked with suppliers, customers, potential competitors, and financial institutions.

A congressional staff study of 29 of the largest industrial firms revealed numerous interlocks with other industrial corporations, banks, and insur-

Table 3.9 Concentration of Deposits Held by Five Largest Banking Organizations, Mid-1969

Concentration ratio	Number of statewide branching states	Percentage of group total	Number of limited branching states	Percentage of group total	Number of unit banking states	Percentage of group total
Over 90%	6	30	—	0	—	0
80%–90%	3	15	—	0	—	0
70%–80%	3	15	—	0	—	0
60%–70%	2	10	1	6	—	0
50%–60%	3	15	3	19	2	13
Total states over 50%	17	85	4	25	2	13
States with less than 50%	3	15	12	75	13	87

Source: "Recent Changes in the Structure of Commercial Banking," *Federal Reserve Bulletin,* vol. 56, no. 3, p. 210, March 1970.

ance companies.[10] One firm, General Motors Corporation, was interlocked with seven of the 100 largest industrials, and with the nation's largest railroad and telephone company. All told, the 63 firms with which GMC was interlocked had combined assets of over $65 billion (in 1962).

A Federal Trade Commission study completed in 1965 revealed numerous interlocks involving the 200 largest industrial firms. Two important characteristics are revealed by the data. One, there is a close correlation between a firm's size and the frequency of interlocks with other large firms. Two, many interlocks involved firms producing closely related products. The top 50 firms had 520 interlocks with firms ranking among the 1,000 largest; 134 of these interlocks were firms producing in the same five-digit SIC product class.

The Federal Trade Commission also studied the interlocks of the larger conglomerates during the 1948–1968 period.[11] They found that interlocking relationships have expanded as this special type of firm grew rapidly in the 1960s. By 1968, each of the conglomerate firms showed many more interlocks with the largest firms, particularly in manufacturing and finance.

In 1968 the staff of the House Subcommittee on Domestic Finance of the Committee on Banking and Currency explored the trust activities of commercial banks. Of the 49 banks surveyed "a total of 768 interlocking directorships with 286 of the 500 largest industrial corporations were found to exist."[12] One bank " . . . reported 401 companies in which it held 5 percent or more of one or more classes of stock. Another bank . . . reported 278 companies with which it has 326 director interlocks."[13]

Thus, the lopsided structure of the American economy is further interlaced with numerous officer and director interlocks in the key economic power centers. The situation is further complicated by the growing shift of individual corporate stockholdings to institutional investments made by mutual funds, pension funds, insurance firms, and the trust activities of commercial banks. Among the major institutional investors, the pension funds hold over $40 billion in stock and are growing at a rate of over $5 billion a year. Mutual funds have stockholdings of about $53 billion, and the commercial bank trust departments administer and control assets of over $600 billion, about half of this is in the hands of a relatively few large banks. It is estimated that these few banks have enough trust and lending leverage to provide effective control of almost 150 of the 500 largest industrial firms. These same 49 banks have placed their representatives on the boards of directors of 286 of the nation's largest firms. Industrial and financial institution interlocks tend to bind together a relatively elite group which shares inside information and decision making in an intricate web of crisscrossing patterns of power.

FARM SIZE AND CONCENTRATION

Growing concentration and size have also been evident in the agriculture sector of the economy. The number of independent farms and the land devoted to farming has continued to decline, as the average size of farms has increased over the years. For example, between 1960 and 1973, the number of farms has declined from about 4 million to 2.8 million, a loss of 29 percent. The average farm size increased from 297 acres to 385 acres, a gain of 30 percent during the same period (see Table 3.10).

A closer look at these substantial changes reveals a most interesting pattern, as it relates to changing concentration and behavior in the agricultural sector. The number of farms under 500 acres declined about one-third during the 1960s, with more than a million farms disappearing as separate independent decision-making units.

Perhaps the most startling and significant finding is that in 1969, the largest farms, those with 2,000 or more acres, comprised only 2 percent of the farms and held 43 percent of all farmland. Thus, the agricultural sector resembles other sectors of the economy and adds another dimension to the pattern of comprehensive concentration.

Food processing and retailing have also become concentrated over the

Table 3.10 Farm Population, Number of Farms, and Land in Farms, 1960–1973

Year	Farm population (thousands)	Number of farms (thousands)	Land in Farms	
			Total (millions of acres)	Average per farm (acres)
1960	15,635	3,963	1,176	297
1961	14,803	3,825	1,168	305
1962	14,313	3,692	1,159	314
1963	13,367	3,572	1,152	322
1964	12,954	3,457	1,146	332
1965	12,363	3,356	1,140	340
1966	11,595	3,257	1,132	348
1967	10,875	3,162	1,123	355
1968	10,454	3,071	1,115	363
1969	10,307	2,999	1,108	369
1970	9,712	2,954	1,103	373
1971	9,425	2,909	1,097	377
1972	9,610	2,870	1,093	381
1973 (prd.)	——	2,831	1,089	385

Source: U.S. Department of Agriculture.

years. While the 1967 Census of Manufacturing tallied over 32,000 food manufacturing firms, the Federal Trade Commission study of the structure of the industry revealed that a scant 50 firms had over 60 percent of the industry's profits and 100 firms had over 70 percent of the profits. In food retailing, there has been a prolonged merger movement which has also produced an imbalanced pattern. It has been estimated that in more than half the nation's 218 standard metropolitan statistical areas, the top four retail chains account for a majority of grocery sales. On a national basis, in 1967, 9 percent of all grocery stores held over 60 percent of the nation's sales. Between the farmer and the consumer there is a concentrated lump which has been gaining an increasing share of the grocery bills across the nation in recent years.

CONCENTRATION AND POWER IN THE STOCK MARKETS

Another area of growing concentration and power is the market for corporate securities. The stock market has become substantially more institutionalized during the past decade, and from all indications this trend will continue in the future unless there are structural changes.

Institutional investors are responsible for about 70 percent of all trading, which results in a distinctly imbalanced market. The institutionalization of the stock market suggests numerous ramifications in a market dominated by large institutional investors due to both legal constraints and practical portfolio reasons. The legal constraint is present because institutions have legal lists they must consider, and most of the firms included on the lists are large firms which have numerous, heavily traded shares outstanding. Thus, there is a restricted population of public companies that receive an inordinate amount of institutional attention.

On the supply side of the stock market, this imbalance tends to create distinct tiers among the various firms with traded securities. For example, at the end of 1972 there were 1,505 firms with stock listed on the New York Stock Exchange, and about 1,100 firms listed on the American Stock Exchange. The over-the-counter market contains about 3,000 firms with stock included on the National Association of Securities Dealers Automatic Quotation system and about 4,000 firms with stock regularly quoted in the National Quotation Bureau pink sheets. Thus, there are close to 10,000 firms with stock traded on a public market.

The top tier of this special market includes firms large enough to accommodate the major institutional investors that desire to establish a meaningful position, and yet maintain liquidity. That is, a situation where an institution can acquire a position adequate for its size without significantly increasing the price in the process and can dispose of a position without precipitating a major price decline in the stock. The number of firms that fit into this catagory is limited. It is estimated that about 300 firms qualify on the size and stock trading criteria.[14] Assuming that another 200 firms may reach this tier in the next few years, an institutionalized market would result in over 70 percent of the trading concentrated in about 5 percent of the firms. A concentrated financial market of this type complicates the position of the vast majority of smaller firms desiring to raise additional equity and long-term debt funds in order to survive and compete with the business giants.

ANOTHER DIMENSION OF POWER AND CONCENTRATION

An important aspect of the political economy in the United States which seldom receives adequate attention is that related to the news media. A major exception is the detailed treatment given this problem by Morton Mintz and Jerry S. Cohen, which is contained in a chapter titled "Hear No Evil, See No Evil, Speak No Evil" in their book, *America, Inc.: Who Owns and Operates the United States*. The authors state that "Concentration in certain industries is easy to describe. When one says that a few companies dominate automobile manufacturing one says the essential fact. Regrettably, simplicity is not an attribute of concentration in news media."[15]

The complication arises because the news media serve both national and distinct local markets, somewhat similar to the situation in commercial banking. One measure of news media concentration is the proportion of cities and towns with daily newspapers having two or more separate owners. Senator Thomas J. McIntyre of New Hampshire has pointed out that in 1910 the proportion was 57.1 percent, in 1930 it was 21.5 percent, and in 1970 it had dropped to 4.1 percent, a significant decline by any measure.[16] Currently, there are 1,483 cities with monopoly ownerships, compared with 64 with competing ownerships. Almost half the 64 competing ownerships are located in cities with populations under 100,000, and about a third are in cities with less than 50,000 people. Even more distressing is the fact that whether a city has single or multiple newspaper ownerships, one or all of the owners are chains or networks. The chains controlled 871 papers in 1967, or about half the nation's total, and accounted for 62 percent of the aggregate circulation and owned 19 of the 25 largest newspapers.

The same general pattern is observed in the broadcasting field. The Federal Communications Commission lists a total of 6,791 commercial broadcasting stations as of January 1, 1969, which appears to suggest more diversity than in newspapers where there are about 1,500 cities with daily papers. However, the imagined diversity is illusionary. In the important television area, there were 666 stations in 1968, and 349 of these were multiple-owned, representing 52.4 percent of the total. Newspapers owned 108 of the stations, which contributes further to the interlocks of control. There are only three national television networks, and 561 stations, or 84 percent of the total, are network affiliated, and the majority are multiple-owned.

The structure of the news media sector of the political economy reveals the relative power of a remarkably small number of people with considerable clout in a sensitive area. In a study made of news media ownership in Oklahoma by FCC Commissioners Kenneth Cox and Nicholas Johnson, one of their findings was "that in spite of the numbers of newspapers and broadcast outlets the control of the greatest share of audience, profit and political power lies in the hands of the very few."[17]

ECONOMIC POWER AND THE POLITICAL SCENE

The process of development and growth of special economic power centers creates the climate and potential for abuses of all types, both economic and political. The pure economic abuses related to pricing, output, and entry decisions in monopolistic and oligopolistic market structures are well and widely known. Lobbying activities for favored legislation or in opposition to restrictions are commonplace, as are attempts to secure protection against price and foreign competition. All these activities are natural and to be expected. The situation would not be too alarming if one had faith that each case would be heard on its merits and with comparable talent advocating each alternative position. Unfortunately, the reality is generally quite different from the theoretical ideal due to an imbalance heavily favoring the economic power blocs in the lopsided economy.

In modern America, the political economy has reached a dangerous stage of development which has only been partially recognized and obviously inadequately treated. As the economy becomes larger with a gross national product exceeding a trillion dollars a year and more, individual firms become multibillion dollar entities, and the stakes become quite high.

Coincident with this development is the high cost of seeking political office at virtually all levels of government. The total costs have increased as the number of voters has increased, which is a function of population gains, voting age changes, and increased registration drives. The expensive mass media of television in national and local areas has assumed a greater importance in the past decade.

Political investment at the national level, especially by big business, translates into overwhelming support for the Republican candidates. The evidence for this lopsided support is gathered in a book *Financing the 1968 Election* by Herbert E. Alexander of the Citizen's Research Foundation.[18] In addition to substantial contributions by bankers and their trade associations, other private interests made substantial "investments" in the campaign. Members of the American Petroleum Institute contributed $429,366 to Republicans and $30,606 to Democrats in 1968. Officers and directors of General Motors gave a total of $114,675 to Republican candidates and $1,000 to Democrats, while the chiefs of Litton Industries, a conglomerate firm, gave $151,000 to Republicans and nothing to Democrats. For thirteen industrial and trade associations, the ratio was eight to one in favor of the Republicans.

Congress has recognized the potential dangers stemming from the high costs of seeking political office. Limitations on campaign expenditures have been enacted; however, a candidate must still raise huge sums of money in order to seek or retain the office with or without federal financing. A national weekly magazine termed the 1972 election as "a national disgrace" terming it a "$400,000,000 election."[19] The scandals arising from that election were the most shocking in the history of the nation and confirm the type of behavior that can be expected in a lopsided political economy. Congressional reaction has resulted in partial funding for Presidential campaigns; however, the political influence of special interests remains firmly in place.

COMPREHENSION CONCENTRATION—A FINAL NOTE

It should be rather obvious, after this relatively brief examination of the various components of concentration and a glimpse at a few of the important sectors of the economy, that America has a broad-gauged, comprehensive concentration of economic power. It is necessary to recognize the scope of the development, since traditionally the focus of professional and legislative attention has been generally more restrictive, i.e., on a few sectors, rather than kaleidoscopic and comprehensive.

NOTES

1 Estes Kefauver, *In a Few Hands: Monopoly Power in America,* Baltimore: Penguin Books, 1965.
2 For another interpretation, see Betty Bock and Jack Farkas, *Relative Growth of the "Largest" Manufacturing Corporation,* New York: National Industrial Conference Board, 1973.

 3 See Stanley E. Boyle and Robert L. Sorenson, "Concentration and Mobility: An Alternative Measure of Industry Structure," *Journal of Industrial Economics,* vol. 19, no. 2, pp. 118–132, April 1971.
 4 William G. Shepherd, *Market Power and Economic Welfare,* New York: Random House, 1970, p. 106.
 5 Ibid., p. 246.
 6 Willard F. Mueller and Larry G. Hamm, "Trends in Industrial Market Concentration, 1947 to 1970," *The Review of Economics and Statistics,* vol. 56, no. 4, pp. 511–520, November 1974.
 7 Ibid., pp. 519–520.
 8 David Schwartzman and Joan Bodoff, "Concentration in Regional and Local Industries," *Southern Economic Journal,* vol. 37, no. 3, p. 344, January 1971.
 9 Ibid.
10 See "Interlocks in Corporate Management," A Staff Report to the Antitrust Subcommittee of the Committee on the Judiciary, House of Representatives, March 12, 1965.
11 See Federal Trade Commission, *Economic Report on Corporate Mergers,* Washington: U.S. Government Printing Office, 1969, p. 203.
12 *Subcommittee on Domestic Finance of the House Committee on Banking and Currency, Commercial Banks and Their Trust Activities: Emerging Influence on the American Economy,* 90th Cong., 2d Sess., vol. 1 (1968), p. 3.
13 Ibid., p. 4.
14 See Frank K. Reilly, "A Three-Tier Stock Market and Corporate Financing," *Financial Management,* forthcoming.
15 Morton Mintz and Jerry S. Cohen, *America, Inc.: Who Owns and Operates the United States,* New York: Dial Press, 1971, p. 95.
16 *Congressional Record,* January 19, 1970, pp. 567–571.
17 See "Broadcasting in America and the FCC's License Renewal Process: An Oklahoma Case Study: A Statement by Commissioners Kenneth A. Cox and Nicholas Johnson on the Occasion of the FCC's Renewal of the Licenses of Oklahoma Broadcasters for a Three Year Term Beginning June 1, 1968."
18 This book is published by D. C. Heath and Company, Boston.
19 See *Time,* pp. 24–30, October 23, 1972.

Chapter 4

Bigness and Concentration for Whom?

Much of the big business mania in the United States has developed from the basic belief that large-scale enterprises are more efficient, more profitable, more inventive, more innovative, and, if that was not enough, that an absolute necessity for large technological investments exists. There appears to be an almost blind faith that scale economies can be realized on an open-end basis through the use of computers and various new management systems. Public concern and doubt have been whisked away by periodic pronouncements such as the Galbraithian view that the power of big business and big labor can be countervailed by big federal government.[1] Or the more recent Galbraithian generalization that very high market concentration and large-scale firms are essential for production efficiency, invention, and innovation.[2]

The countervailing power hypothesis has repeatedly failed in its promise and has proved to be a discretionary method of operation which can be highly discriminatory in application. A contemporary example has been the growing role of government in aiding large firms and key industries with either outright grants, guaranteed loans, import quotas, price supports, antitrust immunity, or other forms of support. The role of government appears more as a partner than a countervailing power.

Focusing on the question of bigness as a positive force in the economy reveals a mixture of costs and benefits, as well as conflicting evidence. On balance, the costs of bigness (even independent of concentration) appear to outweigh the benefits. Thus, the question, "bigness for whom?" is appropriate.

BIGNESS AND PROFITABILITY

The suggestion that mere *size* of firm influences the rate of return has long intrigued economists, as evidenced by the periodic and increasing number of studies on the subject.[3] An examination of these studies reveals that there are mixed results and a lack of consensus of the validity of the hypothesis.

Earlier studies have not always employed industry control variables when attempting to isolate the effect of size. Some researchers have examined the size-profitability relationship within individual industries; however, the industry categories have been far too broad. One recent study pooled observations drawn from diverse industries and sought to control for interindustry differences by including the industry's concentration ratio as an explicit variable. Clearly, a size-profitability relationship can assume economic significance if established within a well-defined industry context, that is, firms producing the same basic goods and/or services. Such a test of the size-profitability hypothesis is presented in Chapter 10 and is related solely to the domestic trunk airlines. The results clearly demonstrate that bigness in size (as applied to the largest airlines) is not related to profitability or efficiency. Another indirect test, consisting of firms in the petroleum industry, is presented in Chapter 8 and reveals that the smaller major firms outperformed the large petroleum multinationals and the larger merger-active petroleum firms.

Perhaps the most interesting recent study, which attempted to isolate "absolute" size of the firm and rates of return, was the work of Matityahu Marcus.[4] A total of 118 industries were examined, and the size coefficient was statistically significant in only 35 of the industries examined. In nine industries the size coefficients were significantly negative, and there was no significance in the remaining 74 industries. The range of variation in the magnitude of the size coefficient was considerable.

Another contribution was the study of John M. Blair, who examined 30 industries for the year 1966.[5] Blair found that in only six of the industries was increasing size accompanied by rising profit rates; in about half of these the increase was due at least in part to substantial monopoly power. In the other 24 industries, either the tendency was in the opposite direction (eight industries) or there appeared to be no relationship at all. Blair concluded that the " . . . profit showings suggest that in only a minority of industries is great size a contributor to efficiency."[6]

Richards C. Osborn, in his study of efficiency and profitability in relation to size, published more than two decades ago, concluded:

Size is considered one of the factors causing differences in relative costs. But unfortunately the statistical evidence is conflicting since large businesses appear to be the most efficient in some fields; next-to-the-largest firms have lower costs in certain industries; and medium-size firms have evidenced the lowest costs in other instances.[7]

Certainly bigness does not appear to be necessary for profitable operation. In fact, the argument that bigness (independent of an industry effect) is necessary for efficiency and profitability does not seem to hold up when a detailed examination of the evidence is undertaken. The data in Table 4.1 list the 10 largest firms in the different business sectors as determined by *Fortune* and their comparative median ranking on profitability and efficiency measures. It is obvious that size (bigness) is no assurance of stockholder benefits.

In addition to the studies of the relationship between size and profitability, there have been a number of studies which have examined the proposition that firms in *concentrated* industries are more profitable than firms in more competitive industries.[8] The bulk of the evidence in the

Table 4.1 Size and Profitability Rankings of the Largest Industrials, Commercial Banks, and Retailing, Transportation, and Utility Companies, 1973

Size rank*	Net income as a percentage of Sales (median rank)†	Stockholders' equity (median rank)	Earnings per share growth, 1963–1973 (median rank)	Total return to investors, 1963–1973 average (median rank)
Big 10 industrials	116	120	259	269
Big 10 commercial banks	—	24	30	15
Big 10 retailers	15	16	28	16
Big 10 transportation	19	28	29	33
Big 10 utilities	—	34	39	39

*Size ranking is based on sales for industrials and assets for the other groups.
†Median rank is for 500 industrials and 50 largest firms in other groups.
Source: Fortune, May and July 1973.

empirical studies since the end of World War II has supported this theory. One of the most extensive studies of the hypothesis was conducted by Norman R. Collins and Lee E. Preston, who concluded:

> Our analysis also appears to validate the continued accumulation and analysis of concentration data as a significant dimension of industry structure. . . . Our results, therefore, would appear to justify serious concern with relatively high levels of concentration wherever they exist and with substantial increases in concentration wherever they occur.[9]

Contrary findings have been reported by Yale Brozen, who utilized a sample of 98 industries for the 1936–1940 period.[10] Brozen, however, omitted industries for which less than three firms could be found; thus his findings should be appropriately discounted.

Thus, the results of studies concerned with size and profitability and those of concentration and profitability appear to produce mixed results. Bigness does not necessarily ensure greater profitability and return on invested capital. These results indicate the existence of both scale economies and diseconomies among large firms. In addition, it may reflect growth-maximizing behavior, with profitability serving as a constraint, rather than as an objective of the firm. The same pattern of firm behavior may well be present in the concentrated areas, regardless of the size of the firm.

BIGNESS AND ECONOMIES AND DISECONOMIES OF SCALE

Even more fundamental than the relationship between bigness and profitability is the determination of scale economies and diseconomies. Unfortunately, the availability of cost data has posed a problem for economic researchers for many years. It is ironic that the proponents of bigness and/or concentration have based much of their justification upon the *assumed* efficiency argument as it relates to the scale of the firm, while the empirical basis is a slender reed indeed.

Recent data gathered in the regulated sector of the economy, especially as related to the airlines and commercial banking, reveal a most interesting pattern which is basically iconoclastic. A study of domestic truck airline size and unit operating expenses (presented in Chapter 10) reveals that the most efficient size is in the range *below* the four largest firms and slightly above the mean size of the four medium-size firms.

Functional cost studies conducted by the Federal Reserve using 1973 data reveal a striking pattern. The most efficient banking firms are those in the smallest size class ($5 million of deposits and under) and the cost curves are upward sloping in the continuum. Clearly, the long-assumed efficiency of bigness has been dealt a mortal blow and indicates the national need for extensive empirical investigation.

The fact that most large firms are decentralized into various multi-plant operations and profit-centers indicates a recognition of the basic difference between firm scale and plant or production scale. Modern technological impact appears to favor a decentralizing movement. Simultaneously, both bigness and concentration have become a function of multiplant operations rather than individual plant size in the manufacturing sector. The same general pattern is apparent in the banking field with the growth of holding companies and branching expansion and in the other sectors of the new industrial order. The progressive shattering of the bigness-efficiency cornerstone and increased recognition of the potential for diseconomies of scale should provide a host of new dimensions to the public and private policy debates in the future as they relate to firms, institutions, organizations, and government units (including municipalities). The potential implications are substantial.

BIGNESS, CONCENTRATION, AND INNOVATION

Much of the misguided belief in the deity of bigness and concentration stems from the Schumpeterian hypothesis expounded about 30 years ago.[11] This hypothesis asserts that the possession of accumulated monopoly rewards, the anticipation of additional rewards in the future, and the security resulting from market power are prerequisites to the assumption of risks and the uncertainties of pursuing innovational activities. The innovations, as defined by Schumpeter, were broad enough to include mergers, new organizations, new advertising campaigns, new products, and new processes. From the point of view of the public interest, only the latter two appear to be particularly relevent.

Recent empirical research by Hamberg, Scherer, Mansfield, Schmookler, Worley, and others suggests that unqualified acceptance of the Schumpeterian hypothesis (and newer interpretations of it) would indeed be a serious mistake.[12] Regarding the assumed compatibility of bigness rather than smallness with inventive output, Scherer finds that ". . . the data suggest that smallness is not necessarily an impediment to the creation of patentable inventions and may well be an advantage."[13] In specific reference to the concentration question, Scherer states that his results imply "that technological output should tend to increase with concentration up to a point, but that it may decline if too much of an industry's output becomes concentrated in the hands of a single dominant seller."[14] In reference to conglomeration or diversification, Scherer finds that " . . . diversification was not per se a structural condition necessarily favorable to patentable invention."[15] Scherer concludes: "These findings among other things raise doubts whether the big, monopolistic, conglomerate corporation is as efficient an engine of technological change as disciples of Schumpeter (including myself) have supposed it to be. Perhaps a bevy of fact-mechanics can still rescue the Schumpeterian engine from disgrace, but at present the outlook seems pessimistic."[16]

The facts indicate that bigness may be inhibiting and that small and medium-sized firms are far more innovative—faster to change, to test new ways, to take risks—than the big corporate colossi. Consider the impressive list of well-known and important inventions presented in Table 4.2. Each was the creative work, not of big corporate laboratories, but of small firms, and even individual inventors—a breed that generally shuns the big bureaucratic organizations. The list developed by Professors Jewkes, Sawers, and Stillerman[17] has been complemented by others[18] who have discovered many additional examples of new products that originated from the work of small firms, sole inventors, or pioneering new entrants into entrenched markets.

The examples are striking and include such things as the incandescent

Table 4.2   Major Inventions Made by Small Companies or Individuals

Air conditioning	Penicillin
Automatic transmissions	Polaroid Land camera
Bakelite	Power steering
Ballpoint pen	Quick freezing
Catalytic cracking of petroleum	Radio
Cellophane	Safety razor
Chromium plating	Self-winding wristwatch
Cinerama	Streptomycin
Cotton picker	Sulzer loom
Cyclotron	Synthetic light polarizer
Domestic gas refrigeration	Titanium
Electric precipitation	Xerography
Electron microscope	Zip fastener
Gyrocompass	Cellophane tape
Hardening of liquid fats	Continuous hot-strip rolling
Helicopter	Crease-resisting fabrics
Insulin	DDT
Jet engine	Shell molding
Kodachrome	Terylene polyester fiber
Magnetic recording	

Source: John Jewkes, David Sawers, and Richard Stillerman, *The Sources of Invention,* New York: St. Martin's Press, 1958, pp. 263–410.

lamp, alternating current, radio telegraphy, the radiotelephone, FM radio, the photoflash lamp, the dial telephone, sound motion pictures, self-developing photography, and electrostatic copying.[19] These inventions stemmed not from the established big firms of industry, but from smaller firms or individuals seeking to "break in" to a market or to expand their position.

An examination of two specific highly concentrated industries dominated by large firms, automobiles and steel, provides additional insight to the significance of the smaller, independent firm in spurring innovation. In autos, most of the basic advances in the past four decades were contributed by relatively small firms. Some examples, together with the name of the innovating firm, are: the all-steel body, Oakland; noiseless rear axles, Packard, with the help of Gleason Gear; the sedan-type body, and subsequently, the low-cost closed car, Hudson; adjustable front seats, Kissell; four-wheel brakes, mechanical and hydraulic, Duesenberg; rubber engine mounts, Nash; automatic spark control, Studebaker; and the natural-grip steering wheel, Hudson. More recent examples include: hydraulic valve lifters, Pierce-Arrow; turn signals, Nash, with help from A. C. Smith; automatic power braking, Pierce-Arrow, with help from Stewart-Warner; making the trunk an integral part of the body, Hudson; spare tire in trunk, Hudson; gear shift on the dash, Reo; overdrive, Studebaker, with help from Borg-Warner; thin-wall Babbitt bearings (enabling higher horsepower), Studebaker and Nash, with help from Cleveland Graphite; power-operated windshield wiper, Studebaker; pressurized fresh-air heating system, Nash; airfoam cushions and the safety hood latch, Hudson; the automobile air-conditioner, Packard; and single-unit body construction, Nash, with help from Budd Company.

A similar pattern exists in steel, where the industry's dominant firms have continually lagged behind their smaller rivals in introducing new products and processes. For example, the oxygen converter is one of the most important advances ever developed in steelmaking. It was invented and used in Europe prior to the Second World War. It was introduced in the United States in the 1950s—not by the big firms, but by McLough Steel, a small, independent firm based in Detroit. A comparable case is continuous casting, a revolutionary process in steel production, which was introduced by ninth-ranked Allegheny Ludlum.

The history of invention and innovation is rich with examples of the key role played by the small organizations or the outsider in stimulating economic and technological progress. The reasons why the small firms have been so creative and the big firms generally so passive are the subject of numerous explanations. However, most reduce to the notion that innovation is so disturbing in its potential impact that it finds its best opportunity in an unbureaucratic environment. Innovations inherently involve risks, and as the size of the organization increases, and the tiers of review multiply, there is a high probability that some member of the chain will turn out to be what C. Northcote Parkinson has called "an abominable no-man."

There is a further explanation of the greater innovativeness of competitively structured industries and markets. When there are a number of participants of different sizes, there is simply a greater probability that innovation will take place. If a new approach to products, services, or pricing does not appeal or occur to one firm, it may to another. The larger the number of firms the more likely it is that a new idea will, like the proverbial spark, find tinder. Creating and preserving a climate favorable to experimentation is critically important to an economy. Such an environment necessitates a number of firms of different sizes aggressively competing for public favor. Increased concentration and bigness may well deaden the prospects for innovation in business and industry, inhibiting its progressivity and suppressing creativity in the process.[20]

Even in the area of labor productivity, a less concentrated structure produces more benefits, as noted by Richard Caves, who stated that " . . . between 1899 and 1955, the industries in which labor productivity rose most sharply were those where levels of concentration *declined*."[21]

BIGNESS AND THE TOP MANAGER'S PAYCHECK

While the evidence suggests that bigness does not necessarily mean higher profits, more efficiency, invention, or innovation, the record does reveal that the top managers of big business firms are rewarded quite handsomely with substantial paychecks. Observers of executive compensation have been telling us for years that top executive income is virtually independent of profitability. For example, McGuire, Chiu, and Elbing conducted a statistical investigation of the correlation between executive incomes, sales, and profits for 45 of the largest 100 industrials, covering the 1953–1959 period. They found that " . . . the evidence presented would seem to support the likelihood that there is a valid relationship between sales and executives incomes as Baumol assumed, but not between profits and executive incomes. . . ."[22]

In another study, Roberts found that the relationship between executive compensation and sales appeared to be stronger than the relationship between compensation and profits.[23] Patton, another student of executive compensation, studied 420 companies for the period 1953–1964 and found: "Company size, of course, is the principal determinant of top executive pay. For every doubling of company size, experience shows that the compensation of top management tends to increase about 20%."[24] Regard-

Table 4.3 Average Chief Executive Remuneration, Age, Service, and Stock Holdings of Top 10 Firms in Selected Business Groups (Ranked by Assets), 1970

	1970 average remuneration	Average age	Average years served With firm	As chief	Average shares owned/ controlled, by value
Big 10 industrials	$338,000	62	31	8	$16,218,000
Big 10 commercial banks	205,000	59	28	4	2,075,000
Big 10 retailing companies	236,000	61	38	5	1,442,000
Big 10 transportation companies	168,000	59	25	7	188,000
Big 10 utilities	166,000	58	27	4	104,000
Big 10 conglomerates	303,000	57	22	7	5,639,000

Sources: *Fortune,* May 1971; and *Forbes,* May 15, 1971.

ing the relationship between profits and executive compensation, Patton states: " . . . the increases between 1953 and 1964 of the companies with the highest paid chief executives (relative to company size) in 1953 were no better than the profit gains turned in by their lowest paid competitors."[25]

The American economy experienced a recession during 1970, and yet an examination of the salaries and bonuses of the chief executives of big business firms reveals an interesting pattern in the lopsided economy. The data on compensation, exclusive of deferred payments and stock options, for the chiefs of the ten largest industrials, commercial banks, retailers, transportation firms, utilities, and conglomerates are presented in Table 4.3.

The average salary and bonus for the industrial chiefs was $338,000, and all held shares in their respective companies with an average value of over $16 million during 1970. The next highest paid group was the conglomerates, where the chief executives of these relatively smaller firms averaged $303,000 for the year, and the chief executive officers held an average of over $5.6 million in stock. The value of the stocks of these particular firms virtually crashed in 1969–1970 after hitting their peak in 1968. Despite this market collapse, the chief executives appear to be bringing home substantial bread while many stockholders are licking their wounds.

The highest paid executive in the United States during 1970 was a conglomerate chief, Harold S. Geneen of International Telephone and Telegraph, with a salary and bonus of $766,755. When asked if chief executive officers are paid too much, Geneen replied: "Maybe if I study this hard enough I'll decide I'm worth $5 million a year and a lot of other guys around here are worth a million each. . . . Somebody recently commented that my objective is to be a million-dollar-a-year man. Wrong. I've set my eye on a *much* higher figure.''[26]

IT&T was ranked eighth in size by *Fortune* and number 132 on net income as a percentage of sales and 133 on net income as a percentage of equity. The rank on earnings per share growth rate for the 1960–70 period was 132, hardly an impressive record on any of these areas of interest to the stockholder.

The officers and directors of IT&T (as a group) received a total remuneration in 1970 of $9,166,721, exclusive of deferred compensation and stock options. As noted in Table 4.4, this is more compensation than the total salary paid the President of the United States, and the Cabinet, plus the 100 United States Senators, the 50 state Governors, the Justices of the United States Supreme Court, the Vice President, and the 50 major regulators combined. These regulators are the Assistant Attorney General in charge of Antitrust; the seven members of the Board of Governors of the Federal Reserve System; the five Federal Trade Commissioners; the Comptroller of the Currency; the five members of the Civil Aeronautics Board; the seven Federal Communications Commissioners; the three members of the FDIC; the five Federal Power Commissioners; the eleven Interstate Commerce Commissioners; and the five Securities and Exchange Commissioners. Adding all the government sectors together, there is still a healthy surplus of over $300,000 remaining in the IT&T account.

Table 4.4 Comparative Remuneration of One Big Business Conglomerate's Officers and Directors and Federal and State Government Officials, 1970

One big business conglomerate:		
Salary and bonuses of 73 officers and directors of International Telephone and Telegraph Company for 1970		$9,166,721
Government:		
President of the United States	$ 200,000	
Vice President of the United States	62,500	
12 Cabinet members ($60,000 each)	720,000	
100 United States senators ($42,500 each)	4,250,000	
50 state governors ($30,000 each)	1,500,000	
9 justices of the Supreme Court Chief Justice ($62,500) and eight Associate Justices ($60,000 each)	542,500	
50 regulators (estimates)	1,500,000	
		$8,774,500

It is interesting to note that in 1973, IT&T was ranked ninth in size by *Fortune* and number 196 on net income as a percentage of sales and 186 on net income as a percentage of equity. The rank on earnings per share growth for the decade 1963–1973 was 315, and the market value of the firm had declined close to a billion dollars from 1970 to 1973. Meanwhile, the total remuneration of the officers and directors had grown to over $11 million, indicating their nests were feathered while the stockholders were being plucked.

It appears that shareholders have been called upon to share their equity positions with top management, in addition to paying salaries and bonuses for the services rendered. In an extensive study of executive compensation patterns conducted by Wilbur S. Lewellan for the 1955–1963 period, it was reported that deferred compensation and stock options combined were worth more than salary over the time period, indicating the importance of the tax laws in the compensation package.[27] The question of the relationship between firm size and top executive pay was tested only tentatively by Lewellan; however, he states that " . . . top executive earnings and employer-company size are directly related . . . a firm's profits seem a somewhat better predictor of the probable magnitude of its senior officers' rewards than do either its assets, its sales, or the market value of its common stock. The connection between executive salaries and bonuses and each of those items is consistently stronger than between the latter and the same individuals' total after-tax remuneration."[28]

BIGNESS AND FAILURE

Another curious but predictable phenomenon in the imbalanced economy was the government action taken to guarantee a bank loan of $250 million for a large industrial firm during the summer of 1971. Congressional action was taken to prevent the failure of a large private firm in the military-industrial complex. Lockheed, a firm with more than 200 former military officers with the rank of colonel or navy captain or above in the executive ranks, received special treatment not generally available to other American firms. Substantial political pressure originating from the office of the President and with the active lobbying support of the Secretary of the Treasury and his assistants (including Charls Walker, former official of the American Bankers Association) led to congressional approval of a guarantee for this private loan held by large banks.

Previous to this event, the large bankers who were creditors to the Penn Central had made a last-ditch attempt to have the government bail out the private rail firm. Only the suddenness of the financial collapse prevented this maneuver. At the time, Congressman George Mahon of Texas mused, "From where I sit, it looks as if we are being asked to bail out the big banks and the big railroad, and the excuse for this is the country cannot afford to let bad business procedures lead to bankruptcy because the bankruptcies might lead to the economic ruination of the country."[29] Since that time, the government has poured substantial funds into this defunct firm.

Big government, big business, and big banking appear to be in an alliance designed to prevent the failure of bigness, in the name of national defense, balance of payments, or employment. IT&T presents an example of using bigness as leverage with the federal government. Following the Hartford Fire Insurance Co. merger, the Justice Department intervened. IT&T argued that it could not divest itself of Hartford without causing harm to the United States economy, the balance of payments, and IT&T investors. The reasoning was simple: once a firm reaches the size of IT&T, any penalty against the firm is also a penalty against the economy. Part of the thinking was that the stock value of IT&T would drop so drastically that it would disrupt the economy.[30] In addition, it was argued that the nation's balance of payments would suffer. IT&T was permitted to keep Hartford and the stock value of IT&T, due to a number of other problems, has dropped drastically, but somehow the economy has managed to survive. However, the lesson is clear, the bigger the firm or loan or violation, the easier it is to get federal aid or subsidy.

Perhaps the old adage should be rephrased to read, "The bigger they come, the harder they fall—*maybe!*" John Cobbs summed up the bigness-failure question in a statement in *Business Week* when he said:

> . . . an increasing number of giant corporations can no longer claim either flexibility or efficiency. They have lost control of their costs, lost their access to capital, misjudged their markets, and diversified into lines of business they do not understand. In desperation they turn to Washington to help, and if they are big enough and shaky enough, they get it. Neither the Administration nor Congress dares allow a major employer to go down the drain—any more than the Kaiser dared to risk one of his expensive battleships.[31]

The problem to the economic system should be clear, that the usual built-in discipline of the system is distorted because of the absolute and relative size and power of certain economic units. The traditional economic outcomes have been diluted and debased for the dubious benefit of a few in what must be identified as another version of a big business welfare program.[32]

THE COSTS OF CONCENTRATION AND BIGNESS

Few people would deny that some economic benefits result from bigness per se. Certainly, large enterprises have made numerous contributions in their time. These benefits have not come without substantial costs, and it is *net* effect of this cost-benefit ratio, as it relates to bigness and concentration, that will receive increasing attention in the future.

While economists have not generated precise data in this area, some costs, as related to particular aspects of the problem, have been estimated. The Washington-based attorney, Ralph Nader, has estimated that the American public is paying about $100 billion a year in excess prices because of the structure and wastes in the economy. In 1970, Frederic M. Scherer estimated the costs of monopoly at 6.2 percent of the gross national product, or $62 billion a year.[33] In the same year, Shepherd concluded that a "conservative estimate of the average effect on efficiency would be 5 percent of costs where market power (concentration) is very high, and 3 percent where it is moderate."[34] Shepherd estimated the total costs to the public to be as much as 5 percent of national income, or close to $50 billion per year at that time.[35]

In addition to the above cost estimates, the inept regulation of major segments of the economy is costing the public many additional billions in excess pricing in transportation, energy, banking, and other basic areas. A national weekly, *Business Week,* estimates the costs to the public at about $130 billion per year or about $2,000 per family. Of this total, $60 billion is allocated to economic regulation with an equal amount for environmental regulation and another $10 billion for health, safety, and product regulations. It is estimated that there are more than 63,000 federal employers with some type of regulatory function. Thus, bigness and concentration have contributed to the growth of a small army of federal regulators attempting to arrive at nonmarket solutions to a variety of problems resulting from an imbalanced industrial order.[36] Even the stockholders of these firms do not appear to reap the rewards of ownership, except in the most serendipitous fashion. The fundamental question—"bigness and concentration for whom?"—appears appropriate.

NOTES

1   John Kenneth Galbraith, *American Capitalism: The Concept of Countervailing Power,* rev. ed., Boston: Houghton Mifflin Co., 1956.
2   John Kenneth Galbraith, *The New Industrial State,* Boston: Houghton Mifflin Co., 1967.

3   See Sidney S. Alexander, "The Effect of Size of Manufacturing Corporations on the Distribution of the Rate of Return," *Review of Economics and Statistics,* vol. 31, no. 3, pp. 229–235, August 1949; William J. Baumal, *Business Behavior, Value, and Growth,* New York: Macmillan, 1959; Norman Collins and Lee Preston, *Concentration and Price-Cost Margins in Manufacturing,* Berkeley: University of California Press, 1968; William T. Crum, *Corporate Size and Earning Power,* Cambridge: Harvard University Press, 1939, p. 226; Ralph C. Epstein, *Industrial Profits in the United States,* New York: National Bureau of Economic Research, 1939, p. 313; Marshall Hall and Leonard Weiss, "Firm Size and Profitability," *Review of Economics and Statistics,* vol. 49, no. 3, pp. 319–331, August 1967; Matityahu Marcus, "Profitability and Size of Firm," *Review of Economics and Statistics,* vol. 51, no. 1, pp. 104–107, February 1969; Joseph L. McConnell, "Corporate Earnings by Size of Firm," *Survey of Current Business,* vol. 25, no. 5, pp. 6–12, May 1945; Richards C. Osborn, "Efficiency and Profitability in Relation to Size," *Harvard Business Review,* vol. 29, no. 2, pp. 82–94, March 1951; and H. O. Stakler, *Profitability and Size of Firm,* Berkeley: Institute of Business and Economic Research, University of California, 1963, pp. 46–52.

4   Marcus, op cit.

5   See John M. Blair, *Economic Concentration: Structure, Behavior and Public Policy,* New York: Harcourt Brace Jovanovich, 1972, pp. 177–185.

6   Ibid., p. 185.

7   Osborn, op. cit., p. 92.

8   See Joe S. Bain, "Relation of Profit Rate to Industry Concentration: American Manufacturing, 1936–1940," *Quarterly Journal of Economics,* vol. 65, no. 3, pp. 293–324, August 1951; Victor Fuchs, "Integration, Concentration, and Profits in Manufacturing Industries," *Quarterly Journal of Economics,* vol. 75, no. 2, pp. 278–291, May 1961; Leonard W. Weiss, "Average Concentration Ratios and Industrial Performance," *Journal of Industrial Economics,* vol. 11, no. 3, pp. 237–254, July 1963; David Schwartzman, "The Effect of Monopoly on Price," *Journal of Political Economy,* vol. 67, no. 4, pp. 352–362, August 1959; Kazuo Sato, "Price-Cost Structure and Behavior of Profit Margins," *Yale Economic Essays,* vol. 1, no. 2, pp. 361–418, Fall 1961; George J. Stigler, *Capital and Rates of Return in Manufacturing Industries,* Princeton, N.J.: Princeton University Press, 1963; Howard J. Sherman, *Macrodynamic Economics,* New York: Appleton-Century-Crofts, 1964, chap. 8; and Norman R. Collins and Lee E. Preston, *Concentration and Price-Cost Margins in Manufacturing Industries,* Berkeley: University of California Press, 1968, and Yale Brozen, "Concentration and Profits," *The Antitrust Bulletin,* vol. 19, no. 2, pp. 381–399, Summer 1974.

9   Collins and Preston, op. cit., p. 116.

10   Brozen, op. cit.

11   Joseph A. Schumpeter, *Capitalism, Socialism and Democracy,* New York: Harper and Row, Publishers, 1942; see especially Chapter 7.

12 See, for example, D. Hamberg, "Size of Firm, Oligopoly, and Research: The Evidence," *Canadian Journal of Economics and Political Science,* vol. 30, no. 1, pp. 62–75, February 1964; Frederic M. Scherer, "Firm Size, Market Structure, Opportunity, and the Output of Patented Inventions," *American Economic Review,* vol. 55, no. 5, pp. 1097–1126, December 1965; Edwin Mansfield, "Size of Firm, Market Structure, and Innovation," *Journal of Political Economy,* vol. 71, no. 6, pp. 556–576, December 1963; Jacob Schmookler, "Bigness, Fewness, and Research," *Journal of Political Economy,* vol. 67, no. 6, pp. 628–635, December 1959; and James S. Worley, "Industrial Research and the New Competition," *Journal of Political Economy,* vol. 69, no. 2, pp. 183–186, April 1961.

13 Scherer, op. cit., p. 1105.

14 Ibid., p. 1117.

15 Ibid., p. 1116.

16 Ibid., p. 1122.

17 John Jewkes, David Sawers, and Richard Stillerman, *The Sources of Invention,* New York: St. Martin's Press, 1958; see especially pp. 263–410.

18 See, for example, David Hamberg, *Essays on the Economics of Research and Development,* New York: Random House, 1966 and Jacob Schmookler, "Inventors Past and Present," *Review of Economics and Statistics,* vol. 39, no. 3, pp. 321–333, August 1957.

19 These examples are from Frederic M. Scherer, *Industrial Market Structure and Economic Performance,* New York: Rand McNally, 1970.

20 I am indebted to Professor Samuel Loescher of Indiana University for providing much of the material presented in this section.

21 Richard Caves, *American Industry: Structure, Conduct, Performance,* 2d ed., Englewood Cliffs, N.J.: Prentice-Hall, Inc., 1967, p. 102.

22 Joseph W. McGuire, John S. Y. Chiu, and Alvas O. Elbing, "Executive Incomes, Sales and Profits," *American Economic Review,* vol. 52, no. 4, p. 760, September 1962.

23 See D. R. Roberts, *Executive Compensation,* New York: The Free Press of Glencoe, 1959.

24 Arch Patton, "Deterioration in Top Executive Pay," *Harvard Business Review,* vol. 43, no. 6, p. 106, November–December 1965.

25 Ibid., p. 114.

26 *Forbes,* May 15, 1971, pp. 186–187.

27 Wilbur S. Lewellan, *Executive Compensation in Large Industrial Corporations,* New York: Columbia University Press, 1968.

28 Ibid., pp. 280–282.

29 See John F. Winslow, "Lets Not Pamper Bigness," *Forbes,* vol. 113, no. 10, p. 81, May 15, 1974.

30 See "Ramsden Report" in Committee on the Judiciary, United States Senate, *Richard G. Kleindienst—Resumed, Part 2,* Washington: U.S. Government Printing Office, 1972, pp. 103–105.

31   John Cobbs, "Ideas and Trends," *Business Week,* p. 16, January 27, 1975.

32   While the federal government also provides aid to some small businesses, during this same time former President Nixon impounded $48 million of the Small Business Administration's direct loan funds. Senator Alan Cranston, chairperson of the Senate Banking Subcommittee on Small Business, estimates that 1,800 small businesses went bankrupt and 10,000 people lost their jobs because of this impoundment. Cranston was also a prime mover in securing the government-guaranteed loan to Lockheed.

33   Scherer, *Industrial Market Structure and Economic Performance,* p. 408.

34   William G. Shepherd, *Market Power and Economic Welfare,* New York: Random House, 1970, p. 196.

35   Ibid., p. 246.

36   See "The Regulators," *Business Week,* pp. 24–28, June 30, 1975.

Part Two

Mergers, Conglomerates, and Performance

This part consists of four chapters which examine various aspects of the corporate merger phenomenon. Periodic waves of combination activity have occurred in the United States since the end of the nineteenth century, contributing to concentration and an array of performance patterns which are both microeconomic and macroeconomic in scope.

Chapter 5 discusses the role of the merger game and various dimensions of these developments. Various aspects of the conglomerate spectacular which added some economic and financial spice to the business scene are examined in Chapter 6. The fundamental and pertinent question "Who wins in the merger game?" is the subject of Chapter 7, which is devoted to an assessment of the impact of these events upon those interested in the outcomes. The concluding chapter (8) presents a case study of an important segment of the petroleum industry and the relative role of multinationalism, merger-active programs, and government policy in the structure, behavior, and performance of this basic industry.

Chapter 5

The Big Get Bigger—The Merger Game

A major contributing factor to the growing imbalance of the economy and the tendency for the big to get bigger is the *merger game*. Of course, internal growth financed by expanding cash flows, particularly during prosperous periods, is a continuous element in the growth process. But reliance on the merger game has been a major contributing factor to the development of lopsided markets and the concentration of substantial economic power in the hands of a relative few. This chapter will highlight the role of the various participants in the merger game.

In nearly every year since 1948, the 200 largest industrial firms have been responsible for about two-thirds of the assets of large firms acquired (firms with $10 million or more of assets). Actually, the big 100 firms accounted for 44 percent of the activity, and the big 200 firms acquired 64 percent of the assets during these two decades. Excluding foreign mergers and joint ventures, the big 200 firms consummated close to 4,000 mergers with combined assets of over $50 billion. Actually the acquired assets are quite a bit higher since data were known for less than 40 percent of the acquired firms. Thus, the merger route has helped the big get bigger and the economy to become more imbalanced in the process.

The big 50 industrial firms acquired $18.4 billion of assets, which is more than three times higher than the $4.8 billion acquired by the firms ranked 51 to 200. This development is at odds with the naïve belief that the existence of the antitrust laws is a major deterrent to merger-induced growth by the largest firms, a subject which will be treated in more detail later.

A graphic presentation in Chart 5.1 shows the share of corporate manufacturing assets held by the 200 largest corporations of 1968 in the selected years 1947, 1960, and 1968. Between 1947 and 1960, these firms'

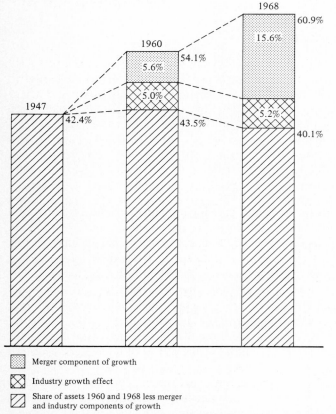

Chart 5.1 Share of assets of 200 largest manufacturing corporations of 1968 and accumulative components of growth; 1947, 1960, and 1968. (*Source:* Bureau of Economics, Federal Trade Commission.)

share of assets rose from 42.4 percent to 54.1 percent. More than half (5.6 points) of the 11.7 percentage points increase is directly attributable to mergers. An additional 5 points are due to the differential industry growth rate.[1] Thus, in this period mergers were more important in the growth of the big firms than the industry effect.

By 1968, the big 200's share of assets had increased to 60.9 percent, or 19 percentage points above 1947. Mergers alone accounted for 15.6 percentage points, and the industry effect accounted for 5.2 percentage points. Thus, if the merger effect is subtracted, the share of the big 200 would have increased only slightly if sole reliance had been on the industry growth effect. It is worth noting that while the industry effect and the merger effect were about equal in the 1947–1960 period, mergers were almost exclusively responsible for the increase in the power of the large firms during the 1960s.

THE MERGER-ACTIVE FIRMS

The use of merger in the growth process of the big 200 industrial firms has not been evenly distributed, since there were varying intensities of activity. In order to determine the relative role of mergers in the growth process, it is necessary to divide the big 200 firms into merger intensity groups[2] (see Chart 5.2). Between 1947 and 1968, the 70 firms which were most active in the merger process increased their share of corporate manufacturing assets from 15 percent to 25.7 percent. Mergers were responsible for 10.1 percentage points and the industry effect contributed about 2.8 points to this rise, indicating that without mergers, the share of these firms would have remained about the same. Subtracting both the merger and industry effects, the share of the firms actually declined from 15 percent to 12.8 percent.

The 74 moderately active firms gained from 12.9 percent to 17.9 percent of the assets. Mergers in this group accounted for almost all the increase, 4.9 percentage points of the difference between the effects.

The remaining least active large firms (56) had the smallest gain, only 2.8 percentage points, with mergers accounting for a mere 0.6 points. With the merger and industry effect removed, the share of these firms remains about the same.

This bit of evidence again confirms the fact that the merger game has been a major contributing factor to the development of the lopsided economy and the rapid growth of particular firms. A brief examination of each distinct wave of mergers and the resulting impact on concentration should emphasize the important historical role of merger activity and how these economic events have put economic power in the hands of the relative few and kept it there over the years.

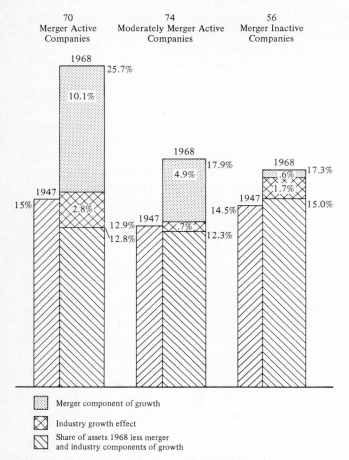

Chart 5.2 Share of assets of 200 largest manufacturing corporations of 1968 and components of growth; 1947 and 1968. (*Source:* Bureau of Economics, Federal Trade Commission.)

MERGER WAVES AND THE STRUCTURE OF THE ECONOMY

The magnitude of merger activity can be measured by the numbers recorded and/or by the amount of assets (or other measures of size) involved. Regardless what measure is used, there have been three clearly evident and distinct waves of merger activity in the economic and business history of the United States.[3] An examination of each major wave and the resulting concentration will help to develop a frame of reference in analyzing these economic events.

The Turn-of-the-Century Wave

An examination of the record of this period leads to the inevitable conclusion that this first giant merger wave set the stage for a highly concentrated economic structure in the United States. It is ironic that this development occurred following the passage of the Sherman Antitrust Act in 1890, which was designed by Congress to prevent just such a happening. Despite congressional intent and the ensuing legislation, business firms found the legislative loopholes and took advantage of the situation.

During the period 1898–1902, there were 2,653 reported mergers, with 1,208 mergers recorded in the year 1899 alone. The merger capitalizations during the period amounted to $6.3 billion, with twin peaks evident in 1899 and 1901. Over $2 billion of activity occurred in each of these years. In relation to the total economy of the period, this was a considerable amount of activity in a brief period of time. According to the 1899 Census of Manufacturers, there were 207,514 manufacturing establishments with a total value of facilities of $11.4 billion, indicating that a few hands had made the grab via the merger route. According to John Moody, there were 318 important industrial consolidations in existence in 1903 with total capital of $7.2 billion and over 5,200 production facilities. [4] Of the total, 236 had been formed in the previous 5 years, accounting for about $6.1 billion of the total capital. [5] Henry R. Seager and Charles A. Gulick, Jr., indicated the relative importance of the large mergers when they observed that " . . . it appears that by 1904 the trusts controlled fully two-fifths of the manufacturing capital of the country." [6] Some individual mergers assumed gigantic proportions such as the United States Steel Corporation combination in 1901 which " . . . reportedly involved 785 plants and $1.37 billion." [7]

There is a general and universal consensus among the various students of the first great wave of mergers that concentration was increased considerably during this period. J. Fred Weston stated that ". . . the merger movement of 1898–1903 resulted in a high degree of concentration in many industries." [8] Jesse W. Markham said that " . . . of all those forces unleashed in the latter part of the nineteenth century that tended to make for larger size and greater concentration, the industrial combination was clearly the most important." [9] George J. Stigler observed, "In this country mergers for monopoly began on a large scale only in the eighties, they reached a minor peak at the beginning of the nineties, and they attained their pinnacle at the end of the century." [10] Of the 92 large mergers studied by Moody, 78 firms controlled 50 percent or more of the output in their industry, and 26 firms controlled 80 percent or more.[11]

The highly concentrated nature of American business which persists to the present time (and is increasing) was the aftermath of this relatively brief but explosive period in American economic history. The vehicle which propelled this development was the corporate merger.

The Late-1920s Merger Wave

An examination of the number of reported mergers reveals that from 1925 to 1931 there were 5,846 mergers, with a peak reached in 1929, when 1,245 mergers were recorded.[12] Measured by these numbers alone, more than twice as many reported mergers occurred during this 7-year period than during the turn-of-the-century wave.

The assets acquired during the 1925–1931 period totaled about $9.6 billion according to a study made by the late Carl Eis. This study also found that the 200 largest firms in 1931 acquired firms with combined assets of $13.7 billion in the 1919–1931 period. The acquired assets of the 200 largest firms equaled 1 percent or more of total industrial assets in each of 7 years—1923, 1925, 1926, and 1928 through 1931.

Gardiner C. Means kept a record of those companies on the list of the 200 largest firms which were acquired by another firm on the same list during the 1922–1929 period. During the 5-year period, 1925–1929, a total of 37 giant firms were merged, involving assets close to $5.4 billion at the time of acquisition. Even this fraction of the total merger activity is close to the total amount of capitalizations recorded in the first major wave.

The share of total manufacturing assets held by the 100 largest industrials rose from 35.6 percent in 1925 to 43.9 percent in 1931. Of this increase, 3.5 percentage points occurred between 1925 and 1929. The assets acquired during this period equaled 3.2 percent of all corporate manufacturing assets. The largest 100 firms' shares rose another 4.3 percentage points between 1929 and 1931, of which about half (2.1 percentage points) is attributable to business combinations.[13]

Mergers appear to have accounted for nearly all the gain of the large firms' share between 1925 and 1929 and about half the increase between 1929 and 1931. The balance of the latter increase was probably due to the failure of many small firms after 1929, according to the Federal Trade Commission.[14] Thus, 2.2 percentage points of the increase reflected a recession-associated development that was corrected upon the return of prosperity, according to the FTC.

On the basis of the available evidence, the late-1920s merger movement was substantial. Even allowing for price-level adjustments and the growth of assets in the manufacturing and mining sector of the economy, the relative volume of activity was considerable.[15] This second great merger wave subsided following the stock market crash and prior to the Great Depression of the 1930s, a situation similar to the conditions prevailing during and after the first merger wave.[16]

The Recent Merger Wave

The recent American merger wave has been the largest and most persistent merger wave in American economic history.[17] Beginning in the mid-1950s, merger activity continued at a relatively high level for 20 years through 1974. Buoyed by a period of prosperity during the 1960s, the peak was reached in 1968, and the wave spilled over to the beginning of the 1970s.

Regardless of the source used to measure the recent merger wave, the magnitude of activity reached an all-time high in both numbers and assets involved. The number of manufacturing and mining firms acquired during the 1955–1973 period was 20,084 as reported by the Federal Trade Commission. About half the mergers (9,557) were consummated in the 1965–1970 period, with the peak of 2,407 reached during 1968.

The number of large firms (those with $10 million and over of assets) acquired during 1955–1970 was 1,439, involving close to $68 billion. In addition, the 200 largest firms[18] were very active, as they acquired or merged 622 of the large firms involving assets of close to $40 billion. Most of this activity was in the 1965–1970 period when the big 200 merged 315 other large firms with assets of over $27 billion, with little government opposition.

From 1960 to 1970, there were 118 industrial firms in the very large ($100 million and over) class acquired with assets of $31.7 billion. The disappearance of these rather large independent decision-making units from an economy with an existing highly concentrated overall structure is distressing. As noted previously, the big get bigger, and one reason is that the 200 largest firms have most of the financial resources. The capital market for corporate assets is quite imperfect and favors this small group of large firms, permitting them to utilize the merger game for growth and/or competitive advantage.

One distinguishing characteristic of the recent merger wave, in addition to its size and longevity, is the comprehensive nature of the activity. In addition to manufacturing and mining, the wave engulfed firms in banking, transportation, insurance, trade, and the services areas of the economy. For example, the Federal Trade Commission recorded 25,425 mergers during the 1960–1970 period using a broader base than manufacturing and mining. In addition, there were 1,483 mergers during the same period involving commercial banks with over $30 billion of assets involved.

Using a more comprehensive approach, W. T. Grimm & Co., reported

26,530 merger announcements during the 1963–1970 period involving many billions of dollars worth of resources. In the year 1968 alone, Grimm reported 4,462 merger announcements with over $43 billion of assets. Another source[19] reported 11,362 mergers in the 1965–1968 period for an annual average of close to 3,000 mergers.

The corporate merger, more than any other economic development, has been responsible for creating the imbalanced economy which has persisted in the United States since the turn of the century. The most remarkable aspect of this development is that three major waves of combination activity have developed following the passage of legislation which presumably was designed to curb this type of economic activity. Each major wave occurred during relatively prosperous times, which are periods when smaller firms have an environment conducive to growth and entrenchment in their respective industries if left alone. Instead of widespread deconcentration in the economy, the merger game has aided oligopolists in maintaining their structured positions in the economy by gobbling up these promising smaller firms and curtailing the "competitive fringe."

THE MOST ACTIVE MERGER MAKERS

The decisions of the few in the American economy are important, as the underlying theme of this book indicates. Again this is apparent when the recent record-breaking merger phenomenon is examined in more depth. As noted previously, the 200 largest industrial firms provided the thrust in the recent merger wave. This is a rather small group of firms; the chief executives of these firms could easily be accommodated at most hotels, motels, and restaurants in virtually any city in the land. Let us divide this group further and examine the role of only 25 firms out of this special group.

Would you believe that the 25 most active merging firms participated in a majority of the activity of the big 200 firms during the 1960s? The 25 most active firms acquired over $20 billion of assets during the brief 1961–1968 period, which is 59 percent of the total assets ($34.2 billion) acquired by the 200 largest manufacturing corporations (see also Chart 5.3). This amount includes assets of firms not only engaged in manufacturing and mining but also firms engaged in wholesaling, retailing, banking, insurance, and other services. The second 25 most active merging firms acquired about $7 billion in assets, or 20 percent of the total amount. Thus, nearly 80 percent of the assets acquired by the 200 largest manufacturing firms were accounted for by the 50 most active firms. The next 50 firms acquired $5.5 billion (or 17 percent), which means that the top 100 merger-active firms were responsible for 96 percent of the activity. Again, the activity is lopsided and can be traced to the activities of a few.

An examination of the first 25 most active firms (see Table 5.1) reveals

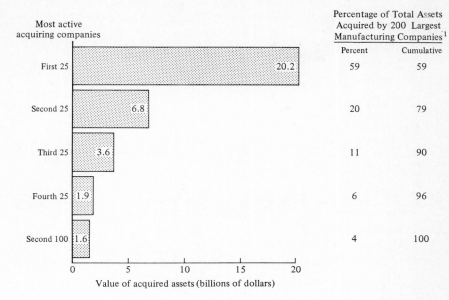

Chart 5.3 Distribution of assets acquired by 200 largest manufacturing corporations 1961–1968. (*Source:* Bureau of Economics, Federal Trade Commission.)

that these firms consummated nearly 700 mergers involving $20.2 billion in assets. This amount is about 150 percent of the total group assets in 1960. Only nine of the group were ranked among the 100 largest industrials in 1960; by 1968 there were 20 of the firms in this group, due mainly to merger activity.

The 25 most merger-active firms can be classified into three general categories: (1) eleven conglomerates, (2) eight petroleum companies, and (3) six firms in the miscellaneous class. The firms in the latter class, notably aerospace and forest products companies, have generally made a few very large mergers displaying a mixture of horizontal and product-extension (or circular) types. The mergers made by these three groups are as follows:

Group	Number	Percentage	Assets (millions)	Percentage
11 Conglomerates	485	70	$10,867	54
8 Petroleum companies	109	16	6,035	30
6 Miscellaneous	101	14	3,325	16
Total	695	100	$20,227	100

Table 5.1 Assets Acquired by 25 Most Active Acquiring Companies among the 200 Largest* Manufacturing Corporations, 1961–1968

Company	Acquisitions 1961–1968 inclusive†		Change in assets of company (millions)			Acquired assets as percentage of change in assets
	Number	Total assets of acquired companies, millions	1960	1968	Change	
Gulf & Western Industries, Inc.	67	$ 2,882	$ 12‡	$ 3,455	$ 3,443	84
Ling-Temco-Vought, Inc.	23	1,901	$ 94	2,648	2,554	74
International Telephone and Telegraph Corp.	47	1,487	.924	4,022	3,098	48
Tenneco, Inc.	31	1,196§	1,734	3,888	2,154	56
Teledyne, Inc.	125	1,026	0‡	1,146	1,146	90
McDonnell Douglas Corp.	8	864	141	1,237	1,096	79
Union Oil Company of California	11	825	734	2,298	1,564	53
Sun Oil Company	3	808	760	2,363	1,603	50
Signal Companies, Inc.	10	770	306	1,228	922	84
Occidental Petroleum Corp.	15	767	7	1,788	1,781	43
Continental Oil Co.	19	686	832	2,537	1,705	40
General Telephone & Electronics Corp.	40	679	2,205	6,157	3,952	17
U.S. Plywood–Champion Papers, Inc.	27	649	210	1,123	913	71
Litton Industries, Inc.	79	609	119‡	1,421	1,302	47
Atlantic Richfield Co.	9	543	820	2,451	1,631	33
North American Rockwell Corp.	6	534	386	1,362	976	55
FMC Corp.	13	497	313	974	661	75
Studebaker-Worthington, Inc.	13	480	164	602	438	100+

General American Transportation Corp.	4	453	414‡	1,204	790	57
Textron, Inc.	50	453	272	892	620	73
White Consolidated Industries, Inc.	28	443	19	620	601	74
Phillips Petroleum Co.	11	440	1,647	2,889	1,242	35
Colt Industries, Inc.	9	437	143	588	445	98
Radio Corporation of America	2	402	816	2,366	1,550	26
Georgia-Pacific Corp.	45	396	295	1,269	974	41
Total 25 companies	695	$20,227	$13,367	$50,528	$37,161	54

Ranks refer to FTC 200 largest manufacturing companies, except where noted, by asset size.

†It should be emphasized that the data shown are compilations based on publicly announced acquisitions of United States and Canadian companies. Foreign acquisitions are not included and asset data are not available for many smaller acquired companies. When a particular company is subject to litigation, it is often found that a number of acquisitions have not been publicly reported. For example, subsequent to the preparation of this table, the Justice Department introduced an exhibit in the IT&T-Hartford hearings (U.S. v. International Telephone and Telegraph Corp. and The Hartford Fire Insurance Company, Civil Action No. 13320) showing IT&T as having made 120 acquisitions from 1961 through 1968. Of this total, 52 were of domestic firms. This number is somewhat larger than the 47 shown above. However, the additional firms included in the Justice list were all small: all had assets of less than $10 million and with one exception had assets of less than $1 million.

‡Including nonconsolidated subsidiaries.

§Tennessee Gas Transmission Co.

The 11 relatively new "conglomerate" firms engaged in 70 percent of the activity of the most merger-active firms and acquired over half the assets (54 percent). The eight petroleum companies acquired 30 percent of the assets. It is worth noting that the 11 conglomerates acquired about one-third of all the assets merged by the 200 largest firms. Thus, a relatively small fraction of the large firms dominated the activity, and the importance of the decisions of a few looms large in the economic spectrum. It is worth noting that while the 11 conglomerates were very active in the merger game, the nonconglomerates were also a dominant force. A more detailed study of the merger-active petroleum firms will be presented in Chapter 8.

Two researchers from the National Industrial Conference Board, Betty Bock and Jack Farkas, have confirmed the merger pattern noted above, that merger is of relative importance as a means of growth for firms moving into the select group of the 200 largest industrial firms. In addition, Bock and Farkas isolated the role of 34 conglomerate firms among the 200 largest firms during the 1958–1967 period and found that " . . . both older and newcomer conglomerates increased their total assets at an average annual rate substantially higher than that of other corporations among the 200 largest of 1967."[20]

THE MAIN STREET TO WALL STREET MOVEMENT

Another dimension of the merger game is the geographical shift in control which results from economic combination activity. Even a cursory examination of the spatial characteristics of the recent merger wave reveals only one real gainer in the geographical merger game—New York.[21] The lopsided shift of economic power to New York, at the expense of the remaining territory, is a significant development.

The New York Activity

All the statistics are swamped by the aggressive activities of firms that headquarter in the Empire State. Data on the number of mergers listed by the leading states and regions are presented in Table 5.2. Two factors stand out: one is that interstate mergers dominated the activity, accounting for 70 percent of the activity. This is to be expected since many firms attempt to diversify geographically, as well as by product line, industry, and so on. The other factor is that the majority of the mergers are consummated by firms headquartered in a relatively few states, with the four leading states (New York, California, Illinois, and Ohio) accounting for 9,600 mergers, or more than half the reported activity. This result may be expected, since these are populous states with most of the nation's industrial, commercial, and financial base.

Table 5.2 Overall Merger Activity by Various Leading States, 1955–1968

	Firms headquartered in state that were acquired			Acquisitions made by firms headquartered in state			Net gain or loss
	Total	By firms outside state	By firms within state	Total	Of firms outside state	Of firms within state	
Nine leading states:							
New York	2,732	1,346	1,386	4,464	3,078	1,386	+1,732
California	2,593	1,541	1,052	2,082	1,030	1,052	–511
Illinois	1,345	910	435	1,829	1,394	435	+484
Ohio	1,105	788	317	1,225	908	317	+120
Pennsylvania	1,103	842	261	1,190	929	261	+87
New Jersey	863	727	136	763	627	136	–100
Texas	854	552	302	822	520	302	–32
Massachusetts	757	578	179	673	494	179	–84
Michigan	755	567	188	644	456	188	–111
Total, nine states	12,107	7,851	4,256	13,692	9,436	4,256	+1,585
Rest of United States	5,787	4,947	840	4,202	3,362	840	–1,585
Total	17,894	12,798	5,096	17,894	12,798	5,096	0
Regions (excluding nine states)							
Northeast (excluding Mass., N.J., N.Y., & Pa.)	702	610	92	555	463	92	–147
North Central (excluding Ill., Mich., & Ohio)	1,630	1,357	273	1,463	1,190	273	–167
South (excluding Tex.)	2,648	2,264	384	1,774	1,390	384	–874
West (excluding Calif.)	807	716	91	410	319	91	–397
Total	5,787	4,947	840	4,202	3,362	840	–1,585

Source: Bureau of Economics, Federal Trade Commission.

Another measure of magnitude which can be used to identify the geographical directions of merger activity is the amount of assets involved. The only available data on this variable are the Federal Trade Commission's records of the merger activity of the 200 largest manufacturing firms. These data are presented in Table 5.3 for the 6 leading states and the remaining 44 states. Again, New York State stands out like a sore thumb, tallying a net gain of 986 firms and assets of over $13.2 billion. The only other states with gains by this measure were California and Ohio, both with small gains. The big losers by this measure were Illinois (minus $2.6 billion) and Pennsylvania (minus $3.6 billion). Michigan also posted a small net loss during the period. It is interesting to note that Illinois had the second largest gain in the number of firms acquired (plus 214), yet was a substantial net *loser* when assets are considered. The remaining 44 states (as a group) were net losers on both counts, an indicated by the number of firms (minus 1,066) and the amount of assets (minus $7.9 billion) involved in the merger activity.

It only takes a brief glance at this table to determine that there has only been one real gainer in the merger game—New York. All the statistics are swamped by the aggressive activities of firms that headquarter in the Empire State. The lopsided activity results in a shift of economic power to New York, at the expense of most of the remaining territory, and is a significant economic development. Certainly merger activity in the recent major wave has contributed to a reversal of a "westward movement" in economic activity, a development which has not been sufficiently recognized.

The Illinois Experience

A more detailed study of close to 2,900 mergers involving Illinois firms during the 1955–1968 period appears to confirm the pattern of direction evident on the national scene.[22] Firms from outside the state merging Illinois firms accounted for 56 percent of the large mergers and 65 percent of the total assets involved in the mergers.

One familiar location stands out in its dominance as the headquarters state of firms that have acquired Illinois firms—New York State, with almost four times as many mergers as the next closest state. Ohio and California lagged behind in importance, followed by Michigan, Pennsylvania, New Jersey, and Wisconsin. There is a predominantly eastward movement of corporate control, with the New York "merger magnet" dominating the activity. Illinois firms acquired more firms in the West and contributed firms to the eastward movement dominated by New York firms.

Table 5.3 Merger Activity of the 200 Largest Manufacturing Corporations, by State and Region, 1948–1968

State	Acquisitions of companies headquartered in state						Total acquisitions by companies headquartered within state		Companies outside state acquired by companies within state		Net gain or loss by state	
	Total		Acquired by companies within state		Acquired by companies outside state							
	Number	Assets (millions)	Number	Assets (millions)	Number	Assets (millions)	Number	Assets (millions)	Number	Assets (millions)	Number	Assets (millions)
Six leading states:												
New York	397	$6,553	179	$4,094	218	$2,459	1,383	$19,781	1,204	$15,687	+986	$+13,228
Michigan	143	1,007	13	114	130	893	83	797	70	683	−60	−210
Pennsylvania	204	5,603	15	241	189	5,362	99	2,000	84	1,759	−105	−3,603
Ohio	225	2,223	52	343	173	1,880	233	2,705	181	2,362	+8	+482
California	433	6,085	138	1,247	295	4,838	456	6,690	318	5,443	+23	+605
Illinois	282	4,556	72	588	210	3,967	496	1,989	424	1,401	+214	−2,567
Total, six states	1,684	26,027	469	6,628*	1,215	19,399	2,750	33,962	2,281	27,335	+1,066	+7,936*
Rest of United States	1,794	22,133	96	1,525	1,698	20,608	728	14,197	632	12,673	−1,066	−7,936
Total	3,478	48,159*	565	8,152*	2,913	40,007	3,478	48,159*	2,913	40,007*	0	0
Regions:												
Northeast (excluding N.Y. & Pa.)	407	4,839	25	313	382	4,526	188	1,883	163	1,570	−219	−2,956
North Central (excluding Ill., Mich., & Ohio)	417	5,024	13	31	404	4,994	143	4,743	130	4,713	−274	−281
South	763	10,666	44	952	719	9,715	266	6,103	222	5,151	−497	−4,563
West (excluding Calif.)	207	1,604	14	230	193	1,374	131	1,469	117	1,239	−76	−1,350
Total regions (excluding six leading states)	1,794	22,133	96	1,525*	1,698	20,608*	728	14,197*	632	12,673	−1,066	−7,936*

*Detail does not add due to rounding. Table excludes 367 acquisitions and $1,423.8 million in assets of companies whose location was not identifiable. It also excludes 63 foreign acquisitions with $593.6 million in assets.
Source: Bureau of Economics, Federal Trade Commission.

The Nebraska Study

A subsequent study of merger activity in Nebraska by Stanley L. Brue confirms the spatial patterns observed at the national level and in Illinois.[23] In discussing the directional flow of corporate control resulting from Nebraska-outstate mergers, Brue observes:

> In the great majority of instances, corporate control flowed into a state with a larger population than that of Nebraska. Furthermore, two of the regions of the United States in which a large portion of all corporate control resided, the Northeast and the Mideast, gained additional decision-making authority at the expense of a state which had relatively little such control. . . . New York gained the largest amount of corporate control during this period. . . . Not only did Nebraska corporate control flow toward larger industrial states, it also tended to flow toward larger urban areas. . . . The outflow of corporate control from Nebraska and from other relatively sparsely populated Midwestern states could have serious economic, social, and political implications.[24]

Thus, the Nebraska pattern confirms the Illinois pattern and indicates a spatial shift in corporate control and capital toward the "merger magnets"—New York and the larger urban areas.

WHY A MERGER GAME?

As noted previously, there is a distinct pattern of merger activity in United States history, with three clearly discernable major waves (see Chart 1.1). Each major wave has developed during periods of relative prosperity accompanied by a buoyant stock market. The primary thrust of a particular merger depends upon whether it is consummated to eliminate a competitor, to broaden a product line, to integrate forward toward consumers or backward toward sources of supply, or for purposes of product or service diversification.

One of the curious aspects of the merger game is why it is so widely utilized during prosperity. Since money has a time value, and a merger with a going concern is a relatively rapid method of achieving an expansion objective, this growth alternative has a special appeal. The problem with this approach is that the payment of premiums is generally necessary to induce cooperation and/or consummation. In addition, there is a certain excitement associated with economic events of this type which appeals to the promoters of the activity. The relative size of the surviving firm is also enhanced, and the leap may be of a quantum nature, depending upon the size of the components. The question of profitability will be discussed in more detail in the next chapters.

The merger game is appealing, and despite the dire consequences which have resulted to individual firms and the economy, the proponents persist. Several years ago, the following statement on mergers appeared during the peak of the recent merger wave:

> A merger is an investment decision that will generally be rationalized on economic grounds, promoted to serve narrow self-interests, and consummated for a variety of noneconomic factors in addition to the usual economic ones. Since the use of merger in the growth process is a hypertonic method of increasing the size of firms, some merging firms will grow faster in size than in profitability. Many firms that have a large percentage of merger-induced growth follow a program of "conspicuous investment" (or expansion) which may have differential effects upon the interests of the various groups involved in these economic events and in the allocation of resources.[25]

Since mergers are consummated in a variety of types and forms, it is difficult to isolate any common overall objective of merger activity. Perhaps the best general objective that can be isolated empirically is size maximization. This is the factor which has appeared rather consistently over time. The growing body of empirical evidence supporting this position will be presented in Chapter 6 for both domestic and international merger activity.

A CONCLUDING NOTE

The big firms continue to get bigger in the imbalanced American economy. A major factor for this continuing development is the *merger game*. Periodic thrusts in activity have developed during periods of prosperity, resulting in major waves of mergers. The impetus is generally provided by a relatively few firms, although substantial activity is widespread, cutting across industry lines in an encompassing development of considerable magnitude. The merger game also contributes to the "Main Street to Wall Street" movement, as the New York merger magnet dominates the action and sucks in control of economic resources from every corner of the nation. Since the use of mergers is a rapid method of adding increments of size, they appear as an attractive method of accomplishing a variety of objectives. The ultimate question of relative success remains and will be examined in the remaining chapters in this part.

NOTES

1 Adjustments were made by the Federal Trade Commission for the industry effect. The asset growth of each of the big firms is normalized to the manufacturing rate of all the big firms. The normalized asset growth of the firms is summed and subtracted from the sum of the unadjusted asset increases of the big firms. The industry effect can be positive or negative.

2 The "merger-active" firms were involved in mergers during the 1948–1968 period with firms having combined assets of at least $200 million. The "moderately active" firms made acquisitions with combined assets in the $50–$199 million range. The "merger inactive" firms made acquisitions of firms with combined assets of less than $50 million.

3 For a more detailed description of each wave, see Samuel Richardson Reid, *Mergers, Managers, and the Economy,* New York: McGraw-Hill, 1968, chaps. 3–6; and John M. Blair, *Economic Concentration: Structure, Behavior and Policy,* New York: Harcourt Brace Jovanovich, 1972, chaps. 11 and 12.

4 John Moody, *The Truth about the Trusts,* New York: Moody Publishing Co., 1904, pp. 453–469.

5 Ibid.

6 Henry R. Seager and Charles A. Gulick, Jr., *Trust and Corporation Problems,* New York: Harper and Brothers, 1929, p. 61. See also Moody, op. cit., p. 487.

7 Jesse W. Markham, "Survey of the Evidence and Findings in Mergers," in National Bureau of Economic Research, Inc., *Business Concentration and Price Policy,* Princeton, N.J.: Princeton University Press, 1955, p. 157.

8 J. Fred Weston, *The Role of Mergers in the Growth of Large Firms,* Berkeley, Calif.: University of California Press, 1953, p. 34.

9 Markham, op. cit., p. 156.

10 George J. Stigler, "Monopoly and Oligopoly by Merger," *American Economic Review,* vol. 40, no. 2, p. 30, May 1950.

11 Moody, op. cit., pp. 453–467.

12 Markham examined the period from 1919–1930, and stated that " . . . nearly 12,000 public utility, banking, manufacturing, and mining concerns disappeared from the American economy through mergers. . . ." Markham, op. cit., p. 168.

13 See data in Federal Trade Commission, *Economic Report on Corporate Mergers,* op. cit., p. 180.

14 Ibid.

15 The wholesale price index was 52.2 in 1899 and 56.1 in 1900, as compared with 100.0 in 1926. See U.S. Bureau of the Census, *Historical Statistics of the United States: Colonial Times to 1957,* Washington, D.C., 1960, p. 117.

16 In the year and a half preceding October 1903, the market value of 100 leading industrial stocks declined by 43.3 percent and there was a recession in 1903.

17 The midyear report by W. T. Grimm & Co., disclosed a slight decline in merger announcements during the first 6 months of 1971; however, merger activity picked up with increased economic activity in the following year.

18 The 200 largest industrial firms for the year 1968.

19 William J. Hudson, Jr., is another collector of merger data.

20 Betty Bock and Jack Farkas, *Relative Growth of the "Largest" Manufacturing Corporation,* New York: National Industrial Conference Board, 1973, pp. 24–36.

21 See Federal Trade Commission, *Economic Report on Corporate Mergers,* Washington: U.S. Government Printing Office, 1969, chap. 7.

22 This material is based upon an unpublished study submitted by the author to the Department of Business and Economic Development of the state of Illinois in 1969.

23 Stanley L. Brue, *Local Economic Impacts of Corporate Mergers: The Nebraska Experience,* New Series no. 43, Lincoln: University of Nebraska, May 1972.

24 Ibid., pp. 64–66.

25 Reid, *Mergers, Managers, and the Economy,* op. cit., p. 128.

Chapter 6

Conglomerate Charades—A Game for a Few

The recent merger wave has been generally billed as a *conglomerate* merger wave. This misconception has served somewhat as a charade relative to a proper understanding of this important economic and business movement. Actually, the misconception developed because of an improper definition made some years ago by a person or a few people at the Federal Trade Commission.

Certainly the initial intention was not to deceive; however, the end result has had this effect. The definition problem is a direct result of an unfortunate practice which began some years ago when the Federal Trade Commission adopted a "residual" approach in classifying conglomerate mergers. Any merger which is clearly not a pure horizontal or vertical merger is designated as a "conglomerate" merger.

The origins of this practice are understandable, since the regulatory agencies were basically concerned (at the time) with the more traditional horizontal and vertical types. The major difficulty of this "residual" approach is that it has resulted in a gross overstatement of the magnitude of the actual number and relative importance of conglomerate mergers in the recent merger wave. For example, data for various periods from 1948–1968 for large firm mergers, utilizing the Federal Trade Commission definitions, are contrasted with the same data defined in a more appropriate manner in Table 6.1. The data in this table were included in a 1969 staff report of the Federal Trade Commission submitted to the Senate Subcommittee on Antitrust and Monopoly which was titled *Economic Report on Corporate Mergers*. Using these data, the report stated:

> Horizontal mergers declined substantially—from 38.8 percent of acquired assets during 1948–51 to 4.2 percent in 1968. But the percentage of geographic market-extension, product extension, and other conglomerate mergers increased from 37.5 in 1948–51 to 88.5 in 1968. This change has been caused in part by current antitrust enforcement policy which has challenged many large horizontal mergers.[1]

This statement is basically misleading since it implies that "conglomerate" mergers dominated recent merger activity and that a contributing factor was antitrust enforcement policy. Both these "myths" will be examined and dismissed later as part of the antitrust "charades" game played with the American public by the regulatory agencies. For example, the same FTC data are presented in Table 6.1 using another set of definitions, and the conclusions that emerge are quite different concerning the major thrust of the recent merger wave.

THE NATIONAL EXPERIENCE BASED ON PROPER DEFINITIONS

Using more realistic definitions, it is observed that both the regular horizontal and the vertical mergers have declined over time. The vertical type did display a spurt during the late 1950s and early 1960s but has declined since 1964. The market extension variety of the horizontal merger type increased during the period until 1968, when these mergers also declined.

The Circular Merger

The one merger type which has dominated merger activity during the recent merger wave is clearly the *circular* merger type, or, using the FTC terminology, the product-extension merger. For some reason, the FTC has neglected the *circular* classification completely, and yet industrial organization economists have identified it and used it in their analyses since the 1920s.[2] The real conglomerate merger has obviously grown in importance

Table 6.1 Distribution of Assets Acquired in Large Mergers by Type and Period, 1948–1968 (Assets in Millions of Dollars)

	1948–1951		1952–1955		1956–1959		1960–1963		1964–1967		1968	
	Assets	Percentage	Assets	Percentage	Assets	Percentage	Assets	Percentage	Assets	Percentage	Assets	Percentage
FTC definition												
Horizontal	210.1	38.8	1,664.8	36.6	1,664.8	27.3	1,187.7	13.3	2,160.0	11.4	525.0	4.2
Vertical	128.7	23.8	523.9	11.5	1,320.6	20.1	2.125.4	23.8	1,691.4	8.9	911.9	7.2
Conglomerate:												
Product extension	202.9	37.5	2,079.3	45.7	2,199.7	35.5	3,383.6	37.8	9,477.0	49.9	4,920.1	39.0
Market extensions			123.9	2.7	325.6	5.0	713.1	8.0	1,649.4	8.7	749.0	5.9
Other conglomerates			162.4	3.6	929.7	14.2	1,533.7	17.1	4,031.0	21.2	5,503.5	43.6
Total conglomerates	202.9	37.5	2,365.6	52.0	3,455.0	52.7	5,630.4	62.9	15,157.4	79.8	11,172.6	88.5
Total	541.7	100.0	4,554.3	100.0	6,567.5	100.0	8,943.5	100.0	19,008.8	100.0	12,609.5	100.0
The relevant definition												
Horizontal:												
Regular	210.1	38.8	1,664.8	36.6	1,791.9	27.3	1,187.7	13.3	2,160.0	11.4	525.0	4.2
Market extension			123.9	2.7	325.6	5.0	713.1	8.0	1,649.4	8.7	749.0	5.9
Vertical	128.7	23.8	523.9	11.5	1,320.6	20.1	2.125.4	23.8	1,691.4	8.9	911.9	7.2
Circular	202.9	37.5	2,079.3	45.7	2,199.7	33.5	3,383.6	37.8	9,477.0	49.9	4,920.1	39.0
Conglomerate			162.4	3.6	929.7	14.2	1,533.7	17.1	4,031.0	21.2	5,503.5	43.6
Total	541.7	100.0	4,554.3	100.0	6,567.5	100.0	8,943.5	100.0	19,008.8	100.0	12,609.5	100.0

Source: Bureau of Economics, Federal Trade Commission.

during the recent wave of activity; however, the relative overall significance was not apparent on a grand scale until the explosive merger year of 1968. This is not to imply that the conglomerate merger type was not significant in the growth of a few individual firms during the recent merger wave (as noted in the previous chapter), but rather that the overall impact was not as obviously visible until the later stages of the recent wave. In addition, a new type of merger developed during the recent merger wave and has not as yet been recognized by the regulatory agencies. This new merger type is discussed below.

The Comprehensive Merger

This is the newest type of merger and is a distinct product of the recent merger wave. It was first identified in the hearing concerned with the request by the Department of Justice for a preliminary injunction in the Northwest Industries–B. F. Goodrich merger case in the spring of 1969. I had the opportunity to serve as a consultant and expert witness for the government in this case. It became apparent to me that the product mix of both firms revealed a pattern indicating that this proposed combination was more than a conglomerate merger. This conclusion developed because there were aspects of *each* merger type in the total combination. For example, both firms were in the chemical business with some overlapping markets, thus there was a horizontal dimension. There were vertical aspects in the transportation and chemical areas. Both firms manufactured pipe and footwear, and product-extension aspects of the circular merger were present since plastic pipe made by Goodrich would add to the steel pipeline made by Northwest through its subsidiary, Lone Star Steel. In the footwear industry, Northwest made boots while Goodrich had a line of rubber footwear. Finally, there were conglomerate aspects because of the unrelated nature of the basic lines of the firms involved, a railroad and tires.

After observing all these relationships, it was evident that this was a special merger type involving each of the traditional types, and thus the term "comprehensive" merger was utilized to describe the proposed merger. If large, diversified firms are permitted to combine in the future, this merger type will become more important due to the increasing diversified nature of many business and financial firms.

In addition, there are other intermediate types of mergers which are not comprehensive, but that include other merger types such as the horizontal merger with vertical aspects, or the conglomerate merger with circular aspects, and so on. This discussion indicates the need for more scrutiny of the relationships between merging firms during periods of intensive diversification.

There are also legal ramifications to the definition problem since many mergers could be challenged on traditional grounds where there is a substantial overlap of products and markets. This situation highlights another important reason for the need of divisional accounting and reporting by firms besides the obvious benefits to stockholders and the financial community arising from more complete disclosure. In addition, there is an obvious need for improvement in the traditional, outmoded, inaccurate, and misleading method used by the Federal Trade Commission to classify mergers. An examination of the FTC definitions of merger types should clarify the current situation and highlight the problem.

The Federal Trade Commission Merger Types

The following definition of merger types has been advanced by the Federal Trade Commission:

> It is traditional to classify mergers into three broad categories: horizontal, vertical, and conglomerate. Conglomerate mergers in turn may be broken into three subcategories: geographic market-extension, product-extension, and "other."
>
> *Horizontal* mergers are those in which the merging companies produce one or more closely related products in the same geographic market; for example, two fluid milk companies in the city of Washington, D.C. *Vertical* mergers are those in which the merging companies have a buyer-seller relationship before merger; for example, an aluminum ingot manufacturer and an aluminum product fabricator. Conglomerate mergers of the *geographic market-extension* type are those in which the acquired and acquiring companies manufacture the same products, but sell them in different geographic markets; for example, a bakery in Washington, D.C., and a bakery in Chicago. Because such mergers frequently closely resemble horizontal mergers, they are sometimes called "chain" horizontals. Conglomerate mergers of the *product-extension* variety are those in which the acquired and acquiring companies are functionally related in production and/or distribution but sell products not in direct competition with each other; for example, a merger between soap and bleach manufacturers. "Other" *conglomerate* mergers involve the union of two companies having neither a buyer-seller relationship nor a functional relationship in manufacturing or distribution, such as a ship builder and an ice cream manufacturer.[3]

While the FTC admits that its classifications are somewhat arbitrary, they are used extensively and give the impression that the recent merger wave has been a "conglomerate" movement, which is a distortion of the actual situation, as noted previously.

MORE REALISTIC DEFINITIONS

For a number of reasons, not the least important being the proper determination of their relative impact, the five types of mergers should be identified in a proper and distinguishable manner which adequately delineates the relationship of the firms involved. The regular *horizontal* merger (which was the leading type in the first two major American merger waves) is the fusion of one or more firms in the same basic industry making and/or selling the same products and/or services. Horizontal mergers may have geographical diversification aspects; that is, firms making and/or selling the same products may be located in different spatial markets (i.e., a bakery serving the New York market acquires another bakery in Chicago). The firms are in the same basic industry, making the same products; however, they are located in and serve different geographic markets.

A *vertical* merger is consummated to provide facilities either to supply goods or services that were formerly purchased (such as a clothing manufacturer buying a textile mill) or to process or distribute goods and/or services at different levels in the distribution process (such as a clothing manufacturer buying a chain of retail clothing stores). Thus the vertical merger may be *backward* or *forward* depending upon the relationship of the firms involved. The manufacturer or distributor buying a source of supply is a backward movement, while the merging of firms directed toward the ultimate consumer is a forward vertical merger.

A *circular* merger involves diversification through product extension; that is, it provides a firm with nonsimilar products and/or services that utilize the same distribution channels. An example would be a razor manufacturer buying a ball-point pen maker, with both products being distributed in the same type of retail outlet. Obviously, the products are nonsimilar since it would be difficult to shave with a ball-point pen, and downright dangerous to attempt to write with a razor, even the safety variety. This product-extension type of merger, the circular merger, has been the dominant merger type in the recent wave as many large firms have engaged in diversification activities by broadening their product lines. This development is an attempt to not only spread risk, but to cement wholesale and retail connections, and to spread advertising, promotion, sales, and research and development expenses over an extended base. The circular merger type is popular with large, established firms searching for a broader arsenal of products and/or services. This development, which began in the industrial sphere, moved into the finance field with the formation of one-bank holding companies on a large scale during the late 1960s in an attempt to accomplish "circular" or concentric objectives.

Easily the most spectacular and highly publicized merger type during the recent merger wave is the *conglomerate* merger. A combination of this type fuses firms with no apparent similarities in producing and/or marketing activities. It is *not* a merger between two bakeries located in different parts of the country. It is *not* a merger between firms where the product line is broadened and the same marketing strategies, channels, and facilities are utilized. Certainly, no one considers a baking company with plants located in various regions or across a nation as a "conglomerate" firm. Nor do we consider a razor blade firm making ball-point pens and deodorants as a "conglomerate" firm. The term "conglomerate merger" should be reserved for combinations of completely unrelated products and/or services.

A fifth type of merger is the *comprehensive* combination involving diversified firms where each of the other merger types is apparent. The evolving industrial patterns should move this less recognized merger type into more prominence in the future when relative prosperity returns.

THE ILLINOIS EXPERIENCE BASED ON PROPER DEFINITIONS

Based upon the alternative definitions of merger types discussed above, close to 2,900 mergers involving Illinois firms were examined and classified.[4] The data are presented in Table 6.2 for the recent period and provide an opportunity to demonstrate the importance of proper definitions. Following the FTC method, horizontal mergers were 7 percent of the total, vertical were 13 percent, and conglomerate mergers were 80 percent.

Using the more accurate alternative method discussed above, horizontal mergers are 26 percent; vertical mergers, 13 percent; circular mergers are ahead by a considerable margin, with 45 percent; and conglomerate mergers accounted for only 15 percent of the total activity. Certainly, the obvious differences would lead to quite different conclusions concerning the preponderence of the various merger types in recent activity.

Since the circular merger category is of such relative importance, an attempt was made in the Illinois study to define more accurate subgroupings. These product-extension mergers were classified as "tight" when the first three digits of the Standard Industrial Classification codes matched for major product lines. Another subgroup was termed "industry-related" when the initial two digits of the four-digit code matched. The term "loose" was used when the firms were classified in different industries but utilized the same distribution channels. The "tight" and "industry-related" circular mergers could be considered horizontal if only the two-digit classifica-

Table 6.2 Classification of Mergers Involving Firms in Illinois by Type of Merger, 1955–1968

Type of merger	1955	1956	1957	1958	1959	1960	1961	1962	1963	1964	1965	1966	1967	1968	Total	Percentage
Horizontal, total	40	46	46	54	47	48	93	51	32	53	48	51	50	86	745	26
Pure	9	14	14	17	12	10	27	6	7	9	12	7	17	31	192	
Geographical diversification	31	32	32	37	35	38	66	45	25	44	36	44	33	55	553	
Vertical, total	16	14	12	13	21	21	27	23	18	27	23	31	44	84	374	13
Forward	9	5	7	4	11	6	12	10	8	17	13	19	26	59	206	
Backward	7	9	5	9	10	15	15	13	10	10	10	12	18	25	168	
Circular, total	60	60	77	63	83	87	94	89	90	93	86	107	143	174	1,306	45
Tight	5	10	7	8	12	4	10	5	12	4	6	7	7	12	109	
Industry-related	18	20	28	25	29	33	30	37	24	43	31	42	42	47	449	
Loosely related	37	30	42	30	42	50	54	47	54	46	49	58	94	115	748	
Conglomerate	12	11	10	15	17	10	22	14	14	14	45	50	66	134	434	15
Unknown	6	—	—	—	—	2	11	—	2	5	17	—	—	1	34	100*
Total	134	131	145	145	168	168	237	177	156	192	219	239	303	479	2,893	
Percentage distribution																
Total*	100	100	100	100	100	100	100	100	100	100	100	100	100	100		
Horizontal	30	35	32	37	30	30	39	30	20	28	22	21	16	18		
Vertical	12	11	9	9	12	12	11	11	12	14	11	13	11	18		
Circular	45	46	50	43	49	52	39	48	58	48	39	45	47	36		
Conglomerate	9	8	7	10	10	6	9	8	10	7	21	21	22	28		
Unknown	4	—	—	—	—	1	—	—	1	3	8	—	—	—		

*Details do not add to total in some cases due to rounding.

Source: Samuel Richardson Reid, "Mergers in Illinois," unpublished report, Springfield: Department of Business and Economic Development, State of Illinois, 1970.

tions are utilized. Thus, the definition problem as related to merger types is important and should not be underestimated, since the results may vary substantially depending upon the relationships of the firms involved.

An examination of the Illinois merger data suggests that the conglomerate merger (when properly defined) is *not* as predominant as it would be using the "residual" approach. It is obvious that conglomerate mergers increased in number and as a percentage of total activity during the 1965–1968 period. The Illinois data reveal that 52 percent of the mergers were interindustry (conglomerate plus the "loose" circular mergers) and 28 percent were conglomerate during 1968. This compares favorably with the findings of W. T. Grimm & Co., for national activity during 1968. Grimm classified 59 percent of all mergers as interindustry and 16 percent as conglomerate acquisitions in 1968. These findings are at odds with the FTC statistic that 88.5 percent of the mergers were conglomerate during the same year.

The approach in this chapter is not intended to be iconoclastic, but rather to focus attention more sharply on the recent merger problem and the fact that appropriate definitions are important for a proper perspective of what is happening in the economy. It is clear that the various regulatory and enforcement agencies which are responsible for compliance with the existing statutes could have taken considerable steam out of the recent merger wave. This could have been accomplished by strictly enforcing the *existing* laws related to the traditional horizontal, vertical, and circular mergers rather than hiding behind the belief that most of the mergers were conglomerate and waiting for a Supreme Court decision on the legality of mergers of this particular type. This critical problem will be discussed in more detail later; however, there are enough precedents in existing law (including the Procter & Gamble–Clorox decision) to aid the regulatory and enforcement agencies in protecting the public interest.

FURTHER EVIDENCE—THE INDUSTRIAL PATTERNS

An examination of the dominant industries in each of the three major waves reveals that the basic industries involved are virtually the same. This fact tends to confirm the finding that there are some common threads to be found in each merger movement and that growing conglomeration has not as yet vastly altered the prevailing industrial relationships. This finding also indicates that antitrust enforcement and regulatory agency surveillance could be directed at particular industrial groupings in a more productive manner.

The leading industries in merger capitalization during the turn-of-the-century merger wave were primary metals, food, transportation equipment, nonelectrical machinery, tobacco products, chemicals, and fabricated metals.[5] During the late 1920s merger wave, the leading industries ranked by merger value were primary metals, petroleum products, food, chemicals, transportation equipment, nonelectrical machinery, and fabricated metal products.[6] During the recent merger wave, the Federal Trade Commission data reveal the leading industries for the period 1948–1968 to be food, paper, chemicals, petroleum, nonelectrical machinery, transportation equipment, and primary metals.[7] These seven industries accounted for nearly two-thirds of the total acquired assets of large firms.

Each wave has been dominated by basically the same industries, and leading industries ranked by the industry of the *acquiring* and the *acquired* firms are the same. This additional evidence indicates and reflects the circular (or product-extension) characteristics of the recent merger wave rather than the much-publicized conglomeration aspects.

THE CONGLOMERATE FIRM—A FORM OF CONSPICUOUS INVESTMENT

While most of the mergers during the recent major wave have been of the *circular* variety, the apparent increase in the use of the pure conglomerate merger has resulted in the expansion and development of so-called conglomerate firms. Most of these newer conglomerates have grown to a relatively large size through utilization of mergers and acquisitions of unrelated firms. These newcomers to the ranks of big business enterprise have generally received their impetus from a dominant individual who engineered numerous financial deals in the process. Some of these individuals were flamboyant types, and thus they attracted considerable attention from the financial and general press, reminiscent of the colorful merger promoters in an earlier era.

The almost universal collapse of the "conglomerate" firms, which occurred at the end of the 1960s, developed so swiftly and with such uniformity that the business and financial community has not yet fully realized the significance of the development. During most of the decade the media, led by *Fortune* magazine, were helping to promote the conglomeration movement by devoting articles and editorial space to the active encouragement of diversification and conglomeration. Investment and commercial bankers, investment advisers, management consultants, some economists, and others were extolling the merits of so-called free-form management and referring to the conglomerates as the "firms of the future" and the "forerunners of the business enterprise system." One conglomerate, Gulf & Western, even adopted the futurist motto: "The 21st Century Company."

The most distressing aspect of the endorsement and encouragement process by the media and others is that conglomeration was so enthusiastically pursued despite the fact that the evidence indicated scant justification for the movement. As an example, in the same issue that *Fortune* devoted an editorial to making a case for conglomerates by praising these firms and referring to the single-product firm as "stuck in cement," it was also reported that the performance of single-product firms (in terms of earnings-per-share growth) was superior to that of the conglomerates.[8] My personal reaction to the *Fortune* editorial appeared in 1968, at the height of the development as follows: "Perhaps it is better to be stuck in cement than in cement, glue, tar, gum, girdles, revolving doors, elevators, mousetraps, molasses, and cells of various types (even the detention variety)."[9]

What Is a Conglomerate Firm?

It is obviously important to properly identify the particular firms which are "conglomerates" in order to determine their relative performance and to assess their impact upon the structure of the economy. Some firms have been quite vocal in their attempts to avoid being tagged a "conglomerate firm," particularly in the current period when this special type and form of diversification has proved to be conspicuously less than successful. Thus, proper definitions are necessary in order to delineate these particular firms from the mainstream of the business community.

A number of definitions evolved in recent times ranging from "a mutual fund with smokestacks" to "the principal gobblers of assets and being at the heart of a fundamentally new economic system which at once resembles traditional private enterprise and the corporate state of fascism."[10] In addition, the president of Gulf & Western related one definition, that "a conglomerate is a kind of business that services industry the way Bonnie and Clyde serviced banks." There is an element of truth in each of these approaches; however, the more professional definitions should be explored.

The Federal Trade Commission has passed along the following definition: "A conglomerate firm may be defined as a company engaged in a number of industrial activities serving more or less distinct markets."[11] Again, this government regulatory agency has confused the issue, although it has remained consistent since it goes on to say that "their conglomerate activities may have taken the form of serving numerous geographical markets in a single line of products or various product markets within a broad industry context."[12] The consistency is that the FTC again confuses the situation concerning the proper definition of a "conglomerate merger." As illustrations of conglomerate firm activities, the FTC states:

For example, large dairy companies are both multi-product and multi-geo-graphic market firms. They produce and sell various product lines within the dairy business and they also serve different local and regional markets. Large steel companies produce and sell a variety of steel products having distinctly different markets. Leading firms in the electrical and chemical industries supply numerous markets within their respective industries.[13]

The Federal Trade Commission definition is obviously inadequate as well as inaccurate for properly identifying conglomerate firms. Most large firms would fit this definition. In their own study of merger-active firms the FTC distinguished between "conglomerates" and petroleum and "others," all of which would fit their definition of a conglomerate firm.

There are a number of other definitions, such as that proposed by Neil H. Jacoby of UCLA, who has stated that "'Conglomerate' is used herein to mean a business corporation producing products or services of several industries that are unrelated with respect to raw material sources, product development, production technology, or marketing channels."[14]

In discussing the economics of conglomerate growth in a paper presented in April 1969, the following definition was utilized: " . . . a 'conglomerate firm' is considered as a 'portfolio corporation' engaged in a variety of nonrelated business activities which may be centralized and/or decentralized within the firm structure. The critical variable in determining a conglomerate firm is the relationship of the various activities."[15] It should be apparent that proper definitions help to identify the particular population of firms in this unique category.

The Conglomerate Firm Population

Prior to examining the recent performance results of the conglomerates, it is worth noting the relatively small population of firms of this distinct type among the total population of business firms. Certainly, if the recent record-breaking merger wave was predominately conglomerate, as the Federal Trade Commission and others would lead us to believe, then the period of prolonged and intensive activity should produce a sizable number of conglomerate firms.

An examination of the evidence leads one to quite the opposite finding, that the number of conglomerate firms is actually quite small relative to the total number of firms in the economy and certainly relative to the vast amount of publicity they have received in the past few years. For example, *Value Line* has identified 15 firms as conglomerates in its surveys. The Stone study uncovered only 15 conglomerates out of *Fortune's* 200 largest firms for 1967.[16] In the Federal Trade Commission study of the 25 most merger-active firms for the 1961–1968 period, less than half (11) were termed by the agency as conglomerate firms. The recent *Forbes* survey revealed only 10 firms in the conglomerate category out of over 550 firms studied, and another 37 firms in their agglomerate group.[17] Thus, the combined groups are still less than 10 percent of the large firms surveyed. The largest number to appear is the 63 conglomerate firms identified in the Weston-Mansinghka study.[18] Certainly, there have been many newer and smaller firms which have been lured into the conglomeration game in recent years; however, the fact remains that when these firms are viewed against the total profile of American business, the number is considerably less than one would expect from the vast publicity given them by the media.

The relatively small number of conglomerates is surprising to not only the casual observer, but also to the seasoned veterans on the business scene. A member of the Board of Editors of *Fortune,* Gilbert Burck (with over 30 years of service and 250 articles about business to his credit), admitted to me that his extended study of conglomerates in the latter part of 1966 uncovered the same finding.[19] Even at that point in time, when *Fortune* was on the conglomerate bandwagon, Mr. Burck admitted that he had found only three of these firms which appeared to be successful. Considering the relatively long period of prosperity, this was an extremely small number of firms.

In summary, the conglomerate firm must be viewed as a special case. These firms are a definite and small minority in the business population and they have received a disproportionately large amount of publicity in recent years. This discussion in no way implies that the impact of these firms has not been substantial, even considering the small population. The situation is nothing more than an extension of the principle that unusual events, groups, people, firms, etc., are more newsworthy than the ordinary. Those who go about their daily business seldom are considered newsworthy.

THE COLLAPSE OF CONGLOMERATES—THE STOCK MARKET TEST

Of obvious interest to observers of the recent merger movement and its conglomeration aspects is the relative *performance* of firms which have played a leading role in this development. As noted previously, the major research in this area casts strong doubts that these firms have operated in the best interests of their shareholders since *size maximization* appeared more dominant than *profit-to-shareholder maximization.*

Despite this evidence, the various proponents of mergers and con-glomeration led the public to believe that not only should superior performance result in prosperous times, but that stability would be achieved in more volatile periods due to the diversified character of these special firms. The stock market decline and recession in 1969–70 provided an excellent opportunity to test the performance of these firms. The height of prosperity and high stock market indexes were reached in 1968. Thus, an examination of the 1968–1970 period will determine the impact of economic conditions on the stability of performance of the conglomerates as measured by stock prices during the 1969–1970 recession.

Chart 6.1 displays the performance of the conglomerate firms and the so-called blue-chip firms. The decline of the conglomerates listed in Table 6.3 is substantial. In 1968, the Dow Jones industrial average rose to a high of nearly 1,000, a gain of about 25 percent over the 1967 low. The conglom-

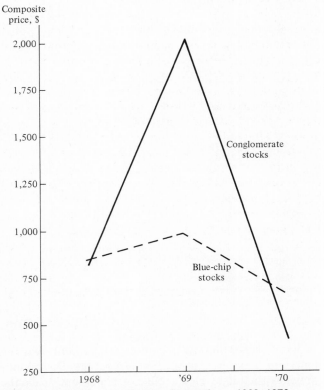

Chart 6.1   High-low stock price fluctuations, 1968–1970.

Table 6.3   Relative Stock Price Performance of Conglomerate Firms, 1968–1970

Firm	1967 low	1968 high	1969–1970 low	Percentage drop, 1968–1970
AMK Corp.	13	105	12	87
ATO	26	74	6	90
AVCO	15	65	9	86
AVNET, Inc.	12	51	6	88
Bangor Punta	24	61	6	89
City Investing	22	69	11	82
Colt Industries	19	66	13	81
Dresser Industries	28	43	22	49
General Host	16	39	7	82
Gulf & Western	30	66	10	83
Indian Head	19	46	14	70
IT&T	36	60	31	49
Kidde (Walter)	46	87	15	83
Kinney National	26	65	21	68
LEASCO Data	12	54	7	87
LTV	49	132	8	93
Litton	80	105	16	85
Loew's	11	63	16	75
Maremont	18	29	7	76
National General	9	46	9	80
National Industries	3	25	4	84
Ogden	16	52	7	87
Penn Central	52	72	6	92
Rapid American	9	46	7	85
Republic Corp.	5	76	8	90
Studebaker Worth	35	61	35	43
Teledyne, Inc.	40	72	13	82
Textron, Inc.	25	45	15	67
Transamerica	29	58	12	80
U.S. Smelting	45	99	21	79
White Consolidated	36	36	8	78
Whittaker Corp.	14	47	5	90
Total	820	2015	387	81

Source: Stanley C. Vance, *Managers in the Conglomerate Era,* New York: Wiley-Interscience, 1971, p. 6.

erates skyrocketed to more than 2,000, for a gain of 150 percent over the 1967 low. Subsequently, in about the same time span, the Dow Jones industrials tumbled to below the 630 level, a decline of 37 percent, while the conglomerates plummeted from the 2,000-plus high to the 387 level, or a

Table 6.4 Market Price Performance of the FTC Merger-active Conglomerates, 1968–1974 and 1970–1974

Eleven merger-active conglomerates	Five-year market price change 1970–1974	Total market value (millions)		Percentage change total market value 1968–1974
		December 1968	December 1974	
Gulf & Western	17.3	$ 877	$ 310	(−64.7)
LTV	(−59.1)	453	77	(−83.0)
IT&T	(−75.3)	3,688	1,381	(−62.6)
Teledyne, Inc.	(−73.2)	1,239	167	(−86.5)
Litton Industries	(−88.5)	1,979	122	(−93.8)
General Tele. & Elec.	(−42.9)	4,604	2,062	(−55.2)
Gen. Amer. Transp.	(−16.4)	561	351	(−37.4)
White Consolidated	(−56.9)	365	91	(−75.1)
Textron, Inc.	(−49.3)	1,177	400	(−66.0)
Colt Industries	(−1.0)	411	160	(−61.1)
FMC Corp.	(−51.0)	1,262	383	(−69.7)
Total	. . .	$16,616	$5,504	(−66.9) average

Source: Forbes, "Annual Report on American Industry," January 1, 1969 and January 1, 1975.

drop of nearly 81 percent. Thus, a kind of "reverse synergy" took place rather than the predicted stability.

Another indication of the conglomerate collapse is apparent in the performance patterns of the 11 "new" conglomerates among the 25 merger-active firms identified by the Federal Trade Commission for the 1961–1968 period. Data related to market price change for these firms in the 1970–1974 period and the change in total market value of these firms in the 1968–1974 period are presented in Table 6.4.

The median decline for these conglomerates was 51 percent, or more than double the 25 percent decline in the Dow Jones industrial average. Another striking result relates to the total market value of these firms. Various theorists of conglomeration have stressed the reduction of risk by diversification as among the attributes of this movement,[20] yet the total market value of these merger-active firms declined from $16.6 billion at the end of 1968 to only $5.5 billion at the end of 1974. A decline of over $11 billion for these 11 firms is truly remarkable by any standard. The total decline in market value represents a loss to the shareholders of an average of $30 million for each conglomerate officer and director in 1974.

It is ironic that the 11 merger-active conglomerates merged assets of other firms valued at almost $11 billion during the 1961–1968 period and suffered an equivalent $11 billion loss in total market value in the post-

merger-active 1968–1974 period. This is a classic case of synergistic schizo-
phrenia.

While the stockholders of the conglomerates were generally experiencing a much higher than average shrinkage in the market value of their
holdings, the total compensation of the officers and directors was increasing. For the 11 merger-active conglomerates identified by the Federal Trade
Commission, officer and director compensation increased from $28 million
in 1970 to over $34 million in 1973. In only 1 of the 11 firms was there a
decline in officer and director compensation, and this resulted from a
substantial thinning of the ranks.

A CONCLUDING NOTE

While a relatively few conglomerate firms made a substantial impact on the
American economy during the 1960s, this development has tended to
obscure other relatively important basic changes taking place in the imbalanced economy. For example, product-related (circular) mergers have
consistently dominated the merger activity. Since most of the conglomerate
firms have not achieved the advantages claimed for them by their ardent
proponents, the investing public has experienced another type of charade
as evidenced by shrinking values. Conglomerate charades have been a
special characteristic of the imbalanced economy in recent years, obscuring
and diverting attention away from the basic nature of the structure of the
American economy.[21] Again, the hands of a few leave their fingerprints on
the economic scene.

NOTES

1 Federal Trade Commission, *Economic Report on Corporate Mergers,* Wash-
   ington: U.S. Government Printing Office, 1969.
2 For example, see Harvey A. Toulin, *Millions in Mergers,* New York: B. C.
   Forbes, 1929, chap. 5; William R. Basset and J. Haywood, *Operating Aspects
   of Industrial Mergers,* New York: Harper & Brothers, 1930, chap. 2; Harry W.
   Laidler, *Concentration of Control in American Industry,* New York: Thomas
   Y. Crowell Co., 1931, p. 444; and Charles S. Tippetts and Shaw Livermore,
   Business Organization and Control, 2d ed., Princeton, N.J.: D. Van Nostrand
   Co., Inc., 1941, p. 481.
3 Federal Trade Commission, *Economic Report on Corporate Mergers,* op. cit.,
   pp. 59–60.
4 This classification was done as part of a study on Illinois merger activity
   completed by the author for the Department of Business and Economic Development of the State of Illinois.

5 See Ralph L. Nelson, *Merger Movement in American Industry, 1895–1956,* Princeton, N.J.: Princeton University Press, 1959, p. 45.
6 See Carl Eis, "The 1919–1930 Merger Movement in American Industry," *The Journal of Law and Economics,* vol. 12, no. 2, p. 276, October 1969. The data are for the 1926–1930 period.
7 Federal Trade Commission, *Economic Report on Corporate Mergers,* op. cit., p. 64.
8 See *Fortune,* February 1969.
9 Samuel Richardson Reid, *Mergers, Managers, and the Economy,* New York: McGraw-Hill, 1968, p. 200.
10 This remark is attributed to H. L. Neiburg; see Robert Dietsch, "Who Owns What?" *The New Republic,* February 22, 1969, p. 14.
11 Federal Trade Commission, *Economic Report on Corporate Mergers,* op. cit., p. 265.
12 Ibid., p. 267.
13 Ibid.
14 Neil Jacoby, "The Conglomerate Corporation," *The Center Magazine,* vol. 2, no. 4, pp. 40–53, July 1969.
15 See Samuel R. Reid, "Conglomerate Growth: Consistency with Economic Theory of Growth," in Leon Garoian, *Economics of Conglomerate Growth,* Corvallis, Ore.: Oregon State University, November 1969, p. 45.
16 See James Stone, "Conglomerate Mergers: Their Implication for the Efficiency of Capital and the Theory of the Firm," unpublished thesis, Harvard University, 1969, pp. 10–11.
17 See *Forbes,* "Dimensions of American Business," Annual Directory Issue, May 15, 1971.
18 J. Fred Weston and Surenda K. Mansinghka, "Tests of the Efficiency Performance of Conglomerate Firms," *The Journal of Finance,* vol. 26, no. 4, pp. 919–936, September 1971.
19 Mr. Burck was personally surprised to find so few firms in the category since the recent merger wave has been termed the "conglomerate" merger wave by the regulatory agencies and others, including *Fortune.*
20 See, for example, Dennis C. Mueller, "A Theory of Conglomerate Mergers," *The Quarterly Journal of Economics,* vol. 83, no. 4, pp. 643–659, November 1969; John Lintner, "Expectations, Mergers, and Equilibrium in Purely Competitive Securities Markets," *The American Economic Review,* vol. 61, no. 2, pp. 101–111, May 1971; Wilbur G. Lewellan, "A Pure Financial Rationale for the Conglomerate Merger," *The Journal of Finance,* vol. 26, no. 2, pp. 521–537, May 1971; H. Levy and M. Sarnot, "Diversification, Portfolio Analysis and the Uneasy Case for Conglomerate Mergers," *The Journal of Finance,* vol. 25, no. 4, pp. 795–802, September 1970. The theoretical aspects of these studies has been challenged by Harold Bierman, Jr. and Joseph L. Thomas in "A Note on Mergers and Risk," *The Antitrust Bulletin,* vol. 19, no. 3, pp. 523–529, Fall 1974.

21 For an interesting discussion of the conglomerate merger situation, see John F. Winslow, *Conglomerates Unlimited: The Failure of Regulation,* Bloomington: Indiana University Press, 1973.

Chapter 7

Who Wins in the Merger Game?

While the merger game is a significant contributor to the imbalanced economy, there are various aspects of the game which are worthy of note. The merger effect can be viewed as a substantial contributor to the concentration of assets, as well as a rapid method of explosive growth in the size of individual firms. The economic consequences of concentration are well known and are beginning to receive renewed attention. The merger effect upon firm size and the relative postmerger performance have not generally been sufficiently recognized by observers and participants in the American business and economic scene. The vast amounts of periodic combination activity attest to this fact of economic life.

Several years ago, in the early stages of the recent merger wave, a paper was presented to the Midwest Economic Association meeting in Chicago which asked a pertinent question in its title—"Mergers for Whom—Managers or Stockholders?"[1] The dichotomy was intentional, since many merging firms grow rapidly through the addition of existing assets to their structure. In addition, large firm size generally means higher executive incomes and more power and prestige for the managers of these firms, at least in the short run. If these investments were rational and efficient, then the owners of the firm (the shareholders) should benefit, in addition to the managers. Income and wealth should be improved relative to alternative forms of investment made by the managers of the merging firms. Employees and others, including the general public, also have a stake in the outcomes of these events. The important question, then, is: Who are the real winners in the merger game?

THE RELATIVE SUCCESS OF CORPORATE MERGERS

It is an interesting fact that a variety of people studying the performance of merging firms, in widely differing time periods and utilizing various statistical methodologies, have almost universally reached the same general conclusion about the relative success (or lack of it) of the merger alternative in the growth process.

Turn-of-the-Century Merger Studies

The best known and most widely quoted study of the performance of mergers during the turn-of-the-century merger wave was by Arthur Stone Dewing, who selected 35 consolidations that were promoted and consummated between 1893 and 1902.[2] Dewing reported three major findings, as follows: first, the earnings of the constituent companies before consolidation were nearly a fifth greater than the earnings of the merged firms for the first year after consolidation, and between a fifth and sixth greater than the average earnings of the 10 years following the merger. Second, promoters' estimates of probable earnings were 150 percent of the actual earnings of the first year, and 200 percent of the actual average earnings during the decade following the consolidation. Third, after sufficient time had elapsed to permit the consolidation to perfect its organization and achieve other anticipated economies, earnings actually diminished, since the earnings of the first year were 7 percent more than the earnings of the tenth year after the consolidation.

Another extensive study of the relative success of mergers was made by Shaw Livermore, whose sample included 328 firms that had merged during the 1890–1904 period.[3] Of the 156 firms classified in the primary group (those with a high degree of market control), Livermore judged less than half (48.7 percent) as successes. His second group contained 172 firms (those which did *not* achieve a high degree of market control), and again Livermore judged less than half (48.4 percent) as successful.

The National Industrial Conference Board conducted a study of the earnings of the 48 consolidations that had a continuous existence from their inception until 1914.[4] The general conclusions drawn from the NICB survey of the record of earnings of these surviving consolidations were these: when whole industries have been bogged down in stagnation, the mergers have been unable to escape the prevalent drift toward ruin; in new industries experiencing rapid growth, the mergers have participated in the general prosperity; the consolidations have *not* been able to avoid sharp declines of profits in years of general business decline; when consolidations have been handicapped by an unmanageable financial structure, they have been unable to adjust to new situations; and business mergers offer no substitute for competent management.

Recent Merger Wave Studies

The first major study comparing the performance of merging firms and nonmerging firms in the industrial sector during the recent wave was originally presented at the Midwest Economics Association meeting in the spring of 1964, and later presented before the Senate Subcommittee on Antitrust and Monopoly.[5] This statistical study included a sample of 478 large industrial firms which were separated in groups depending upon the intensity of their merger activity during the 1951–1961 period. The underlying hypothesis of this study was based on the Berle and Means observations regarding the separation of control from ownership and changes in corporate behavior and performance stemming from this independence.[6] The results of the tests indicated that the interests of managers and stockholders in these large publicly held firms tended to be more independent or conflicting rather than complementary, as was generally supposed.

The same pattern was revealed when nonmerging firms were compared with 430 merging firms following various types of growth-by-merger strategies (i.e., horizontal, vertical, circular, and conglomerate).[7] Merging firms (particularly the conglomerates) clearly had the largest growth in the size-related variables (sales or revenues, assets, and employees),[8] while the nonmerging firms displayed a superior performance in the profits-to-stockholder variables.

Another study of the relative success of merging and nonmerging firms in the current period was made by Eamon M. Kelly.[9] This study compared 20 matched pairs of firms in the same industry which had merged (Group A) with others with little or no merger (Group B). Kelly's nonparametric tests revealed that half the firms in each group led in the increase of market price of common stock. The "nonmerging" firms led in rate of return, earnings per share, market price of common stock, and profit margin. The merging firms led in price/earnings ratio and capital turnover (net sales per share of common stock). Kelly's findings suggest that merging firms maximize sales per share rather than earnings per share.

Joel Segall made a study of the profitability of 58 mergers in the 1950–1959 period involving firms listed on the New York Stock Exchange.[10] Segall examined changes in stockholder wealth positions as measured by stock price changes and cash dividends. The firms were studied before and after the date 6 months prior to the merger announcement. The study revealed only slight evidence that the mergers were profitable when measured in this manner. Puzzled by these findings, Segall stated:

> It may be that more powerful tests will show that mergers are profitable to somebody over some period when measured in some fashion. It seems doubtful, though, that mergers will ever be, on the average, extremely profitable. The difficulty is that we can continue to see mergers in large numbers all about us. How are mergers to be explained if they are not profitable?[11]

A more recent study of the profitability of mergers is contained in a dissertation by Eugene O. Poindexter, who studied a sample of 134 mergers formed between 1956 and 1963 through the exchange of common stock or securities convertible into common stock, and a sample of 111 nonmerged companies in the same industries in the identical time period.[12] Poindexter measured the rates of change in the average earnings per share 5 years before and after merger relative to the rates of change in the average earnings per share of a sample of other firms in their respective premerger industries. An alternative method of determining profitability was utilized which measured the percentage increases or decreases in the average market values of the shares of common stock 3 years after merger relative to the average market values 3 years prior to merger as compared with changes in the average market values of the shares of common stock of a sample of other firms in their same industry. An examination of the coefficients of determination provided by the regression analysis reveals that the average annual profitability of the merging firms had slightly lower earnings per share, and only slightly higher market values of common stock, a differential accounted for by a relative increase in the price/earnings ratios accorded to merging firms by the market in this time period. Among the merging firms, Poindexter found that those involved in vertical and conglomerate mergers averaged higher earnings per share and market value than firms engaged in horizontal mergers.[13] These findings led Poindexter to conclude that "the evidence offered by the analysis suggests that for acquiring companies merger is no more profitable than growth through internal investment."[14]

A limited study of firms engaging in different types of mergers during the early part of the current wave was conducted by H. Igor Ansoff and J. Fred Weston.[15] This study included two small groups: five firms involved in concentric mergers and seven firms in conglomerate mergers. Ansoff and Weston defined "concentric" mergers as those involving a common thread in the relationship between the merging firms, and conglomerate mergers as those combining unrelated product lines. In testing for stability of sales and profits for the 1957–58 recession, they found that the decline in these variables was smaller for the group utilizing the concentric strategy. These firms also performed better than the conglomerate firms in the 1952–1959 period in growth of earnings per share and market price per share.

The Ansoff-Weston study is generally credited with introducing the "synergy" concept to the business lexicon. This is the so-called $2 + 2 = 5$ concept expressed so frequently in the popular business press during the recent merger wave. Subsequent empirical research has all but demolished this concept, as will be noted below.

J. Fred Weston has also attempted to prove that conglomerates are "efficient" firms. Weston and Surenda K. Mansinghka examined a specially selected group of conglomerate firms and compared them with two random samples of large firms taken from a different universe—*Fortune's* 500 largest industrials and the list of the 750 largest firms.[16] The time period used was 1958–1968, and 1960–1968, that is, from a recession period to the peak of prosperity. The previous findings of Ansoff and Weston had noted the relatively poorer results of the conglomerates during the 1957–58 recession period. Subsequent tests of the Weston-Mansinghka samples for the 1960–1970 period reveal that the conglomerates excelled only in the size-maximizing process during this period. The decline in the market price of the stock of the conglomerates was substantially larger than the random samples, and the results were statistically significant at a high level.[17]

Another abortive attempt to prove that the conglomerates were successful was undertaken as a thesis project in the economics department at Harvard University by James M. Stone in 1969.[18] This study was prompted by the visit of a conglomerator to the Harvard campus who was in search of evidence to support the conglomerate position. Mr. Stone studied two groups of firms, the 15 conglomerates which he identified and the remaining firms which were considered nonconglomerates. The three size-related variables all strongly favored the conglomerates and were statistically significant, while two of the three profits-to-stockholder variables were statistically significant and strongly favored the nonconglomerates. Mr. Stone neglected this empirical evidence, stating that "earnings per share growth cannot be equated with stockholder benefits."[19] Instead, Stone attempted to prove the "efficiency" of the conglomerates by using Ling-Temco-Vought as a case study. The ink was hardly dry on this thesis when the 1969 results for LTV showed a $38.3 million loss. The 1970 performance was even poorer, with an LTV loss of $69.6 million for the year. The work of Mr. Stone is academically curious and intellectually depressing, to say the least.

By contrast, another thesis of considerably higher quality and contribution was completed by Thomas F. Hogarty at the State University of New York at Buffalo in 1969.[20] Hogarty presented some of the findings of this study and other recent research to the Senate Subcommittee on Antitrust and Monopoly in November 1969.[21]

Hogarty reported on the profit performance of 43 firms active in the merger process. These firms represented a broad spectrum of American industry, as they were spread over 29 three-digit industries and ranged in size from $2 million to over $700 million in assets. Two-thirds of the firms had a premerger growth in sales (exclusive of merger) which was at least as large as that of their respective industries. Hogarty found that only 14 of the 43 merging firms had an investment performance superior to that of their respective industries.[22] This result led him to state that "clearly active acquirers are less profitable than ordinary firms, at least in the long run . . . this result implies that stockholders do not generally benefit from active acquisition programs; in fact, relative to similar opportunities, they lose on the average."[23]

Hogarty also investigated to determine if mergers generally produce synergy. The answer was *no,* since only a minority achieved it, which prompted Hogarty to conclude that "this sort of result is hardly indicative of widespread opportunities for synergy . . . since these 43 firms were, prior to merger, healthy, typical representatives of their respective industries, it seems fair to conclude that synergy through merger is beyond the reach of the ordinary industrial firm."[24]

A businessman, John Kitching, examined 69 acquisitions made by 20 companies in the 1960–1965 period.[25] This study included the results of the mergers for a 2- to 7-year postmerger period and was based upon interviews with executives of the acquiring firms. The interviews were divided into two parts. The first dealt with top management's qualitative assessment of the success or failure of the acquisition program as measured against the original strategy; the second focused on the financial results actually obtained. Even using this naturally biased and subjective type of analysis, a considerable number of failures were identified. Kitching found the greatest incidence of failure occurring in the *concentric* mergers; ironically, this merger type is expected to produce synergistic benefits (according to Ansoff and Weston). The major difficulty with synergy is that the proponents of this concept do not identify what variable(s) are affected. If the managers of merging firms are realizing profit and earnings per share growth, then synergy would contribute to stockholder welfare. If, instead, synergy refers to size growth (sales, assets, and so on) without a corresponding gain in profitability, the interests of the stockholders are adversely affected. Most current research findings indicate that size synergy resulting from mergers is more certain and that profits synergy appears more serendipitous. In discussing success, Kitching identified the critical element for success not as the potential amount of synergy to be realized in combining two companies but rather as the existence or absence of ''. . . 'managers of change'—people who can catalyze the combination process.''[26]

Baruch Lev and Gershon Mandelker have attempted to measure some of the microeconomic consequences of a selected group of 69 merging firms.[27] The objective of this study was to attempt to isolate the merger effect by comparing for each firm the period of 5 years before and the postmerger period of 5 years after the merger year. For each of the merging firms, a comparable matching firm was selected which was supposed to be a nonmerging firm. While this is a desirable statistical methodology, it suffers from some serious deficiencies as it relates to the pattern of recent merger activity. The important merging firms have been engaging in combination activity on a more sustained basis than was evident at the turn of the century and during the late 1920s. Thus, it is virtually impossible to isolate a representative sample of firms with "clean" before and after periods.

An examination of the Lev-Mandelker sample reveals that both the merging firms and "control" firms were involved in 846 reported mergers, with the majority consummated during the so-called clean before-and-after periods. The so-called nonmerging control group engaged in 312 mergers. One matched pair had Georgia-Pacific as the merging firm, compared with U.S. Plywood–Champion Papers as the "nonmerging" control firm. Both these firms were among the 25 merger-active firms identified by the Federal Trade Commission for the 1960s. The so-called nonmerging firm acquired assets valued at $649 million during the 1961–1968 period, which was three times more than the firm's assets in 1960. There also was no attempt to distinguish between the various types of merger utilized (i.e., horizontal, vertical, circular, conglomerate, etc.). Another problem in the Lev-Mandelker study was the averaging of the variables in the before-and-after periods, which tends to obscure the performance pattern, especially when additional merger activity is introduced. In short, it is not surprising that Lev-Mandelker found little or no differences between the groups in attempting to measure the microeconomic consequences of merger.

The International Experience

An extensive study of the performance of merging firms in Sweden was conducted by Bengt Rydén for the 1946–1969 period. Rydén studied the performance pattern for 62 Swedish manufacturing and construction firms and found the fastest-growing firms were also the most merger-active. In the words of Rydén, "The most merger-active firms have expanded their sales more rapidly than the less merger active. . . . The correlation between merger activity and profitability (measured by the movement of stock prices) is more complicated. No such association could be detected for any of the investigated firms.''[28] Rydén further found that those firms who owe relatively little of their expansion to mergers have seen their stock prices go up much more than firms for whom mergers have contributed a large or very large part of their expansion. Rydén also examined various hypotheses related to the causes of merger and found the highest explanatory value attributed to the restraint-of-trade motive and the lowest to the technical-economies-of-scale-in-production motive, although none of the variables were statistically significant. Since the size variable was significant, the motive for merger appears again to be size maximization rather than benefit to the shareholder.

A major comprehensive merger study, designed to test a variety of merger hypotheses, was conducted by Douglas L. Henderson as a doctoral thesis in Australia.[29] Henderson tested a variety of aspects of the merger problem as they relate to the valuation of the firm, risk-return characteristics, financial performance, growth rates, and so on in his two-volume thesis. Henderson empirically tested the hypotheses utilizing a sample of 48 Australian firms. The matched-pair technique was utilized in this study also; however, in contrast to the United States experience in the recent merger wave, the Australian mergers were less frequent and thus more suitable to "clean" before-and-after periods. In contrast to the Lev-Mandelker study, Henderson did not average the before-and-after periods, instead, he examined the year prior to the merger year and the first, second, and fifth full years in the post-merger period.

The results of the Henderson study are striking. His general conclusion was that mergers have a significant effect in reducing shareholder utility and the internal strategy of expansion (i.e., nonmerger) was far superior to any of the three merger strategies (horizontal, vertical, and diversified). In addition, all the merger strategies indicated a decline in financial performance. Henderson examined the diversification question and concluded as follows:

> The principle behind diversifying by merger is that given the correct selection of suitable firms whose returns correlate negatively with the existing firm, the risk of the acquiring firm should be reduced. However, the result of the diversifying sample was to increase risk for the shareholders of both acquiring and acquired samples . . . the most suitable strategy for expansion of the firm, from the shareholders' point of view, is the 'internal' method, where firms expand without resort to merger. Merger strategies, whether horizontal, vertical or diversified, all resulted in a decline in performance when the pre-merger results were compared to the post-merger activity.[30]

An extensive study of the relative performance of merging firms in Canada for the 1960–1970 period has been conducted by S. N. Laiken.[31] This study consisted of 369 Canadian-based firms listed on the Toronto Stock Exchange. A variety of variables were examined relating to size, profitability, and changes in the capitalization rate. The pattern of results confirms the tendency of merging firms to add size dimensions on a more consistent basis than profitability. Laiken observes that "the four measures of size used tend to confirm on a consistent basis a positive association with external growth through merger . . . merging firms did not show a consistently greater increase in profit margins . . . than did nonmerging firms."[32]

A study of the performance of acquiring and nonacquiring firms in the United Kingdom has been conducted by Ajit Singh of Cambridge University.[33] This study compared the relative profitability of an acquiring firm in the year of the acquisition and 1 and 2 years after the merger with the combined (weighted average) relative prior profitability of the firms involved before the merger. The results clearly demonstrate that, both for individual industries and for all industries together, there was a decline in the relative profitability of the acquiring firms in the year of the takeover and 1 and 2 years later. In the third year after merger, 77 percent of the firms recorded a relative decline in profitability.

A British magazine, *Management Today* (May 1970 issue), reported on a study of the earnings records of the 30 largest United Kingdom firms that were involved in one or more important mergers in the 1960s. The survey revealed that only a small proportion of the firms performed well in terms of growth of earnings per share. The study concluded that the biggest potential losers were the shareholders in the acquiring firms, who were ignored by management in the quest for expansion.

These various studies, concerned mostly with industrial firms, have demonstrated that there is a considerable amount of variance in the post-merger performance of firms following this growth strategy. This implies that the risks to the stockholders and the economy are (on the average) considerably more than generally acknowledged or realized. A rather consistent pattern of results is revealed in these numerous studies, which demonstrates the lack of a strong postmerger profit position for merging firms. Actually, the most sophisticated empirical research reveals that mergers are less successful (on the average) than the alternative strategy based on pure internal growth which provides new production capacity to the firm and industry.

A lesson should be learned from history, for a similar situation prevailed during a previous period of prolonged prosperity in the United States (a long merger wave followed by a depression), as reported in the NICB study published in 1929:

. . . these mergers did not prove exceptionally profitable. . . . The majority did not achieve a conspicuous success as profit-makers. . . . In the popular mind the notable profit records of single large consolidations tend to be magnified. Such companies stand out as the striking examples of what consolidation can accomplish. What is commonly overlooked is the fact that concerns like these represent the exceptions rather than the rule among consolidations.[34]

PERFORMANCE STUDIES IN THE REGULATED INDUSTRIES

The major studies of the performance of mergers and merging firms in the regulated industries have focused on the commercial banking field, and the findings have been substantially the same as in the industrial and commercial field. For example, two studies by Cohen and Reid isolated the effects of mergers on the interests of managers, stockholders, and also the public, since banking is considered a regulated industry.[35]

These studies included a nationwide sample of 165 large banks, as well as other samples of banking firms in particular geographical areas.[36] Variables related to size, profitability, and service to the public were utilized in the analysis of variance tests. The results indicated that, on the average, merging banks became larger in size, less profitable for stockholders, and did not exhibit any advantages in servicing the public interest. Studies of the performance of multiple-bank holding companies (who generally concentrate on merger in the growth process) also conclude that these establishments are not generally efficient.

Bank holding company performance was examined by Robert J. Lawrence in a study for the Board of Governors of the Federal Reserve System.[37] Examining a sample of banks acquired by holding companies and matching them with comparable independent banks, Lawrence found that mergers did not generally lead to increased efficiency or improved earnings performance. Lawrence also found that "customers of the subsidiary banks would probably be paying higher service charges on their demand deposit accounts but would not be receiving significantly higher interest payments on their time deposits."[38] In addition, Lawrence stated that "It is also likely that the acquired bank would lose autonomy as the holding company took over some of the decision-making."[39] This finding confirmed the same pattern observed by Gerald C. Fischer in his earlier study of the performance of this type of banking institution.[40] Fischer found that banks acquired by holding companies typically did not gain in profitability relative to their competitors and, in fact, that profitability often declined in the short run due to increased expenses. A study of bank holding company performance in New England by Steven J. Weiss which included mergers during the 1956–1967 period again confirms the same pattern.[41] Weiss found that the capital positions of the acquired banks did not improve in the postmerger period and that "comparative figures also fail to indicate any significant overall impact of affiliation on the earnings performance of acquired banks."[42] Thomas R. Piper and Weiss also studied a nationwide sample of bank holding companies for the post-World War II period and found that "On average, the acquisitions have been breakeven propositions for the holding companies and have not furthered the interests of their stockholders. The mean profitability for the 102 acquisitions studied was only 1% above the breakdown level. Fifty-three percent of the acquisitions were, in fact, unprofitable; their incidence was spread across most of the holding companies."[43]

Another study of the impact of bank mergers upon the performance of merging banks in the Fourth Federal Reserve District (Cleveland and surrounding territory) during the 1960–1965 period was conducted by David L. Smith.[44] This study demonstrated that "the increases in current operating expenses at merging banks more than offset the increases in current operating revenues; consequently, the ratio of net current operating earnings to total assets actually declined."[45] The change was statistically significant at the 1 percent level. Smith continues by observing the following:

> On balance, the evidence strongly suggests that merger did not enable merging banks to increase their profitability *rates* more than nonmerging banks. Such a finding has important implications for an analysis of the motives behind bank mergers, since it is often held that banks merge because they find it profitable.[46]

The merger-for-profit motive is rather generally held despite the vast array of evidence presented here which strongly disputes this belief. As an example, Governor George Mitchell, one of the advocates of a concentrated banking structure, has stated that "It suffices to assume the motive to merge is profit. In fact, if we really take the enterprise system seriously, we *must* assume that it is the profit motive that assembles resources to meet needs and that it is ordinarily an efficient and workable apparatus for this purpose."[47] The substantial and growing body of empirical evidence suggests this assumption should be accepted with substantial caution, if accepted at all. Additional evidence concerning the performance of merging and nonmerging banking firms will be presented in Chapter 12.

All these studies indicate that while mergers add *size* dimensions to individual firms, it does not necessarily follow that profitability and efficiency are realized. The classic example of this situation among regulated firms is the Penn Central merger in the transportation field. The staggering losses resulting from this combination have been distributed among numerous private and public interests. Meanwhile, service and safety have declined, and rates have continually increased. It is difficult to find a rationale for the creation of economic units of this dimension since the bigger they come, the harder they may fall, depending upon the government. The Penn Central merger was originally proposed to save two railroads suffering profit problems, yet prior to the consummation of the merger, each of the roads achieved record profits independently, which eliminated the original need for the merger. History is replete with examples as people seem to continually develop bigger and bigger organizations seemingly without regard for the natural and inevitable consequences—financial, economic, social, and environmental.

A logical explanation for the consistent pattern of a lack of success registered by merging firms (compared particularly with nonmerging firms) would be that these firms are merging with less profitable firms. This situation is also frequently cited as a justification for combination activity. In a recent major empirical study, Stanley E. Boyle found that the opposite pattern prevailed; he concluded:

> We have pointed out that some economists and others have argued that merger may well be a welcome alternative (from an efficiency point of view in the transfer of corporate assets) to bankruptcy, with its attendant disintegration of corporate assets and identity. If these arguments are taken seriously, the acquiring firms might well be awarded a medal of merit for their service to the economy. A careful examination of the facts, however, showed that less than 10 percent of the large corporations which have been acquired over the past 20 years have been at "death's door."
> To be sure, some companies were losing money and others were earning rather low rates of return at the time of their acquisition. At the other extreme, however, almost 50 percent of them were earning a rate of return of 10 percent or more after taxes. These are not charity cases. Not only were these firms profitable in the year prior to acquisition, but the majority of them had experienced increases in their absolute dollar levels of profits and assets in the five years prior to their acquisition. As a group, they enjoyed a rate of return about equal to that being earned by all corporations over the period under examination. Moreover, they had experienced increases in their assets which were slightly greater than the average for all manufacturing corporations between 1950 and 1968.[48]

In summary, a substantial, consistent, and growing body of major empirical research studies concerning the relative performance of merging firms reveals a significant body of evidence which strongly suggests that mergers are a suboptimal method of allocating resources.[49] The implications for private and public policy should not be ignored during this period when the concept of "bigness" is being questioned and examined in a variety of ways. The cost of bigness appears to outweigh its benefits in business, banking, transportation, education, government, farming, cities, and so on. In addition, the cost of mergers to the national economy is substantial and is examined below.

THE MERGER GAME AND THE NATIONAL ECONOMIC GOALS

The substantial and growing body of evidence examined above suggests that the corporate merger, as an economic event, is generally a major flop. Except for the fact that studies of executive compensation indicate that size of the firm is more critical than profitability in explaining levels of pay, and since mergers add size dimensions, some managers may have temporary benefits. The other interested parties in merger activity generally gain little or nothing, or even lose in the process of the game. Since premiums are usually paid for the shares of the acquired firm, these stockholders have some chance of gain, particularly if they sell the new securities within a reasonable time.

At the macro level of the economy, it is a fact that mergers generally add nothing to the accomplishment of national economic goals. Actually, they usually have major detrimental effects. An analysis of the impact of mergers on the economy was presented prior to the peak of the recent merger wave in a previous book, *Mergers, Managers, and the Economy*. The subject was important then and has assumed additional significance in view of the current economic mess in America.

The President of the United States is responsible by law to use the power of the office to attain the nation's economic goals. This mandate was contained in the Employment Act of 1946, which legislation provided the President with an important three-member council of economic advisers to assist in attaining the goals of full employment, economic growth, and reasonable price stability. Let us examine the role of the merger game in accomplishing these important goals.

Economic Growth and the Merger Game

The impact of spending by a business firm may contribute nothing to the economic growth objective since the expenditure is for *existing* capacity and will *not* show up in the national income accounts as business investment spending. Most mergers, particularly the larger mergers, involve an exchange of stock in the transaction. Of the large mergers consummated in the 1964–1970 period, 83.5 percent were stock transfers, compared with only 11.7 percent cash transactions; the balance were a combination of stock and cash. The relatively few mergers involving cash may have a different effect, depending upon the spending patterns of the recipients of the cash. This effect could be seriously adverse if the recipients of the cash use most of the funds for consumer expenditures rather than reinvestments in the business community, particularly during periods of rising demand when mergers usually take place. Thus, mergers make little, if any, contribution to the economic growth goals since these investments are for *existing* assets rather than for new productive capacity.

Full Employment and the Merger Game

The act of merger (by itself) does *not* contribute to the full-employment objective in the economy, since the employees involved may remain with the same firm or with the new owners. In other words, new jobs are not created by the merger act per se. Actually, the evidence suggests that many executives and other employees lose their jobs in the process. Jon G. Udell, in his study of postmerger employment patterns in Wisconsin, found that firms acquired by conglomerates had close to 12 percent annual employment gains before merger and after the merger the annual decline was about 2 percent during the relatively prosperous 1963–1967 period.[50]

The ultimate effect of a merger upon employment creation depends upon the relative success and the eventual *internal* expansion of the firm. The fact that the number of employees in merging firms generally increases faster than in nonmerging firms does not indicate that more jobs have been created by merging firms. An acquiring firm instantly adds size dimensions, including the assets and employees of the merged firm, and does *not* change aggregate employment (or capacity) at the time of the merger.

Reasonable Price Stability and the Merger Game

The contribution of the merger game to the accomplishment of the reasonable price stability objective is, of course, difficult to measure. Prices tend to rise when capacity utilization rates are high, and/or when market structures become concentrated and when firms base their pricing policies on target rates of return rather than market conditions. Thus, in some sectors of the economy prices may rise even when capacity utilization rates are low or declining.

Since mergers do not add new capacity to an industry, it is likely that during periods of strong aggregate demand the capacity constraints will eventually cause prices to rise. Since a merger results in the acquisition of existing capacity (which is in various stages of obsolescence), the relative costs of operation may also be higher than if a similar (or even smaller) expenditure had been made on new, modern capacity with the increased potential for realizing *productivity* gains.

Increased productivity gains are particularly important during periods of rising labor costs, and the most logical method of achieving these benefits is through replacement and expansion investment in *new* plant and equipment. Productivity is the key to economic growth, price stability, and increasing wages and jobs, and merger contributes virtually nothing to the process.

If the much discussed "efficiencies" and "expected" economies of scale which are generally associated with merger activity were actually realized, then these economic events would be contributing to price stability or declines, and/or quality improvements, increased profits, and other benefits to the general public. Unfortunately, the cupboard is bare.

Mergers and Pollution Control

The effects of big power centers on the quality of life in America will be examined in more detail later. However, one important facet is the pollution problem. A dimension of this problem is business investment spending on *existing* plants and equipment, most of which are not new and are usually the biggest contributors to the pollution problem. If we assumed that American industry had invested the equivalent amount spent in the merger game on *new* plants and equipment during the past decade, a giant step toward a curb on pollution would have been realized. This is one more mark against the merger game and should be rightfully recognized as another aspect of this economic nonsense which has preoccupied so many business people during recent years.

Top Managers and the Merger Game

While the substantial body of evidence presented in this chapter casts doubt on the probabilities of success for corporate mergers, it does appear that the personal interests of some managers are served. For example, in the previous chapter it was noted that a relatively few firms which have been active in the merger process had played a significant role during the recent merger wave. Data related to top management compensation and stock holdings in 1970 for the 25 merger-active firms including the 11 new conglomerates (as identified by the Federal Trade Commission) are presented in Table 7.1.

The average and median remuneration (salary and bonus excluding deferred compensation and stock options) of both the most active acquirers and the "new" conglomerates was considerably above the median salary of $139,000 of the more than 700 chief executives of the largest United States

Table 7.1   Remuneration, Age, Service, and Shares Controlled by Chief
Executive Officers of the 25 Most Active Merging Firms (1961–1968) and
the New Conglomerates (1961–1968), for the Year 1970

	1970 salary and bonuses*	Age	Years served With firm	Years served As chief	Shares owned/ controlled by value
FTC 25 merger-active firms (1961–1968)					
Average	$244,000	57	22	7	$7,872,000
Median	$225,000	56	23	5	$2,154,000
FTC 11 new conglomerates (1961–1968)					
Average	$275,000	55	20	8	$5,540,000
Median	$250,000	57	17	9	$1,950,000

*Excludes deferred compensation and stock options.
 Sources: The firms are listed in the FTC *Report on Corporate Mergers* (Washington, D.C., 1969, pp. 260–
261), and the personal data are from *Forbes,* May 15, 1971 issue.

corporations listed by *Forbes*. Less than a third of the chief executives on
the *Forbes* list held $2 million or more of stock in the firm, yet the average
and median amounts exceed this figure for the merger-minded managers.
The personal income and wealth positions of the managers indicate that
there are some personal winners among the top managers in the merger
game.

MAJOR MERGER WAVES AND BUSINESS CONDITIONS

An important question that economists have neglected over time is that of
relating the impact of major merger waves upon business conditions *following* the peak of activity. It has been recognized that an economic environment of relative prosperity and a buoyant market for securities has contributed the impetus for major waves of merger activity. Since the peak of each
merger wave has preceded a collapse in business conditions (see Chart 1.1),
it appears that these massive microeconomic developments have a discernable macroeconomic impact which has not been recognized. The problem
is necessarily complex and requires a multidimensional approach to con-
nect the variety of facets related to the merger phenomena.

In order to untangle the maze of merger facets, it is necessary to begin
with developments during the thrust of the wave. An important development is related to the financial aspects of the merger activity. In examining
the forms of merger, a consolidation or an acquisition will generally involve

an exchange of securities which will alter the capital structure of the surviving firm. Even if cash is utilized, the capital structure of the surviving firm will most likely change in a short period to adjust for the drain of working capital caused by the combination. The surviving firm needs to service either an expanded debt and/or an equity base. While the service of the debt base is rather straightforward, the equity-base service requirements are more complicated. Even though dividend payments are not legally required, the merging firm must be cognizant of rates of return, earnings per share, and price/earnings ratios, since these financial indicators are utilized for a variety of purposes, i.e., calculating the cost of capital to the firm, arranging merger terms, securing working capital, and so on. In short, the mere act of financing merger activity causes a multiplicity of debt and equity problems which are sensitive to the condition of the money and capital markets and the performance of the firm. The debt component adds risk dimensions, while the equity component may become seriously diluted in the merger process, especially when premiums are paid. Rapid growth during boom periods tends to mask many of the problems inherent in the combination process, problems which become pronounced with changes in macroeconomic policies or firm performance.

An examination of the performance pattern of 39 diversified industrial firms which were major participants in the recent merger is illuminating. This sample is contained in the *Report of the Federal Trade Commission on Rates of Return in Selected Manufacturing Industries 1961–1970* and covers the period 2 years *prior* to the 1968 merger peak and 2 years *after* the peak.[51] The average firm size, measured by total assets, and the average rate of return for these firms are presented in Table 7.2 and Chart 7.1. The data are quite revealing since it is apparent that the rate of return of these diversified firms was declining *prior* to the 1968 merger peak, while

Table 7.2 Changes in the Average Firm Size and Rate of Return for 39 Diversified Manufacturing Firms, 1966–1968 and 1968–1970

| | | Total assets (millions) | | | |
1966	1968	Percentage change	1968	1970	Percentage change
$576	$1,273	+121%	$1,273	$1,102	−13%

| | | Rate of return | | | |
1966	1968	Percentage change	1968	1970	Percentage change
15.2	13.0	−14%	13.0	8.7	−33%

Source: Data obtained from *Report of the Federal Trade Commission on Rates of Return in Selected Manufacturing Industries 1961–1970*, Washington, D.C., 1972, pp. 58–65.

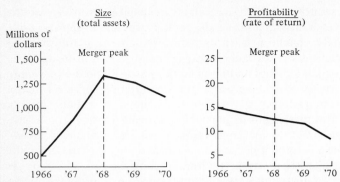

Chart 7.1 Changes in the average firm size and rate of return for 39 diversified manufacturing firms, 1966–1970.

the assets were growing at a hypertonic rate of 121 percent in a 2-year span of time. The average firm size increased from $576 million in 1966 to $1.3 billion in 1968, a net gain of almost $700 million per firm. Following the merger peak, the rate of return declined 33 percent, and this disappointing performance was accompanied by a net decrease in asset size of minus 13 percent. The contrasting pattern in these 2-year periods *prior* to the merger peak and in the postpeak period is stunning and revealing.

The data suggest two related, yet separate developments. One is the tremendous strain that is put on the money and capital markets as the peak in the merger wave is approached. The relatively sudden burst in demand for capital is reflected in both interest rates and the diversion of funds to suboptimal allocations. Since most of the capital is expended for existing assets in various stages of obsolescence, there is a question of the qualitative nature of the acquisitions. Meanwhile, there is no new quantitative addition to the nation's productive capacity which creates a strain on *existing* capacity and generally increases costs in the process. In short, both financial *and* productive capacity are strained in the process. Situations of this type may prompt macroeconomic intrusions into the economy, as evident in the United States in the recent postmerger-peak period.

The second related development is that pertaining to the declining rate-of-return phenomenon simultaneous with a substantial surge in average firm size. This development suggests managerial and productive diseconomies stemming from the postmerger problem of integrating formerly independent behavioral systems, knowledge constraints, control and budgetary complications, and productivity and related problems. The resulting amalgam drains capital and leads to cutbacks due to the shrinkage of available debt and equity pools. There are a number of other dimensions which have been omitted in the interests of brevity and that are in the process of theoretical development and empirical testing. In short, massive merger waves of a hypertonic nature strain the economic system to an extent that they have a microeconomic impact on business conditions. The pattern has been obvious even prior to the substantial development and influence of monetary and fiscal policy, that is, at the turn of the century and in the late 1920s.

WHO WINS?

It is difficult to imagine any game with so few winners than the merger game. The surest winners are the promoters who take their piece of the action and leave the scene. The vast amount of empirical evidence collected over the years using different samples, time periods, hypotheses, and statistical techniques (both parametric and nonparametric) indicates a general lack of success for mergers and merging firms. At the micro level of the firm, there is a lot of wasted motion, money, and resources played out on a game that should be regarded as economic nonsense.[52]

Even the "Main Street to Wall Street" movement of corporate control has its mixed blessings, since any benefits accruing to New York from these spatial shifts may be offset by numerous costs to New Yorkers in urban problems associated with increasing masses of people commuting to and working in the growing office complexes in the metropolitan area.

The merger game has an equally serious impact on the attainment of the national economic goals and becomes a form of aggregate nonsense at this level. In summary, the best hope for eventual reasonable price stability, sensible economic growth, and the creation of employment opportunities lies in convincing managers, legislators, regulators, and other government officials (and the public) that the *qualitative* as well as the quantitative aspects of business capacity are important in the economy.

NOTES

1 This paper was later published as part of my testimony before the Senate Subcommittee on Antitrust and Monopoly, see *Economic Concentration*, Part 5, Washington, D.C., 1967, pp. 1914–1939.
2 Arthur S. Dewing, "A Statistical Test of the Success of Consolidations," *Quarterly Journal of Economics*, vol. 36, no. 4, pp. 84–101, November 1921.
3 Shaw Livermore, "The Success of Industrial Mergers," *Quarterly Journal of Economics*, vol. 50, no. 4, pp. 68–96, November 1935.
4 National Industrial Conference Board, *Mergers in Industry: A Study of Certain Economic Aspects of Industrial Consolidation*, New York: NICB, 1929.

5   See Committee on the Judiciary, Senate Subcommittee on Antitrust and Monopoly, *Economic Concentration,* Part 5, 89th Congress, 1st Session, Washington, D.C., 1967, pp. 1914–1939 and Samuel R. Reid, *Mergers, Managers, and the Economy,* New York: McGraw-Hill, 1968.

6   See Adolph A. Berle, Jr., and G. C. Means, *The Modern Corporation and Private Property,* New York: The Macmillan Co., 1932.

7   Samuel R. Reid, "The Conglomerate Merger: A Special Case," *Antitrust Law and Economic Review,* vol. 2, no. 1, pp. 141–166, Fall 1968.

8   While the number of employees in the acquiring firm grew faster, the number of jobs generally declines causing a *net loss* in employment opportunities. For evidence on this development, see Jon G. Udell, *Social and Economic Consequences of the Merger Movement in Wisconsin,* Madison: University of Wisconsin, May 1969.

9   Eamon M. Kelly, *Profitability of Growth through Mergers,* University Park: The Pennsylvania State University, 1967.

10 Joel Segall, "Merging for Fun and Profit," *Industrial Management Review,* vol. 9, no. 2, pp. 17–29, Winter 1968.

11 Ibid., p. 28.

12 Eugene O. Poindexter, *The Profitability of Industrial Merger,* unpublished doctoral dissertation, Syracuse University, 1970. An abstract is available in the *Journal of Finance,* vol. 25, no. 5, pp. 1182–1183, December 1970.

13 Horizontal mergers include firms in the same industry such as railroads, airlines, or steel manufacturers. This finding confirms the previous empirical research on this aspect of the merger problem.

14 Ibid., p. 1183.

15 H. Igor Ansoff and J. Fred Weston, "Merger Objectives and Organizational Structure," *The Quarterly Review of Economics and Business,* vol. 2, no. 3, pp. 49–58, August 1962.

16 J. Fred Weston and Surenda K. Mansinghka, "Tests of the Efficiency Performance of Conglomerate Firms," *The Journal of Finance,* vol. 26, no. 4, pp. 919–936, September 1971. See also Samuel R. Reid, "A Reply to the Weston-Mansinghka Criticism Dealing with Conglomerate Mergers," *Journal of Finance,* vol. 26, no. 4, pp. 937–946, September 1971.

17 See Samuel R. Reid, "A Reply to the Weston-Mansinghka Criticism Dealing with Conglomerate Mergers," op. cit., p. 945.

18 James M. Stone, "Conglomerate Mergers: Their Implications for the Efficiency of Capital and the Firm," unpublished thesis, Economics Department, Harvard University, 1969.

19 Ibid., p. 54.

20 Thomas F. Hogarty, "The Success of Industrial Mergers," Buffalo: State University of New York at Buffalo, unpublished dissertation, 1969.

21 The presentation appears in *Economic Concentration,* part 8, op. cit., pp. 4647–4656.

22 Assuming reinvestment of cash dividends, without reinvestment only 10 of the 43 could be considered successful.

23 Hogarty, op. cit., p. 4649.

24 Ibid., p. 4650.
25 John Kitching, "Why Do Mergers Miscarry?" *Harvard Business Review,* vol. 45, no. 6, pp. 84–101, November–December, 1967.
26 Ibid., p. 91.
27 Baruch Lev and Gershon Mandelker, "The Microeconomic Consequence of Corporate Mergers," *Journal of Business,* vol. 45, no. 1, pp. 85–104, January 1972.
28 Bengt Rydén, *Mergers in Swedish Industry,* Stockholm: Almqvist & Wiksell, 1971, p. 297.
29 Douglas L. Henderson, "Analysis of Company Mergers in Australia," Sydney: University of New South Wales, unpublished dissertation, 1974.
30 Ibid., p. 334.
31 S. N. Laiken, "Financial Performance of Merging Firms in a Virtually Unconstrained Legal Environment," *The Antitrust Bulletin,* vol. 18, no. 4, pp. 827–851, Winter 1973.
32 Ibid., pp. 846–856.
33 Ajit Singh, *Takeovers: Their Relevance to the Stock Market and the Theory of the Firm,* London: Cambridge University Press, 1971, especially pp. 161–166.
34 National Industrial Conference Board, op. cit., p. 171.
35 Kalman J. Cohen and S. R. Reid, "The Benefits and Costs of Bank Mergers," *Journal of Financial and Quantitative Analysis,* vol. 1, no. 4, pp. 15–57, December 1966, and K. J. Cohen and S. R. Reid, "Effects of Regulation, Branching, and Mergers on Banking Structure and Performance," *Southern Economic Journal,* vol. 34, no. 2, pp. 231–249, September 1967.
36 The relative performance of banks located in Virginia and New York State was examined because of major changes in state laws tending to encourage mergers. The nonmerging banks achieved a superior relative performance.
37 Robert J. Lawrence, *The Performance of Bank Holding Companies,* Washington, D.C.: Board of Governors of the Federal Reserve System, June 1967.
38 Ibid., p. 24.
39 Ibid.
40 Gerald C. Fischer, *Bank Holding Companies,* New York: Columbia University Press, 1961.
41 Steven J. Weiss, "Bank Holding Companies and Public Policy," *New England Economic Review,* pp. 3–29, January–February 1969.
42 Ibid., p. 22.
43 Thomas R. Piper and Steven J. Weiss, "The Profitability of Multibank Holding Company Acquisitions," *The Journal of Finance,* vol. 29, no. 1, p. 173, March 1974.
44 David L. Smith, "The Performance of Merging Banks," *The Journal of Business,* vol. 44, no. 2, pp. 184–192, April 1971.
45 Ibid., pp. 190–191.
46 Ibid., p. 191.
47 George W. Mitchell, "Mergers among Commercial Banks," in Almarin Phillips (ed.), *Perspectives on Antitrust Policy,* Princeton, N.J.: Princeton University Press, 1965, p. 241.

48 Stanley E. Boyle, "Pre-Merger Growth and Profit Characteristics of Large Conglomerate Mergers in the United States: 1948–1968," in *Conglomerate Mergers and Acquisitions: Opinion and Analysis,* 44 St. John's Law Review (special ed., 1970), p. 169.

49 See Samuel R. Reid, "Is the Merger the Best Way to Grow?" *Business Horizons,* vol. 12, no. 1, pp. 41–50, February 1969.

50 Jon G. Udell, *Social and Economic Consequences of the Merger Movement in Wisconsin,* Wisconsin Economy Studies Number 3, Madison: Bureau of Business Research and Service, May 1969, pp. 5–27.

51 See Federal Trade Commission, *Report of the Federal Trade Commission on Rates of Return in Selected Manufacturing Industries 1961–1970,* Washington, D.C., 1972, pp. 58–65.

52 For a discussion of managerial motives in mergers, see H. Levinson, *The Great Jackass Fallacy,* Cambridge: Harvard University Press, 1973, especially chap. 7, pp. 108–125.

Chapter 8

The Petroleum Industry: A Case Study of Bigness and Power

The petroleum industry presents a case study of bigness and power in American industry. It provides an illustration of some of the companies among the 50 largest industrial firms and is represented by 18 firms among the 100 largest. The five largest firms are multinational firms which exert considerable economic and political power on a worldwide basis. The industry presents a particularly interesting case study in that it consists of a variety of large firms and is also a concentrated industry, since the four largest firms dominate a large part of this integrated industry.

In addition to multinational economic activity, the industry also had a considerable amount of merger activity of each type during the 1960s. This development has been generally overlooked, as attention was generally focused on the conglomerate firms in the recent merger wave. Yet there are more merger-active firms in the petroleum industry than any other single industry. The widespread gasoline and heating oil shortage in the United States, which appeared in 1973, suggests that the investment activities of these large firms, including the merger game, may well have been a contributing factor to this national problem in addition to the Arab embargo. Finally, the roles of a variety of government policies deserve special attention as they apply to this basic industry.

PETROLEUM COMPANY MERGER ACTIVITY

The petroleum industry has been at the forefront of the merger movement during the past couple of decades and particularly during the peak period of the 1960s. As discussed previously, mergers and acquisitions represent a special form of capital budgeting, since decisions to expand via combination will add capacity to the surviving firm but add nothing to industry and aggregate capacity. The reason for this effect is that mergers and acquisitions involve *existing* capacity rather than *new* additional firm, industry, and aggregate capacity. Unfortunately, this is one facet of merger which has not received sufficient attention, despite its importance to the economy.

The petroleum industry in the United States presents an interesting illustration of capital budgeting activities as they relate to mergers and acquisitions. Among the 25 most merger-active firms identified by the Federal Trade Commission for the 1961–1968 period, eight were large petroleum companies.[1] These eight petroleum firms acquired more than $6 billion of assets in this relatively brief yet explosive period, and they were second only to the 11 conglomerates that dominated merger activity during this time. While the eight merger-active petroleum firms engaged in all types of mergers during the period, most of the activity involved horizontal mergers, including some of the major firms in the industry. Among these mergers (and the assets of acquired firm) were: Union-Pure ($766 million of assets); Sun-Sunray ($750 million of assets); Atlantic-Richfield's partial acquisition of Sinclair ($1.9 billion of assets); and the acquisition by Phillips Petroleum of the Western Division of Tidewater Oil for nearly $400 million. In addition, over $1.2 billion of assets were involved in mergers of independent petroleum producers, refiners, and marketers. Other acquisitions consummated by firms in the merger-active group included leading coal companies, chemical companies, and major diversified firms.[2]

Petroleum Mergers and Domestic Refining Capacity

The Petroleum Industry Research Foundation has attributed one of the major causes of the recent fuel oil and gasoline shortages directly to the lack of adequate domestic petroleum refining capacity.[3] As shown in Table 8.1, the United States had the smallest percentage gain in refining capacity of any region of the world during the 1961–1972 period. In addition, the

Table 8.1   World Crude Oil Refining Capacity Changes, 1961–1972 (Thousands of Barrels per Stream Day)

World sector	Refining capacity		Capacity change	Percentage change
	Jan. 1, 1961	Jan. 1, 1972		
Africa	122.5	902.4	+779.9	637.8
Asia-Pacific	1,431.7	6,817.7	+5,386.0	376.2
Europe	4,476.1	16,982.8	+12,506.7	279.4
Middle East	1,481.8	2,851.3	+1,369.5	92.4
Western hemisphere (excluding the United States)	3,185.7	6,134.1	+2,948.4	92.6
Canada	1,002.3	1,444.5	+442.2	44.1
United States	10,400.0	13,284.9	+2,884.9	27.7
Total	22,100.1	48,417.7	+26,317.6	

Source: Oil and Gas Journal, p. 104, December 25, 1961; and p. 73, December 27, 1971.

relative position of the United States as the leading country in petroleum refining declined significantly during this period. In 1961, the United States had almost half (47 percent) the available capacity; by 1972, this share had declined to 27 percent. Europe and Asia-Pacific each added more actual capacity during the period, and their percentage gains exceeded ten times that of the United States. In the process, Europe became the leading petroleum refining area in the world, increasing its share from 20 percent in 1961 to 35 percent in 1972.

Lagging growth in domestic petroleum refining capacity can be traced directly to the capital budgeting decisions of the major firms in the industry and to governmental policy which influenced these decisions. The data in Table 8.2 clearly indicate the capacity effect that merger-active programs had on the firms involved and on the industry. The domestic refining capacity of the merger-active firms increased 110 percent in the 1961–1972 period. However, when capacity is adjusted for the merger effect, the actual growth of these firms was less than 2 percent for the entire period. Merger-adjusted growth is calculated by adding the refining capacity of merged firms for the initial year, which is 1961 in this study. The net result is that these eight basically domestically oriented firms expended substantial amounts of funds combining *existing* firms and capacity rather than for additional new modern refining capacity, and this development added to the nation's energy crisis. The combined growth of the multinationals and the merger-active firms in domestic capacity was a mere 20 percent in the 1961–1972 period, while their collective foreign capacity increased 192 percent.

Table 8-2 Domestic and Foreign Refining Capacity Change by Groups of U.S. Petroleum Firms, 1961–1972 (Thousands of Barrels/Stream Day)

Group	Domestic refining capacity					Foreign refining capacity		
	1/1/61	1/1/61 Merger-adjusted*	1/1/72	Percentage change 61-72	Merger-adjusted 1961–1972 (percentage)	1/1/61	1/1/72	Percentage change
Multinationals†	3,600.3	3,708.8	4,882.4	35.6	31.6	3,379.3	9,648.5	185.5
Merger-active‡	1,149.3	2,373.8	2,413.0	109.9	1.7	138.4	629.6	354.9
Other large§	1,960.6	2,338.5	3,299.4	68.3	41.8	200.5	411.4	105.2
Other smaller¶	423.8	495.4	1,096.0	158.5	121.2	none	60.0	

*Merger adjusted means that the capacity of the firms acquired by merger are added to the surviving firm for 1961.
†Includes Exxon, Mobil, Texaco (includes half interest in Cal-Tex), Gulf, and Socal (includes half interest in Cal-Tex).
‡Includes Continental, Arco, Tenneco, Phillips, Occidental, Union, Sun, and Signal.
§Includes Standard (Ind), Shell, Cities Service, Ashland, Std. (Ohio), and Getty.
¶Includes Amerada Hess, Marathon, Kerr-McGee, American Petrofina, Commonwealth, and Clark.

Multinational Investments and Domestic Refining Capacity

The five largest firms in the industry (Exxon, Mobil, Texaco, Gulf, and Standard of California) are also among the leading multinational firms in the world. All five petroleum multinationals rank among the top 15 multinational firms in the world. Foreign sales as a percentage of total sales are: Exxon (50 percent), Mobil (45 percent), Texaco (40 percent), Gulf (45 percent), and Socal (45 percent). The relative changes in domestic and foreign refining capacity of this group of firms, as shown in Table 8.2, clearly indicate a substantial shift in expansion away from the United States in investments for refining capacity. The multinationals had a modest domestic gain of 36 percent (32 percent when adjusted for mergers), and a foreign capacity gain of 186 percent during the 1961–1972 period. The actual foreign capacity gain of the multinationals was more than twice the *total* United States gain in the period.

The merger-active petroleum firms had the largest percentage increase in foreign refining capacity, 355 percent; their net domestic growth (on a merger-adjusted basis) was only one-twelfth their actual foreign increase. Thus domestic mergers and foreign investments by the major firms in the industry are linked to the relatively slow rate of growth in domestic refining capacity since the early 1960s. The economic and political realities of the 1970s have mitigated this development somewhat since pricing policies and other developments have prompted domestic conservation of refined petroleum products and a search for alternative sources of energy.

RELATIVE PERFORMANCE OF THE MAJOR PETROLEUM FIRMS

Since expansion alternatives, mergers, and foreign investment are part of the capital budgeting process, an examination of the performance patterns of firms emphasizing particular strategies should be of interest. While refining capacity investments are only a part of the operations of these integrated firms, they constitute a major and critically important aspect of the petroleum business.

A basic performance hypothesis would assume that firms engaging in major merger programs and/or concentrating on multinational investments would be maximizing the relative net present value of their shareholders' wealth. An examination of the performance characteristics of these firms in the pre–energy crisis period reveals a varied pattern.

Data for the various firms grouped according to their operating or size characteristics are presented in Table 8.3. Included in the data are the results of tests of an analysis of variance in the group means for these 25

Table 8-3 Means of the Growth and Profits-to-Stockholders Variables for 25 Major Petroleum Firms and Groups

	8 merger-active	17 others	F-ratio†	5 multi-national	20 others	F-ratio†	8 merger-active	5 multi-national	6 other large	6 smaller	F-ratio†
Size-related variables*											
Sales, 1961–1971	7,557.1	354.0	2.19	137.0	288.7	1.41	7,557.1	137.0	499.2	390.5	0.67
Assets, 1961–1971	2,395.0	228.1	2.23	137.1	256.6	3.46$^{(.10)}$	2,395.0	137.1	217.7	314.4	0.68
Employees, 1961–1971	1,891.6	69.4	2.37	16.7	82.4	2.22	7,891.6	16.7	116.1	66.5	0.72
Profits-to-stockholders variables											
Net income, 1961–1971	(−801.5)	230.8	2.49	99.7	223.1	0.86	(−801.5)	99.7	222.1	348.8	0.78
Earnings per share, 1961–1971	(−296.1)	191.8$^{(.10)}$	3.51$^{(.10)}$	90.8	162.0	0.30	(−296.1)	90.8	159.8	307.9	1.20
Market price, 1961–1971	85.3	164.5	0.95	66.2	165.9	0.97	85.3	66.2	155.1	255.9	1.28
Dividends, 1961–1971	1,283.8	1,380.9	0.01	111.6	801.1	0.78	1,283.8	111.6	1,983.2	1,836.3	0.37
P/E, 1961	22.05	16.05	1.34	12.18	16.47	1.29	22.05	12.18	14.33	21.00	0.98
P/E, 1971	11.46	16.59	1.82	10.44	18.62	4.46$^{(.05)}$	11.46	10.44	18.18	10.12	1.92
Net income as % of sales, 1961	9.65	10.15	0.03	11.24	8.42	0.90	9.65	11.24	8.85	10.53	0.13
Net income as % of sales, 1971	4.38	6.84	3.46$^{(.10)}$	9.16	5.75	8.78$^{(.01)}$	4.38	9.16	5.93	5.80	2.76$^{(.10)}$
Net income as % of equity, 1961	8.00	10.47	1.34	11.4	9.81	0.21	8.00	11.14	8.42	11.97	0.98
Net income as % of equity, 1971	5.66	10.05$^{(.05)}$	4.51$^{(.05)}$	11.56	8.97	1.53	5.66	11.56	7.62	11.23	2.34
5-yr. return on equity	11.04	13.75	2.13	12.58	13.29	0.09	11.04	12.58	11.05	17.43	4.01$^{(.05)}$
5-yr. return on total capital	7.65	10.84$^{(.01)}$	10.20$^{(.01)}$	10.76	10.09	0.23	7.65	10.76	9.17	12.57	7.01$^{(.01)}$
5-yr. market price change	(−2.55)	18.26	1.39	(−2.32)	21.43	1.14	(−2.55)	(−2.32)	8.60	45.07	2.04
Debt/equity, 1971	0.55	0.41	1.41	0.20	0.49	7.95$^{(.01)}$	0.55	0.20	0.35	0.65	4.36$^{(.05)}$
P'/assets, 1961	(−0.19)	0.07	3.04$^{(.10)}$	0.07	(−0.03)	0.36	(−0.19)	0.07	0.06	0.08	0.93

*All the variables for the 1961–1971 period list the mean percentage change for that period. The other variables with a single year listed, i.e., 1961 or 1971, are the mean figures for that year. The 5-year variables include the mean figure for the 1966–1971 period. The sources of the data are Fortune's 500 Largest Directory for 1971 and 1961, and Forbes Annual Directory, May 15, 1972. Data for firms not listed in the Fortune 1961 Directory were obtained from Moody's Industrial Manual, 1962.

†The F-ratios shown for each variable are based on one-way analysis of variance tests of the significance of the observed differences in group means for that variable. The italicized F-ratios are those for which the probability is less than 0.10 that the observed differences could be the result of chance; in these cases, the significance levels are shown in parentheses as superscripts to the F-ratio.

major firms, which are among the 500 largest industrial firms in the United States. The overall performance pattern revealed by this study indicates that the smaller "major" firms (which are domestically oriented) outperformed the larger major firms, which appeared more interested in foreign investments and/or domestic merger activity in their expansion strategies. An examination of the performance patterns of each group of firms is presented below.

The Performance of the Eight Merger-Active Firms

When the performance of the eight merger-active firms is compared with the balance of the major petroleum firms, it is evident that this special group had substantial gains in each of the size-related variables; however, the differences were not statistically significant. An examination of the profits-to-stockholders variables indicates a different pattern of performance. Each of the five profitability variables that were statistically significant, that is, earnings per share growth, 1961–1971, net income as a percent of sales, 1971, net income as a percent of stockholder equity, 1971, 5-year return on total capital, and profits (P') to beginning of the period assets, favored the remaining groups of non-merger-active firms. While the price/earnings ratio of the non-merger-active firms increased slightly during the period, the ratio of the merger-active firms in the industry was cut almost in half. If there is such a thing as merger-induced synergy,[4] it appears more related to size maximization than to profitability in this pre–energy crisis period.

The Performance of the Petroleum Multinationals

A comparison of the five large multinational firms with the balance of the major firms reveals a varied pattern. These giant firms grew less than the balance of the firms and the profits-to-shareholders performance was also lackluster during this period. The price/earnings ratio declined for this group; the difference was statistically significant in 1971.

Two other variables were also statistically significant and reveal an important difference between the large multinationals and the balance of the industry. The relatively low debt/equity ratio of the multinationals indicates that these special firms did not trade on their equity to the same degree as the other firms in the industry. The profits-to-shareholders variables reflect this development in their lackluster performance. In addition, the multinational group had a significantly higher net income as a percentage of sales in 1971, indicating a higher profit margin on sales. On balance, the multinationals experienced slower size growth, a generally poorer performance as related to stockholders' interests, and a significantly higher profit margin on sales than the balance of the major petroleum firms.

The Performance of the Other Major Firms

The two groups of major petroleum firms that had the largest increase in domestic refining capacity in the 1961–1972 period (see Table 8.2) also had the best overall performance on the variables related to stockholders' interests. In addition, both groups grew more in relative size than the large multinationals and less than the hypertonic merger-active firms (see Table 8.3).

Of particular interest is the group of "smaller" major firms, since this group had the largest gain in net income, earnings per share, and market price of common stock over the 1961–1971 period. This group also had the highest price/earnings ratio in 1971, the highest debt/equity ratio in 1971, the highest 5-year return on stockholders' equity, and the highest 5-year return on total capital. In addition, this group of smaller major firms had a substantially larger increase in the payment of dividends to their shareholders than either the group of large multinationals or the merger-active group.

The data, as they relate to changes in petroleum refining capacity and economic and financial performance, indicate that the large multinationals and the merger-active firms did *not* produce relative benefits for their shareholders in the pre–energy crisis period. In addition, part of the shortfall in domestic refining capacity can be traced to the investment activities of these firms. These developments emphasize the importance of capital budgeting activities, as they relate to alternative expansion programs and the role of government and private interests in the process.

THE IMPACT OF GOVERNMENT POLICY

The role of government policy and industry practices as they relate to the capital budgeting process in the petroleum industry are worthy of examination, since widespread private and public interests are involved. The shortfall in domestic refining capacity and the decline of the United States as the leading petroleum refining center during the past decade are significant developments. The influence of government policy has been profound, and the role of the industry in the formation of this policy (or absence thereof) has been considerable over the years. Some of the many and varied dimensions of this problem are examined below.

Import Quotas

In 1959, President Eisenhower clamped mandatory controls on foreign crude oil imports into the United States to prevent price competition from the then cheaper Middle Eastern crude oil. As this policy came under attack in the 1960s for maintaining artificially high domestic prices, the petroleum industry fought to defend it. The heaviest threat to the mandatory import restriction came in 1969 when a cabinet-level task force headed by George Shultz recommended scrapping the import quota in favor of a tariff system. In a series of statements filed with the task force, the oil companies, without exception, strongly recommended the continuation of the import quota policy. Bowing to the recommendations of the industry, rather than accepting the findings of the task force, President Nixon declined to scrap the import quota program.[5] This government policy was changed only after it became apparent that shortages were imminent in early 1973 following the reelection of President Nixon. The imposition of the mandatory import crude oil program made foreign investments in refineries to serve the growing European and Japanese markets more attractive to the multinationals since the then cheaper foreign crude oil could be utilized in these expanding markets, and prices were comparatively higher overseas.

Tax Policy

Government tax policy relating to special benefits at the crude oil level has encouraged pricing policies which favor the crude level and squeeze the refining level—discouraging new investments at this critical stage by the major firms. Petroleum firms have enjoyed a special 22 percent oil depletion allowance, ostensibly to encourage exploration of new oil sources in the interests of national defense. In addition, there are allowances for intangible drilling costs, including wages and rental fees for equipment, which can be deducted from taxable income immediately, rather than spreading the deductions over the period of years that the well is in operation. The Treasury Department estimates that these deductions saved the oil firms about $600 million in federal income taxes during 1972.

Special treatment for tax purposes of foreign profits has encouraged multinational development in foreign areas. Following a ruling in 1950, tax and royalty payments to foreign nations can be written off as a tax credit on a dollar-for-dollar basis against federal tax liabilities. This foreign tax and royalty policy has been especially beneficial to the large firms making foreign investments; for example, in 1971 the five multinationals paid an average of about 4 percent of their net income in federal income taxes. Special treatment of foreign tax credits has encouraged foreign investment in refining as well as crude oil exploration and other operations.

Another aspect of tax policy relates to taxes collected at the retail level. Gasoline taxes channeled into highway trust funds have encouraged more wasteful consumption of energy while public mass transit and research on alternative energy sources have been neglected.

Antitrust Enforcement

Another important area of government policy affecting this industry is antitrust policy. It is no secret that the Antitrust Division of the Department of Justice and the Federal Trade Commission were lax in their enforcement policies during the period when the major petroleum mergers were consummated.[6] Mergers involving major firms generally went unchallenged in that era.[7] Antitrust actions related to pricing behavior and other noncompetitive practices were also conspicuously absent. Thus, the index of law enforcement as it relates to this industry has been quite low on a variety of matters related to structure and behavior.

Environmental Restraints

Governmental recognition of the importance of environmental considerations upon the quality of life also irritated an industry which had enjoyed an almost *carte blanche* privilege to pollute the atmosphere and water in selected areas of the nation. While this recognition was a positive step by the government to protect the public interest in the environmental area, the industry has appeared to resent these constraints, which have contributed to some extent to the curtailed domestic refining expansion in recent years prior to the energy crisis.

The constraints also contributed to increased demand, as many utilities converted from coal to oil for boiler fuel. A strategy designed to force the relaxation of environmental controls in the face of an energy crisis appears to be gaining advocates in public and private circles. Congress passed the trans-Alaska pipeline legislation following a 3-year delay; clean air standards have been relaxed to encourage more coal consumption; and attempts have been made to overcome local opposition to refinery siting in the wake of the so-called energy crisis.[8] Thus, the role of government has many prongs, some of which are contradictory, as they relate to the need to protect the environment and simultaneously encourage domestic energy self-sufficiency.

INDUSTRY STRUCTURE

Traditionally, the large integrated petroleum firms have avoided price competition at the retail level. Instead, huge expenditures have been made on *non*–price competitive programs such as advertising and service station locations. While attempts were made by the large firms to put "tigers in our tanks" and final filters on the pumps, the nonintegrated independent retail petroleum firms emphasized *price* competition. Much to the dismay of the

Table 8.4   United States Gasoline Market Share of the Top 10 Firms, 1968–1972

Rank	Firm	Percentage of United States gasoline market					Change, 1968–1972
		1972	1971	1970	1969	1968	
1	Texaco	8.1	8.4	8.1	8.3	8.5	−0.4
2	Shell	7.1	7.3	7.9	8.2	8.3	−1.2
3	Standard (Md.)	6.9	7.0	7.3	7.5	7.6	−0.7
4	Exxon	6.9	7.1	7.4	7.6	8.0	−1.1
5	Gulf	6.5	6.7	7.1	7.6	7.5	−1.0
6	Mobil	6.4	6.4	6.6	6.7	6.7	−0.3
7	ARCO	4.9	5.5	5.5	5.7	5.8	−0.9
8	Standard (Cal.)	4.7	4.7	5.0	5.2	5.3	−0.6
9	Phillips	4.1	3.9	4.0	4.0	4.0	+0.1
10	Sun	3.9	4.1	4.1	4.3	4.4	−0.5
	Total	59.5	61.1	63.0	65.1	66.1	

Source: Oil & Gas Journal, p. 29, May 14, 1973.

larger firms, the independents had increased their market share of the domestic retail gasoline market each year in the decade prior to the 1973 shortages. The combined market share of the 10 leaders in retail gasoline sales declined from 66.1 percent in 1968 to 59.5 percent in 1972. The only major firm among the top ten to increase its market share was Phillips Petroleum, which used price competition in some sections of the country, and also converted a substantial number of its stations to secondary brands and sold higher volumes at independent prices (see Table 8.4).

The independents, which held about a quarter of the domestic retail gasoline market prior to 1973, were a thorn in the side of the majors. Government policy again aided the majors during the important initial stage of the shortage period. Voluntary controls persisted at the retail gasoline level, even after mandatory controls were imposed on other petroleum products, and scores of independent small businesses (over 20,000 stations) were forced out of business by the combined efforts of big business and big government. It was this strong independent competitive fringe that helped to hold retail gasoline prices in line prior to the induced shortages. The cost of this loss to the nation is not calculable, but is substantial. The key to success in forcing this important segment to fold was the voluntary gasoline allocation policy which permitted the majors to supply the outlets of their choice, particularly their own stations. Private actions aided by government policy permitted the majors to protect their retail marketing investments at the expense of small businesses and consumers.

"ENERGY CRISIS"—PRICES AND PROFITS

Prior to the so-called energy crisis, retail gasoline and oil prices were relatively stable for many years. This condition was due mainly to the existence of the independent competitive fringe and the decline in petroleum refinery labor costs reflecting increased productivity. For example, the average price for a gallon of regular-grade gasoline in the United States had increased from 31.1 cents per gallon in 1960 to 34.8 cents in 1969, a gain of 12 percent. During the same period, the average operating costs of domestic refineries increased only 8 percent, and this was due mainly to increased prices paid for crude oil and for royalty payments. Labor costs at the refinery level declined from 50.3 cents per barrel in 1960 to 47.7 cents in 1969. By contrast, during the first 9 months of 1973, wholesale prices of fuel increased over 60 percent, and future price increases have been assured by the government.

The profit performance of the major petroleum firms during the early phase of the energy crisis was spectacular, despite periodic imposition of retail price controls. The five multinationals had combined profits in 1973 of over $6 billion compared to 1972 profits of about $4 billion. The median gain in profits for the multinationals was 54 percent and the median return on common equity in 1973 was 16 percent. The merger-active group had a median profit gain of 46 percent, and their median return on equity was 10.5 percent in 1973. The largest gain in profits was recorded by the "smaller" majors, with a median profit increase of 185 percent, and a rate of return of 19.4 percent in 1973, as this group continued to outperform the larger firms in the industry. This result suggests that the larger firms in the industry may be realizing diseconomies as related to scale, integration, or diversification (either product or spatial), or a combination of each on a relative basis.

It is also interesting to note that the major petroleum firms have defended their substantial profit increases during the initial stage of the so-called energy crisis based on the need for additional capital to finance expansion and oil exploration. Simultaneously, Gulf Oil announced plans to acquire a large insurance firm and the world's largest circus. Mobil Oil, in announcing plans to invest $1.5 billion in 1974 on expansion and exploration, said it hoped to spend more than half the total—$803 million—to acquire Marcor Corporation, which operates the Montgomery Ward merchandising empire and owns Container Corporation of America. Thus, a substantial part of the greatly expanded profits are not going for new energy sources, but rather to diversification into nonallied industries. Even a casual observer realizes that there is no oil in a department store or under a circus tent.

SUMMARY OF THE MERGER-RELATED IMPACTS

This examination of some of the merger-related impacts in the petroleum industry reveals some distinct patterns related to firm growth effects, capacity effects, and performance effects in the petroleum industry.

Firm Growth Effect

The eight merger-active firms acquired over $6 billion of assets in the 1960s and increased firm size substantially in the process. The mean growth rate of these firms was over 20 times that of the other major firms in the industry. Some examples of growth of assets are Occidental, $14.6 million in 1961 to $2,580.0 million in 1971; Atlantic-Richfield, $898.1 million to $4,704.1 million; Union Oil, $761.5 million to $2,564.8 million.

The Capacity Effect

While the domestic petroleum refining capacity of the merger-active group increased 110 percent in the 1961–1972 period, the growth was considerably less, a mere 2 percent, when adjusted for *merger* activity. The data clearly reveal the effect that mergers have upon firm and industry capacity growth. When a firm acquires, or merges with, another firm in the same industry—a horizontal merger—the firm adds existing capacity and grows in the process. At the same time, industry capacity remains constant. One of the factors which contributed to the petroleum refining shortfall in the United States has been the substantial combination activity of the merger-active group in this industry.

The Profit Performance Effect

The poorest profitability performance among the major petroleum firms during the 1961–1971 period (prior to the energy crisis) was recorded by the merger-active group of firms. Each of the profit-related variables that was statistically significant favored the non-merger-active group of firms. In short, the merger-active petroleum firms have not performed as well as the other major firms in the industry in either the pre–energy crisis period or in 1973, the initial year of the energy crisis.[9]

A CONCLUDING NOTE

Mergers are special economic events with a number of dimensions, each of which has an impact of varying degree upon growth, capacity, and performance, in addition to the competitive effect. The petroleum industry presents a special illustration of these varying impacts, since this industry spawned more merger-active firms than any other industry during the recent major merger wave. In addition, government policy has contributed to the petroleum rip-off in a variety of dimensions. The role of government, as it relates to antitrust and regulatory policies, will be examined in more detail in the next part.

The combined economic and political power of the few large multinational petroleum firms, together with the producers' cartel, the Organization of Petroleum Exporting Countries, has left an indelible mark upon the world economy in recent years. Administered pricing, restrictive output, and international and domestic political pressure have been the hallmarks of their behavior. Individuals conserve energy and end up paying higher prices for their sacrifice. Increased conservation leads to increased administered prices in order to maintain or expand the level of revenues in a classic case of big business and big government cooperation. History may well judge these economic and political developments to be the most massive public rip-off ever perpetuated in commercial affairs. The appropriate question remains—bigness and power for whom?

NOTES

1   These eight firms and their relative rank among the 25 most merger-active firms are: Tenneco (4), Union Oil (7), Sun Oil (8), Signal Cos. (9), Occidental (10), Continental (11), Atlantic Richfield (15), and Phillips Petroleum (22).
2   Continental acquired Consolidation Coal, the leading domestic bituminous coal company. Occidental acquired Island Creek Coal Co., the third largest firm and Maust Coal and Coke Co., while Socal acquired Old Ben Coal Corporation. Both Tenneco and Signal Companies made numerous conglomerate mergers during the period, diversifying into other industries.
3   Domestic demand for petroleum products prior to conservation measures and higher prices was about 17 million barrels a day, while refinery capacity is about 13 million barrels at full capacity.
4   Synergy is the so-called 2 + 2 = 5 effect, where the whole is supposedly greater than the sum of the parts; see H. Igor Ansoff and J. Fred Weston, "Merger Objectives and Organization Structure," *The Quarterly Review of Economics and Business*, vol. 2, no. 3, pp 49–58, August 1962.
5   The petroleum industry was a major contributor to the campaign to reelect President Nixon in 1972. Some large firms in the industry have admitted publicly to having made illegal political contributions in that infamous campaign.
6   See "Taking the Crusade Out of Antitrust," *Business Week*, pp. 59–62, May 20, 1967.
7   The Department of Justice did challenge the Arco-Sinclair merger in 1969, and a consent decree settled the litigation in August 1970.

8   The Governor of New Hampshire actively promoted state legislation which
    would have permitted the state to override local control of zoning ordinances to
    permit construction of a petroleum refinery. Citizens in the town of Durham had
    expressed their opposition to the seacoast refinery proposal by an overwhelming
    vote of 1,254 to 144 to reject the $600 million project in their small town. The
    state legislature upheld "home rule" in a historic vote during a special session in
    March 1974.

9   As a group, the eight merger-active petroleum firms performed better than the 17
    other firms (conglomerates and miscellaneous) in the Federal Trade Commission
    list of the 25 most merger-active firms, for the 1970–1974 period. Most of the
    major mergers were horizontal, and the industry profit performance was
    reflected in these results, although this group did not perform as well as the
    "smaller" major firms.

Part Three

Antitrust, Regulation, and the Public Interest

This third part of the book examines the role of antitrust and regulation and the performance patterns that have emerged over time. The initial chapter (9) is devoted to a broad glance at the basic regulatory structure and an examination of the effectiveness of the antitrust arsenal and its application to the merger game.

The important transportation segment and its regulation is the subject of Chapter 10. Particular emphasis is placed on the railroads and airlines, a couple of key components in the overall system.

The last three chapters of this part (11, 12, and 13) are a comprehensive examination of regulatory developments in the commercial banking field. Chapter 11 focuses on regulatory behavior as related to the massive bank holding company movement and its impact on structure. The separate regulatory pattern which has emerged concerning approved bank mergers is examined in Chapter 12. The last chapter of this part (13) discusses the problem of identifying the public interest and the role of the regulators. These banking chapters are more technical than other sections of the book, and it is recommended that those with minimal or slight interest in banking skim over Chapters 11 and 12 and concentrate on Chapter 13, prior to beginning Part Four.

Chapter 9

The Regulatory Sham: What Ever Happened to the Public Interest?

The six largest business firms in the United States have combined assets of over $185 billion dollars and operate in regulated industries.[1] Two-thirds of the 50 largest American business firms come under the direct influence of public regulators. These 33 giant firms control over $412 billion of resources, or 78 percent of the exclusive group's assets, as noted below.

	Assets (billions)	Percentage	
		Of firms	Of assets
33 regulated firms	$412,637.6	66	78
17 private firms	116,512.4	34	22
Total, 50 largest firms	$529,150.0	100	100

How does this preponderence of control of resources in the hands of firms in regulated industries square with the rather common belief that America has a competitive, free enterprise economic system? The obvious answer is that there is no squaring and that the regulatory agencies are regulating business into a system quite contrary to that which was in the minds of our founding fathers.

In addition, numerous congressional mandates have been virtually ignored by these agencies. This is a serious charge that can only be responsibly made if there is evidence to support the charge. The evidence is available and some will be presented in this chapter with more to follow in the later chapters. First, let us examine the basic regulatory structure as it applies to business in the United States. After reviewing the structure, the performance record of the more important agencies will be examined as it relates to the promotion and protection of the public interest.

REGULATORY STRUCTURE

The major regulatory structure of the United States and the appropriate business sector is as follows:

Business Sector	Regulatory agencies	Regulators—number of people
Commercial banking	Board of Governors of Federal Reserve System	7
	Comptroller of the Currency	1
	FDIC	3
	Subtotal	11
Transportation	Interstate Commerce Commission	11
	Civil Aeronautics Board	5
	Subtotal	16
Utilities	Federal Communication Commission	7
	Federal Power Commission	5
	Subtotal	12
Other regulation		
Industrials and others	Federal Trade Commission	5
	Antitrust Division, Dept. of Justice	1
	Securities and Exchange Commission	5
	Subtotal	11
Total		50

The above is the basic regulatory structure; however, it should be understood that there are a number of overlaps, as well as other agencies, both at the federal and state levels, involved in the regulatory process.

One important fact emerges from this simple presentation of the structure—only *50 people* are basically responsible for this important activity. All are politically appointed, and *none* are *elected* by the public whose "interest" they are *supposed* to represent. The decisions made by each of these appointed commissioners and board members have an important impact on the structure of the industries, the size and power of individual firms, and most pertinently, the pocketbook of individual citizens of the nation.

Hundreds of billions of dollars of assets and revenues are in the control of the regulated firms, and a handful of politically appointed people (in some cases from the industry being regulated) are expected to protect the public interest. This is an incredible situation which is structurally unsound and predictably unworkable in the imbalanced economy and which needs serious consideration by Congress.

Unfortunately, there is considerable variance in the quality of the appointees to these positions, and the public generally knows very little about the actions taken by the commissioners, governors, or members on a collective, as well as an individual, basis. To its credit, the Board of Governors of the Federal Reserve System has published the votes of the board (as well as individuals) on most bank merger and many holding-company applications. The data are utilized for the analysis presented in Chapters 11 and 12; however, as a general rule, a considerable amount of secrecy is involved in many important decisions made by these groups. In other words, these agencies do not fully submit themselves to public scrutiny.

Certainly one of the most ineffective of the agencies has been the Interstate Commerce Commission (however, it is only a matter of degree, since all have been rather ineffective). This agency approved (and even helped to promote) the largest merger in history, which also turned out to be the biggest financial failure in economic history. *Fortune* magazine stated that "the path to the ICC passes through politics, as the backgrounds of the present members suggest."[2] These are the backgrounds of the 11 members of the Interstate Commerce Commission:

    1 Chairman—for many years an administrative assistant to a Senator

    2 Vice Chairman—a former congressional liaison officer for the ICC, who was sponsored by the late Senator Everett Dirksen

    3 Formerly minority staff director for the House Appropriations Committee

    4 Lyndon Johnson's college roommate and later an executive of L.B.J.'s Texas television stations

    5 A protégé of the late Senator Walter George of Georgia

    6 Served as lieutenant governor of Kentucky

   7 Campaign manager for Senator George A. Smathers of Florida,
who now works for the railroads
   8 Long active in Democratic politics in West Virginia
   9 Once an aide to Governor of Ohio
   10 Former Republican Congressman
   11 Long-time postal official

   It is no wonder that an expert who has spent more than a decade
studying this agency closely, economist George W. Hilton of UCLA, says,
"In the most literal sense, the I.C.C. doesn't know what it's doing."[3]
Certainly, the public has paid a high price for this ignorance as service has
declined, fares and prices have continued to rise, deterioration is rampant,
safety endangered, and now rail passenger service has been nationalized.
Examples are so numerous that volumes could be filled with evidence of
regulatory collapse at this agency. Most rail commuters are quite familiar
with the scenario concerning this mess, as it surrounds them virtually
every working day.
   In summary, the *few* that have control of the majority of assets in the
regulated industries, amounting to hundreds of billions of dollars, are
supposed to be regulated by another *few* who are politically appointed and
usually less than aggressive in their promotion of the public interest. This
latter point will be discussed below.

THE PERFORMANCE OF THE REGULATORS

In 1970, nearly $200 billion, an outlay equivalent to nearly a fifth of the
nation's gross national product, and almost as much as the gross national
product of Japan, was spent by Americans moving people and goods
around on the regulated transportation system. Despite these huge revenues, the 50 largest transportation firms, taken together, lost money in
1970. Thus, it appears that in the transportation sector of the economy,
ineffective regulators and inefficient management of large firms have
teamed to create a substantial mess. Even the newer and more glamorous
airlines have suffered, and this industry appears to be heading for future
problems not too dissimilar to their railroad brethren in the transportation
field. A more detailed treatment of the airlines and their regulators, the
Civil Aeronautics Board, will be examined separately in the next chapter.
   In the commercial banking field, there are three separate regulatory
bodies, including the Board of Governors of the Federal Reserve System,
the Federal Deposit Insurance Corporation, and the Comptroller of the
Currency. In addition, individual states have regulatory agencies for financial institutions. The record of all these agencies in the area of approved

bank mergers is incredible. Since the passage of the Bank Merger Act of 1960, the combined approval rate has been 97 percent of the applications. Bank holding company applications are handled solely by the Board of Governors of the Federal Reserve System, which has approved over 90 percent of the applications. This situation will be treated in more detail in the following chapters.

In addition to regulatory decisions on operating matters, the record of law enforcement has also been dismal. The remainder of this chapter will be devoted to the analysis of the breakdown of law and order on business and economic matters, particularly the enforcement record and policies concerning the antitrust laws. Future chapters will deal with commercial banking and transportation matters.

LAW ENFORCEMENT—THE ANTITRUST RECORD

In recent years, antitrust policy has been under attack from both extremes of the political spectrum, that is, the left and the right. John Kenneth Galbraith sees antitrust as a "charade" acted out to delude the public into believing that the market is still alive and well in the United States.[4] *Fortune,* the magazine of big business, speaks for the big business community when it pleads for more "realistic" antitrust, which to *Fortune* means restricting antitrust to price fixing and other hard-core restraints of trade. In its 1966 "proposition" for a new antitrust approach, the editors would have the law provide "that mergers—horizontal, vertical, or conglomerate—are entirely legal unless they sprang from a manifest attempt to restrain trade."[5] In explaining why *Fortune* felt obliged to put forward the proposition, the managing editor said that the work of Max Ways (a member of *Fortune's* board of directors) demonstrated that "the concentration of power feared by generations of trustbusters is just not in the cards."[6] This ostrich-type observation is curious in view of the accumulated evidence on this subject.

Actually, an examination of the law enforcement record as it relates to antitrust cases and merger activity reveals little more than a superficial attempt at law enforcement and hardly justifies the *Fortune* proposition for more lenient laws. In fact it is difficult to conceive of a more lax enforcement policy than that of the federal government in this economic area.

It is a curious fact of economic life, as noted previously, that each of the major waves of merger activity has developed *following* the passage of an antitrust law. The record clearly shows that the turn-of-the-century wave developed following the passage of the Sherman Act in 1890; the late-1920s wave was recorded following the passage of the Clayton and Federal Trade Commission Acts in 1914; and the recent wave rolled on virtually unabated

Table 9.1   Number of Reported Mergers and Acquisitions in Manufacturing and Mining, 1895–1974

Sherman Antitrust Act (1890)		Clayton and FTC Acts (1914)		Celler-Kefauver Antimerger Amendment (1950)	
Year	Annual total	Year	Annual total	Year	Annual total
1895	43	1915	71	1951	235
1896	26	1916	117	1952	288
1897	69	1917	195	1953	295
1898	303	1918	71	1954	387
1899	1,208	1919	171 (438)*	1955	683
1900	340	1920	206 (760)*	1956	673
1901	423	1921	487	1957	585
1902	379	1922	309	1958	589
1903	142	1923	311	1959	835
1904	79	1924	368	1960	844
1905	226	1925	554	1961	954
1906	128	1926	856	1962	853
1907	87	1927	870	1963	861
1908	50	1928	1,058	1964	854
1909	49	1929	1,245	1965	1,008
1910	142	1930	799	1966	995
1911	103	1931	464	1967	1,496
1912	82	1932	203	1968	2,407
1913	85	1933	120	1969	2,307
1914	39	1934	101	1970	1,351
		1935	130	1971	1,011
		1936	126	1972	911
		1937	124	1973	874
		1938	110	1974	
		1939	87		
		1940	140		
		1941	111		
		1942	118		
		1943	213		
		1944	324		
		1945	333		
		1946	419		
		1947	404		
		1948	223		
		1949	126		
		1950	219		

*Data not comparable.

Source: Ralph L. Nelson, *Merger Movements in American Industry 1895–1956*, Princeton: Princeton University Press, 1959, p. 37; Federal Trade Commission, *Report on Corporate Mergers and Acquisitions*, Washington, D.C., 1955; and Federal Trade Commission, Bureau of Economics.

following passage of the antimerger amendment to the Clayton Act in 1950[7] (see Table 9.1). Obviously, not all mergers are against the laws as now constituted, yet the aggregate impact of these major waves has contributed to the creation and maintenance of the imbalanced economy. In fairness, it should be recognized that each law has influenced merger activity (during each of the major waves) in varying degrees. In the following sections, each merger wave will be examined separately in an attempt to isolate some of the factors contributing to this development.

The Turn-of-the-Century Merger Wave

It is ironic that the Sherman Act of 1890, which was directed at monopoly and monopoly practices, not only failed to halt monopolization and increased concentration of industry, but has been considered by some scholars to be a partial cause of the development. A business school professor, Jesse W. Markham, has remarked that "The Sherman Act of 1890 made collusion illegal and put an end to the trustee device, thereby forcing industrialists seeking market control to resort to complete fusion of their separate companies."[8] This attempt to escape the prohibitions of the law was aided by the interpretations of the courts, among other factors. Walter Adams blames both the executive and judicial branches of government for the development of the first merger wave; in discussing the crucial *E. C. Knight* decision by the courts, he states:

> Yet it was this decision which provided the first significant test of the Sherman Act's effectiveness in combating mergers. It was this decision ("manufacturing is not commerce"), which reassured lawyers and businessmen that mergers in manufacturing and mining were quite safe under the new law. It was this decision—combined with President Cleveland's subsequent statements that made trusts a state rather than a federal problem—which served as a powerful impetus to the merger movement of the late 1890's. On the basis of the available evidence it appears that public policy—both the favorable ruling in the Knight case and the "adverse" dictum in the Northern Securities case—had a profound influence on the scope and limits of this admittedly gigantic merger movement.[9]

Another factor which contributed to the ineffectiveness of the first antitrust law during this period was the fundamental change in the corporation laws which took place at about the time the antitrust legislation was passed. It became legal for one corporation to acquire and hold the stock of another corporation, a development which effectively defeated the purpose of the legislation.

A distinguished economist, Arthur R. Burns, summed up the situation when he said that "although federal antitrust legislation has been on the books since 1890, there is little doubt that we have failed to achieve a competitive system at all closely resembling that which was in the minds of the economists of the last century and which provided the background for the legislation."[10] The interpretations of the courts during this period should be considered as a contributing factor to the ineffectiveness of the Sherman Act in curbing this development in the American economy.

A seldom recognized fact suggests that the *economic* environment was more of a deterrent to combination activity in this period than the *legal* environment, a development which persists to the present time. The first great merger wave came to a halt following the stock market collapse at the turn of the century and the sharp recession of 1903.[11] The important *Northern Securities* decision was not rendered until 1904, after the recession and at a time when the first major wave had all but dissipated.[12]

The Late-1920s Merger Wave

After the first great merger wave had subsided, the Clayton and Federal Trade Commission Acts were added to the books in 1914, more than a decade after the initial peak of activity. These new laws appear to have contributed to a change in the form of merger following their passage. An examination of the data from Ralph L. Nelson's study of the time period 1895–1920 provides some evidence.[13] The acquisition merger replaced the consolidation merger after 1914 as the most prevalent form of merger. However, due to the size of the consolidations, the consolidation merger continued to have a slightly higher percentage of merger capitalizations.[14]

During the merger wave of the late 1920s, the acquisition merger continued to dominate the activity. This development suggests that the mergers of the period were not necessarily designed to create monopolies, but rather to establish or reinforce oligopolistic positions, increase control over sources of raw materials and/or distribution channels, and to diversify in product lines or geographically.[15] George J. Stigler attributes this change to the existence of the Sherman Act (which had failed to curb the first wave); he states that "the Sherman Law seems to have been the fundamental cause for the shift from merger for monopoly to merger for oligopoly.[16] Stigler further states: "Sometimes its workings were obvious, as when Standard Oil was dismembered and when the leading banking mergers were prevented from combining. More often, its workings have been more subtle: the ghost of Senator Sherman is an ex officio member of the board of directors of every large company."[17] Since the Sherman Act was on the books during the period when mergers for monopoly were being consummated at the turn of the century, it seems superfluous to consider this act as the prime reason for the change. More relevant factors were the *Northern*

Securities decision in 1904, plus the new acts passed in 1914, as well as the lack of relative success of the early consolidations.

Despite the new judicial decisions and the additional output of legislation, a second great merger wave took place in the 1920s, reaching a peak in 1929. Close to 30 years had passed since the first wave, and a new generation was participating in the growing prosperity of the "roaring twenties." These developments caused a change in the public attitude concerning mergers and the concentration of industry. Willard L. Thorp recognized this when he said:

> There has been an amazing shift in public attitude towards the concentration of economic activity since the years before the war. Certainly, from 1890 to 1914 it was the prevailing opinion that any such trend as that outlined above was contrary to the interests of the public. *Today the only persons who appear to be disturbed by the announcement of the merger are those directly involved whose jobs or income may be threatened.* (Emphasis added.)[18]

Following the peak of merger activity in 1929, the bottom dropped out of the economy. It is ironic, yet true, that the public (including the legislators) did not attempt to isolate the impact of the second major merger wave upon the collapse of prosperity. The attention of the public was diverted and directed elsewhere. The reaction after the stock market crash (which signaled an end to prosperity as well as the merger wave) was directed more at promotional abuses rather than mergers per se. The result was no change in the antitrust laws, yet a rash of new legislation was passed by Congress. As Markham observed: "It is not surprising, therefore, that the public's reaction to the merger movement of the 1920's was not more rigid enforcement of the Sherman Act, but the enactment of the Securities Act of 1933, the Securities Exchange Act of 1934, and the Holding Company Act of 1935."[19]

Thorp, a major student of the second merger wave, concluded that the Supreme Court was a factor in the movement. He said:

> I suppose the first reaction of an individual not familiar with the developments in this field to this statistical display would be to inquire how such a degree of consolidation is possible in the country of the Sherman Antitrust Law, the Bureau of Corporations, the Clayton Act, The Federal Trade Commission, the "big stick" of Roosevelt, and thousands of board feet of antitrust plants (sic) in party platforms. The truth of the matter is that the Supreme Court has played a practical joke on the legislators.[20]

Many theories and factors have been advanced to help explain the second merger wave, yet the fact remains that it did take place despite the fact that there were antitrust laws on the books regarding merger activity. A second merger wave was not deterred by the existence of the antitrust laws. Again the *economic* environment was more of a deterrent than the *legal* environment, since merger activity declined substantially during the depression years.

The Recent Merger Wave

In 1950, following the ripple of merger activity in the early post-World War II period, Congress passed legislation designed to plug the loophole that existed in section 7 of the Clayton Act concerning the purchase of assets.[21] The passage of the Celler-Kefauver Amendment (referred to as the *"anti-merger amendment"*) coincided with the beginning of the third great merger wave, which peaked in 1968. Again, there was the passage of a major piece of legislation designed to curb merger activity prior to the beginning of the recent wave of mergers, which was the largest and most persistent of the major merger waves.

During the period of 1950–1969 there were close to 30,000 recorded mergers among manufacturing and mining firms as reported by the Federal Trade Commission.[22] Over 1,400 of the acquired firms had assets in excess of $10 million, and the total assets of these firms amounted to more than $63 billion, with the majority of assets being acquired by the 200 largest firms.[23] *Fortune* reported that all but 14 of the 500 largest firms had been involved in mergers during the 1955–1965 period.[24] As previously noted, few firms have been hindered in their growth plans by the passage of the so-called antimerger amendment. Rather than concentrating solely on horizontal or vertical mergers, a number of these firms have utilized diversification mergers, both circular and conglomerate, in the growth process, to become either conglomerate firms or "portfolio-type" holding companies.[25]

No attempt was made by the Federal Trade Commission or the Antitrust Division prior to the Nixon administration to determine if the existing antitrust laws could be used to attack the "conglomerate" or "comprehensive" types of merger. Aided by a favorable economic environment, that is, a prolonged period of prosperity, the recent wave set new records for magnitude and longevity. America may discover someday whether or not it is possible for the *legal* environment to contain merger waves in the absence of significant changes in the economic environment. The record to date suggests that enforcement has been an exercise in futility and that the antitrust laws are at a crossroads concerning their relevance as related to merger activity. The pattern of consistency was preserved when the recent wave subsided due mainly to the recession in 1969 and 1970. Again, the *economic* environment prevailed rather than the *legal* environment.

SOME EXPLANATORY REASONS FOR THE FAILURE OF THE ANTITRUST LAWS TO CURB MERGER WAVES

The record of enforcement and the effectiveness of the antitrust laws in curbing mergers is rather dismal to say the least. Recognition of some of the factors which have contributed to this condition should improve our understanding of this rather ominous situation.

Legal Loopholes

It should be obvious to even the most casual observer of these events that business people, along with their legal counsel, have uncovered loopholes in the existing laws. When collusion was made illegal, the trust device was abandoned in favor of complete fusion through consolidation. When the purchase of stock became illegal, then assets were acquired. Rather than expand via merger with a direct competitor, firms have merged with an industry-related firm in another geographical market, or achieved diversification through the process of merging firms in other industries, some related and some not, as a method of skirting the laws.

Judicial Decision

Since the effectiveness of any law depends heavily upon the interpretations of the courts, key judicial decisions are of prime importance. Certainly the early decision in the *E. C. Knight* case ("manufacturing is not commerce") was a dominant reason for the failure of the Sherman Act to contain the first great merger wave. Later judicial decisions strengthened the law concerning its application in individual cases, yet even the addition of new laws, as well as new judicial decisions, has not prevented the formation of major waves of merger activity. It was expected that the merger cases initiated by the Antitrust Division related to "conglomerate" and "comprehensive" mergers in the early enthusiasm of the Nixon administration would provide an opportunity for additional judicial decisions concerning the existing antitrust laws. The government lost all the major cases in federal district courts and no appeals were made to the Supreme Court, eliminating the possibility of judicial decision coming to the rescue on the legal issues surrounding conglomerate mergers. As noted previously, there are sufficient judicial precedents to support a rigorous enforcement policy related to the dominant *circular* merger type.

Enforcement Policies

Another major factor contributing to the ineffectiveness of the existing antitrust laws to curb merger waves is the relatively *lax* enforcement policy of the responsible agencies. An examination of the data presented in Table

Table 9.2   Number of Reported Mergers in Manufacturing and Mining and Merger Cases Instituted and/or Tried by the Department of Justice and the Federal Trade Commission under Section 7 of the Clayton Act, 1914–1969

Year	Mergers	Justice Dept.	FTC	Year	Mergers	Justice Dept.	FTC
		Cases initiated				Cases initiated	
1914	39	—	—	1942	118	1	—
1915	71	—	—	1943	213	—	—
1916	117	—	—	1944	824	—	—
1917	195	1	—	1945	333	1	—
1918	71	—	1	1946	419	—	—
1919	438	—	4	1947	404	—	—
1920	760	—	—	1948	223	—	—
1921	487	—	2	1949	126	2	—
1922	309	—	—	1950	219	—	—
1923	311	—	1	1951	235	—	—
1924	368	—	—	1952	288	—	1
1925	554	—	—	1953	295	—	—
1926	856	3	—	1954	387	—	2
1927	870	1	1	1955	683	5	3
1928	1,058	—	2	1956	673	6	12
1929	1,245	2	1	1957	585	1	6
1930	799	—	—	1958	589	5	3
1931	464	—	—	1959	835	10	3
1932	203	—	—	1960	844	11	13
1933	120	—	1	1961	954	18	2
1934	101	—	—	1962	853	12	1
1935	130	2	—	1963	861	7	5
1936	126	—	—	1964	854	15	3
1937	124	—	—	1965	1,008	18	11
1938	110	—	—	1966	995	13	12
1939	87	—	—	1967	1,496	10	7
1940	140	1	—	1968	2,407	24	10
1941	111	2	—	1969	2,246	20	11
Total					29,732	191	118*

*In addition to these cases reported, there were another 53 which the FTC brought and which were dismissed without opinion, 1918–1947.

Source: Merger Data from the Federal Trade Commission: The data on section 7 cases is from American Bar Association, *Merger Case Digest, 1967,* Chicago: American Bar Association, 1967, and from the agencies for the period 1966–1969.

9.2 indicates that enforcement has been considerably *less* than aggressive. It is surprising to discover how few cases (related to merger) have actually been instituted by the government's antitrust enforcement agencies. The Justice Department and the Federal Trade Commission have initiated and tried only about 300 cases under section 7 of the Clayton Act during the period from 1914 to 1969, a period when almost 30,000 mergers were reported in the manufacturing and mining sectors of the economy and many thousands more in other sectors of the economy.

A partial explanation for the small number of cases initiated prior to 1950 is the wording of the legislation and the courts' interpretation of it, which eliminates cases involving the purchase of assets. Since 1950, the law specifically includes the acquisition of properties and thus closes this loophole. Yet the absolute number of cases initiated by the government since the change is still relatively small when viewed against the profile of merger activity.

It is interesting to note that there were *no* section 7 cases initiated in a total of 31 years by the Department of Justice or by the Federal Trade Commission. In only 19 of the 56 years was more than one case initiated by the Antitrust Division; and the Federal Trade Commission had more than one case in only 18 years during the period. The enforcement index, when measured in this manner, is obviously quite low.

Even in the area of bank mergers (where the Antitrust Division has been relatively active in recent years) only a small percentage of these basically horizontal mergers have been challenged. B. J. Klebaner recognized this when he stated that "Altogether the Attorney General brought 8 bank merger complaints to court during the 69 month life of the unamended act. Fewer than 1% of the acquisitions of the period were challenged. . . ."[26] This apparent laxity is partly by design, but it is also closely related to the appropriations and appointments problem discussed in the next section.

Congressional and Executive Branch Indifference

Another reason why merger waves have not been curbed by the antitrust laws is the difficulty of getting Congress to act in the absence of a crisis (unless prodded by vested interest groups). There is a considerable amount of evidence which suggests that Congress and the executive branch are not really committed to the proposition that the antitrust laws should be vigorously enforced or made more effective.[27] Evidence of this proposition is readily available upon examination of the appropriations and the appointments made to the regulatory agencies responsible for enforcement activities. The following statement, which appeared in a government report, is indicative of the problem. Notice the meager amounts of labor power and funds devoted to the merger problem, as reported two decades ago:

> In the Department of Justice, the Legislation and Clearance section of the Antitrust Division has primary responsibility for merger investigation. . . . Of

the 16 attorneys assigned to this Section, *6 spend from 80 to 95 percent of their time on merger work: 3 from 50 to 60 percent of their time.* In addition, 3 attorneys from other sections and 5 economists are utilized on a part-time basis.

The Federal Trade Commission's merger activities, on the other hand, are now being handled by a special 12-man task force of attorneys and economists which was established on April 6, 1955, for the single purpose of working on mergers and developing means of speeding their investigation . . . Between July 1, 1954, the date of the reorganization of the Federal Trade Commission, and February 11, 1955, for example, *total funds expended by the Commission for field investigations of merger cases amounted to $90,640,* which included the cost of project attorneys, accountants, economists, and statisticians in Washington, as well as attorneys in field offices. *Trial or merger* cases during this period consumed $33,861. In short, of the Commission's total appropriation of $4,178,000 for the fiscal year 1955, *$124,501 was expended on merger activity in the 7-month period beginning July 1, 1954.*[28] (Emphasis added.)

Appropriations place a constraint upon the resources which can be utilized in the enforcement process. While the situation has improved somewhat in recent years, a business weekly observed that " . . . Justice has the resources to oppose only about 20 mergers."[29] Limited resources prompt policy decisions within the agencies to try cases where there is a high probability of a favorable decision for the government, or "landmark" cases which will provide new judicial interpretations. In this type of situation, numerous potential challenges must be abandoned because of the "limited resources" problem, which contributes some credence to the "charades" theory of antitrust.

Appointments can also be an effective method of reducing the force with which the antitrust laws are applied. Much depends upon the degree of dedication and tenacity which the people in these responsible positions bring to their jobs. Even with insufficient appropriations, there has been a great variance in the manner in which those responsible for antitrust enforcement have performed. The attitudes of the executive branch of government concerning the importance of the antitrust laws to the structure and performance of the economy will be reflected in the appointments made to these agencies. There has been considerable variance in the types of individuals in these government posts over the years, as would be expected. They have ranged from hard-hitting, practical people concerned with the problems of concentrated industry to passive theorists attempting to formulate merger guidelines while merger waves burn larger totals into the record book.[30]

Special Interest Groups

The existence of very powerful and affluent special interest groups must also be considered. These groups maintain active lobbyists in government halls at the national and state level. The things that they can accomplish are truly amazing and should be more universally recognized. For example, lobbyists representing banking interests succeeded in getting Congress to overrule the Supreme Court regarding certain bank merger decisions.[31] Never underestimate the power of any group which can reverse the rulings of the highest court in the land. Some Congresspeople willingly cooperate and actively help these vested interests.[32] The pressures that special interest groups can apply and the temptations that they dangle before public officials and others (including some academic people) are not to be underestimated or dismissed lightly.

These two factors combined—the influence of powerful special interest groups and the problem of congressional appropriations—were responsible for the fact that what promised to be one of the most important and revealing studies ever attempted concerning American business was never completed. This was the ill-fated 1,000-firm study proposed by the Bureau of Economics of the Federal Trade Commission in 1962.[33] This study would have provided invaluable information to researchers, government officials, business people, lawyers, and other interested individuals or groups. The purpose of the study was to determine the merger activity and the web of intercorporate relations between large firms. The study was halted due to pressure brought to bear by certain members of Congress (notably Gerald Ford of Michigan), and various threats, including that of withholding the funds necessary to operate the FTC, were applied. This latter threat was the tactic which caused the FTC to give in and abandon the study.[34] This is an example of how the legislative branch (or a small number of people in this branch of government) can and do operate for special interest groups. There is a bit of irony to all of this since Congress and the courts, as well as top-level task forces, have since lamented the lack of data and studies concerning mergers and the conglomerate firms which have resulted from some of this activity.

Lack of Contemporary Interest by Economists

Economists have consistently displayed a pattern of lagging professional interest during periods of substantial merger movements. This unfortunate development has been documented in detail elsewhere.[35] Particularly distressing is the recently released report of the Task Force on Productivity and Competition commissioned by President-elect Nixon in the fall of

1968.[36] Admittedly, this group was functioning under severe time constraints; however, the report failed to treat the subject assigned, except in a most superficial manner. In addition, the recent merger movement was virtually neglected except for the recommendation that the Antitrust Division ignore conglomerate mergers and conglomerate enterprises pending a conference to gather information and opinions on the effects of the conglomerate phenomenon.[37]

Another group, the Task Force on Antitrust Policy, was appointed by President Johnson in December 1967 to study the antitrust laws and determine how antitrust policy might be strengthened by new legislative or administrative measures. This task force was dominated by lawyers and law professors and submitted its report to the President on July 5, 1968; however, the contents were not released until May 21, 1969.[38] This report is far more thorough and relevant and its recommendations more specific than the so-called Stigler Report mentioned above. This report by the Task Force on Antitrust Policy will be discussed in more detail in the final chapter.

Political Pressure and Chicanery

Another distressing aspect of the antitrust enforcement policy is the lack of independence of the agencies responsible for enforcement from overt political pressure or, even worse, political chicanery. Examples abound concerning the use of political pressure or advantage involving antitrust matters. One major example of politics entering the antitrust area was the Justice Department decision not to proceed against the merger by Warner-Lambert with Parke, Davis & Company. Warner-Lambert is represented by the law firm that President Nixon and Attorney General Mitchell were associated with prior to their moving to Washington. The actual decision to drop the action in this large horizontal merger was made by Mitchell's deputy, Richard Kleindienst, in what must be considered a political game. Law and order for the poor and the "radicals" appears to have been a different policy than law and order for big business friends of the administration. In this case, the FTC did take belated action to curb the merger, but the pattern is clear even to the casual observer.

The largest individual shareholder in Warner-Lambert Co., a firm with over $1 billion in sales, is Elmer H. Bobst, the man for whom President Nixon tossed a gala birthday party at the White House. Mr. Bobst, long active in Republican politics, was responsible for placing President Nixon with the law firm that represents Warner-Lambert Company. While the decision not to file an action in this very large horizontal merger (Parke, Davis & Co., had assets of about $400 million in 1970) may be viewed as favoritism, it is an example of antitrust arbitrariness based upon political consideration.

Political chicanery was also readily apparent in the settlement by consent decree of the antitrust action involving the IT&T takeover of the Hartford Fire Insurance Company. The record in this case reveals a bleak chapter in the enforcement history of the Antitrust Division of the Department of Justice. The interplay of economic and political power was dramatically illustrated by the involvement of top-level people in business, government, and law enforcement. The existing practice of clearing the initiation of antitrust actions with the White House obviously creates the potential for political abuse and chicanery.

A CONCLUDING OBSERVATION

An examination of the record leads to the inevitable conclusion that antitrust law enforcement has been ineffective in curbing major waves of merger activity despite the fact that it may have influenced the size and shape of the waves. Ironically, a major piece of legislation designed to curb mergers and the practices which may arise from them was passed *prior* to each wave. The Sherman Act was passed in 1890, preceding the first great wave at the turn of the century; the Clayton and Federal Trade Commission Acts were passed in 1914, following the first wave and prior to the late-1920s merger wave; and the so-called antimerger amendment to the Clayton Act became law in 1950, prior to the recent wave of merger activity.

Recognition of the fact that the antitrust arsenal has not effectively curbed major waves of merger activity would be an honest step toward a goal of enforcing or revising these laws as they relate to merger activity. While the antitrust arsenal is impressive, it appears that its practical and potential power has been emasculated at times by judicial decision; pressures from special interest groups; political pressure and chicanery; and insufficient congressional appropriations and concern.

The *economic* environment appears to have been a more pragmatic deterrent than the *legal* environment. It appears that the "charades" theory of antitrust has some validity when major waves of merger activity are examined. At a time when the relevance of various customs, laws, and institutions is being questioned by new generations of citizens, it appears that the antitrust laws and the enforcement policies related to them will eventually be subject to their scrutiny.

Firms under direct regulation, as well as the unregulated firms in the private sectors of the economy, have used merger to grow to giant size over the years. Despite the antitrust laws, even the limited market competition that remains will not survive unless the public exerts pressure for enforcement of the rules of law prohibiting certain courses of conduct and demanding the maintenance and attainment of effectively competitive market structures in *a new economic America*. The basic problem with depending upon antitrust law enforcement, besides its infrequent use, is the turtlelike pace at which the litigation proceeds. Yet the importance of these laws to the system is critical if anything like a competitive, free enterprise system is to be restored and preserved in the future.[39]

NOTES

1 These firms and their 1970 assets in billions of dollars are: AT&T ($49.6), Bank America ($29.7), Prudential ($29.1), Metropolitan ($27.9), First National City Bank ($25.8), and Chase Manhattan Bank ($24.5).

2 Dan Cordtz, "It's Time to Unload the Regulators," *Fortune,* vol. 84, no. 1, p. 65, July 1971.

3 Ibid., p. 65.

4 J. K. Galbraith, *The New Industrial State,* Boston: Houghton-Mifflin Co., 1967, p. 187.

5 "A Fortune Proposition," *Fortune,* vol. 73, no. 3, p. 129, March 1966.

6 "The Editor's Desk," *Fortune,* vol. 73, no. 3, p. 101, March 1966.

7 A. D. H. Kaplan made a similar observation more than two decades ago; see his article, "The Current Merger Movement Analyzed," *Harvard Business Review,* vol. 33, no. 3, p. 91, May–June 1955.

8 Jesse W. Markham, "Survey of the Evidence and Finding on Mergers," in National Bureau of Economic Research, Inc., *Business Concentration and Price Policy,* Princeton, N.J.: Princeton University Press, 1955, p. 167.

9 Walter Adams, "Comment" (following Markham's paper), National Bureau of Economic Research, Inc., *Business Concentration and Price Policy,* Princeton, N.J.: Princeton University Press, 1955, pp. 189–190.

10 This statement appeared in Dexter M. Keezer, "The Effectiveness of the Federal Antitrust Laws: A Symposium," *American Economic Review,* vol. 39, no. 4, p. 691, June 1949. This article contained a number of statements made by leading lawyers and economists concerning the antitrust laws. It appears that there has been little advancement in the past 25 years in this area since most of the statements would still be applicable.

11 Markham recognized this development when he said " . . . the merger-creating industry did not thrive for long. Bankers, industrialists, and the stock-buying public, on whose support the promoter relied, soon had their expectations shattered. In the eighteen-month period preceding October, 1903, the market value of 100 leading industrial stocks shrank by 43.4 percent. Much of this shrinkage was undoubtedly a downward adjustment of stock prices to reflect the difference between expected and actual earnings. The result was the 'Rich Man's panic' of 1903, by which time the early merger movement had run its course." Markham, op. cit., p. 166.

12 For more discussion on this point see Samuel Richardson Reid, *Mergers, Managers, and the Economy,* New York: McGraw-Hill, 1968, pp. 7–8.

13 Ralph L. Nelson, *Merger Movements in American Industry: 1895–1956,* Princeton, N.J.: Princeton University Press, 1959, p. 60.

14 Ibid., p. 60. Part of the reason for this is that Nelson defines a "merger capitalization" as follows (p. 18): "Conceptually this designation comes closest to being the sum of the sizes of the merging firms."

15 Both the vertical merger and diversification mergers began to be used on a large scale during this second wave. Joseph P. McKenna, in his article, "The Current Merger Movement," *Review of Social Economy,* vol. 16, no. 1, March 1958, pp. 12–13, states that "the vertical merger was much more common during the period of the twenties." Markham also observed (p. 171) that " . . . a large portion of the mergers formed in the 1920s brought together firms producing totally different lines of products, the same products in noncompeting territories, or firms engaged in different states of fabrication."

16 George J. Stigler, "Monopoly and Oligopoly by Merger," *American Economic Review,* vol. 40, no. 2, p. 31, May 1950.

17 Ibid.

18 Willard L. Thorp, "The Persistence of the Merger Movement," *American Economic Review,* Supplement, vol. 21, no. 1, p. 88, March 1931.

19 Markham, op. cit., p. 173.

20 Thorp, op. cit., p. 78.

21 It is estimated that there were slightly over 2,000 mergers involving an estimated $5 billion in assets during the 1940–1947 merger ripple. See Reid, op. cit., p. 73.

22 See Table 8.1. It is estimated that during the first merger wave (1898–1902) there were 2,653 reported mergers and during the second wave (1925–1931) a total of 5,846 reported mergers.

23 See Federal Trade Commission, *Current Trends in Merger Activity, 1969,* March 1970, p. 12.

24 See Carol J. Loomis, "The 500: A Decade of Growth," *Fortune,* vol. 74, no. 1, July 15, 1966, p. 214.

25 For a statistical comparison of the relative growth performance of firms using conglomerate mergers as well as firms following other growth strategies, see Reid, op. cit., pp. 177–205.

26 Benjamin J. Klebaner, "The Bank Merger Act: Background of the 1960 Version," *Southern Economic Journal,* vol. 34, no. 2, p. 252, October 1967. The Antitrust Division has been slightly more active since 1966 and has challenged about 3 percent of the approved bank mergers; see Oscar R. Goodman, "Antitrust and Competitive Issues in United States Banking Structure," *The Journal of Finance,* vol. 26, no. 2, pp. 615–646, May 1971.

27 It should be recognized that there are a number of individuals and organizations that favor either the abandonment or curtailment of the existing antitrust laws. For example, *Fortune* magazine has proposed that antitrust be restricted to price fixing and other hard-core restraints of trade. See "A Fortune Proposition," *Fortune,* vol. 73, no. 3, p. 129, March 1966.

28 Committee on the Judiciary, *Corporate and Bank Mergers,* Interim Report of the Antitrust Subcommittee, House of Representatives, 84th Congress, 1st Session, Washington, D.C., 1955, p. 17. Increased appropriations to the antitrust agencies does not necessarily mean increased effectiveness. The budgets of these agencies have generally been increasing during the 1960s while their formal caseloads have declined. For example, the FTC had a budget of $4.2 million in fiscal 1965 and it has increased in the past decade.

29 See *Business Week,* June 14, 1969, p. 49. Until the mid-1930s, the Antitrust Division of the Department of Justice got along on annual appropriations of less than $300,000. This would cover the costs of only a few cases a year. The division had to pick arbitrarily no more than a dozen cases a year for intensive investigation and trail. Once a given year's funds were committed, any conscious violators of the antitrust laws were guaranteed immunity for the time being, and open offenses might never be brought to trial for lack of appropriations made available to the Antitrust Division.

30 Prior to appointment as chief of the Antitrust Division of the Department of Justice, Donald F. Turner wrote an article, "Conglomerate Mergers and Section 7 of the Clayton Act," *Harvard Law Review,* vol. 78, no. 7, May 1965. In the article he stated (p. 1322) that " . . . a quick survey of the three broad categories of mergers would suggest the following relative hierarchy of rules: hardest on horizontal merger, easier on vertical, and least severe on conglomerates." The peak of the merger wave was attained during Turner's tenure at the Antitrust Division.

31 Public Law 89–356, amending the Bank Merger Act of 1960, was signed by President Johnson on February 21, 1966. This new legislation permits the responsible agency to approve a proposed merger "whose effect in any section of the country may be to substantially lessen competition, or to tend to create a monopoly, or which in any other manner would be in restraint of trade, clearly outweighed in the public interest by the probable effect of the transaction in meeting the convenience and needs of the community to be served." The Attorney General now has only 30 days after approval of a merger in which to initiate an action under the antitrust laws. As part of this bill, some bank merger cases which had received an "adverse" decision by the Supreme Court were exempted.

32 Recent studies by two newspapers (the Washington Post and the Washington Star) of information supplied the House Committee on Standards of Official Conduct under new ethics legislation ". . . show about two-thirds of the 435 House members have outside interests in financial institutions." See "Banking Leads in Personal Interests of Congressmen," *American Banker,* May 8, 1969, p. 1. Ten members of the House Banking and Currency Committee have ties with financial institutions, mostly commercial banks.

33 See the testimony of Willard F. Mueller, Committee on the Judiciary, Senate Subcommittee on Antitrust and Monopoly, *Economic Concentration,* 89th Cong. 1st Sess., 1965, pp. 520–521.

34 Ibid.

35   See Samuel R. Reid, "Mergers and the Economist," *Antitrust Bulletin,* vol. 14, no. 2, pp. 371–384, Summer 1969.

36   *Report of the Task Force on Productivity and Competition* (mimeographed), February 1969. The members of this group were George J. Stigler, Chairman, W. W. Bowman, Jr., R. H. Coase, R. S. Crampton, K. W. Dam, R. H. Mulford, R. A. Posner, P. O. Steiner, and A. O. Stott.

37   The proceedings of a conference held April 30, May 1, 1969, in Kansas City on this subject are available in Leon Garoian, *The Economics of Conglomerate Growth,* op. cit.

38   *Report of the Task Force on Antitrust Policy* (mimeographed), July 5, 1968, The members of this group were Phil C. Neal, Chairman, W. F. Baxter, R. H. Bork, C. H. Fulda, W. K. Jones, D. G. Lyons, P. W. MacAvoy, J. W. McKie, L. E. Preston, J. A. Rahl, G. D. Reycraft, R. E. Sherwood, and S. P. Posner, Staff Director.

39   In a speech delivered to the National Press Club on the occasion of the eighty-fifth anniversary of the Sherman Act in June 1975, Attorney General Edward H. Levi stated that the "paramount importance" of the antitrust laws was as "a viable alternative to more severe, more interfering, more bureaucratic forms of Government regulation." Because of this, he said the antitrust laws must be enforced vigorously and at times dramatically so that the public can see "splendid demonstrations" of their power against large corporations. In addition, he proposed the creation of a short-lived Presidential commission perhaps every five years, made up of lawyers, economists, and other experts from outside the government, "which would report on the concentration and structure of American industry from the standpoint of apparent anticompetitive or monopoly behavior." See *New York Times,* June 20, 1975, pp. 45–50.

Chapter 10

The Transportation Mess

Another important and basic area of the economy, the transportation complex, where Americans spend about $200 billion a year for services, has also experienced a flurry of merger activity. The activity during the 1960s centered on the railroads, and in the early 1970s, the urge to merge has affected the newer airline firms. Actually, mergers are not new to either of these regulated transportation industries. Among the railroads, there were 520 approved mergers, involving a score of rail firms, since the mid-1920s.[1] Among the domestic trunk airlines, the number of firms has declined from 38 to the current low of 10 carriers since the inception of regulation in 1938.

Certainly, in the transportation industries, the relative size of the approved mergers is more relevant than the number of these events. The largest approved merger in the history of business involved two large competing rail firms. This combination created a firm with over $7 billion of assets and $2 billion of revenues in 1968. It appears ironic that a decade of discussion took place prior to approval and further that during this decade, each of the firms, the New York Central and the Pennsylvania, achieved record profits independently. Following approval (and even promotion) by the regulatory agency involved, Penn Central's common stock moved above $86 per share, reflecting an expectation of synergistic benefits, in addition to the promised annual savings of over $80 million, due to the combination.[2] Within a year or so, when the merger miracles (i.e., divine synergy) failed to appear, the stock price steadily slumped and on that fateful June 8, 1970, when the $7 billion holding company petitioned for bankruptcy, the stock price plunged to a pathetic $5⅝ per share. On the basis of the 23.1 million shares then outstanding, this decline represented a paper loss of nearly $2 billion, the largest such single-firm loss in recent economic history.

In the past five years since the bankruptcy, the merged firm has lost $1.5 billion; it has not paid one cent of interest to more than 100,000 holders of its bonded indebtedness; it has cut back its payroll to 76,000 workers from 95,000, while 742 of its executives have left for other jobs. To continue operating, the merged firm has relied on outright government grants and guaranteed loans. Meanwhile, its plant has deteriorated so greatly that many of its trains are under slow orders, holding speeds to 6 to 10 miles an hour. This transportation mess is in the process of being transferred to ConRail, the new carrier organized by the United States Railway Association, another federal agency organized in 1973, which will surely drain more from the public purse.

THE PENN CENTRAL PROBLEM

It will be years before the tangled financial mess surrounding the failure of the Penn Central merger is known to the public; however, a staff report of the House Committee on Banking and Currency has uncovered some distressing facets of the situation.[3] These facets reveal some of the abuses which can arise when large financial institutions, such as commercial banks, have inside information generally obtained through interlocking directorates.

The staff report reveals highly unusual trading patterns by a select group of institutional investors, including Chase Manhattan National Bank and Morgan Guaranty Trust Co., both of which maintained interlocking directorates with the railroad. In addition, these banks held a combined total of about $85 million of the Penn Central's debt, and each was a member of the steering committee involved in the attempt to secure a government loan guarantee. Thus, each bank was in a preferred position to secure inside information. This is particularly true of the Chase Manhattan.

since the person most acquainted with the operations of the railroad—the president, Stuart Saunders—was a member of the board of directors of Chase Manhattan during the critical period prior to the financial collapse.

The staff report identifies certain inside events and negotiations which were not known to the general public, but available only to a highly select group of insiders. Three major events are singled out which occurred during the period May 19 through May 27, 1970. The events are listed as follows:

1 On or about May 19, Stuart Saunders, Chairman of the Board of Penn Central, discussed the possibility of a Government guaranteed loan with Secretary of the Treasury, David Kennedy.

2 On May 21, David Bevan, chief financial officer of the Penn Central, met with banking representatives. Discussion included P.C.'s postponement of the $100 million debenture offering and its intent to seek a Government guaranteed loan.

3 On May 27, the Board of Directors of the railroad met at 11:00 a.m. Directors were informed of decision to postpone the debenture offer . . . This was a private board of directors meeting and no announcement was made to the public about the failure of the debenture offering until 26 hours later, at 1:20 p.m. on May 28.[4]

The report notes that over half the sales of Penn Central stock recorded during the May 19 to May 27 period belonged to Chase Manhattan, the Allegheny Corporation Group, and five other institutional investors. On May 19, 77 percent of the sales recorded were made by the institutions studied and on May 27, the transactions conducted by this group apparently accounted for all the sales of Penn Central stock. Thus, the public has been the loser in a variety of ways from this approved merger. A few commercial bankers added insult to injury by using inside information to conduct a massive shell-game which apparently deceived the public.

Another notably large approved merger created the Burlington Northern through merger of Great Northern; Northern Pacific; Chicago, Burlington and Quincy; and Spokane, Portland, and Seattle railroads. This approved combination resulted in the union of four railroads with about 27,000 miles of track, vast timber and mineral resources, total assets in excess of $3 billion, and a dominant transportation firm covering a substantial region of the nation.

Regulatory approval of this huge merger is the direct result of the recent "permissiveness" of the Interstate Commerce Commission, aided by the Supreme Court. As far back as 1893, the Great Northern attempted to gain control of the Northern Pacific, but was effectively blocked for 77 years by various rulings of the Supreme Court. Within less than a year following the collapse of the Penn Central, the Supreme Court granted unanimous approval to the creation of another rail giant, thus reversing its previous judicial position.

THE RAIL MERGER PERFORMANCE RECORD

The demise of the Penn Central looms large on the record sheet when appraisal of the anticipated public interest benefits from approved mergers is undertaken. Great efforts have been and will be made to establish that the Penn Central is *sui generis*—a financial calamity without parallel. Indeed, one ardent proponent of combinations, J. Fred Weston, has already under-taken such an analysis and after a review of his efforts, the reader is put in the uneasy position of wondering if the merger had actually taken place.[5] Be assured that the merger *did* take place and that it was by no means a hasty marriage, nor even a "shotgun" wedding. A decade of promotional effort went behind this huge flop.

The proponents of this giant merger spewed forth glowing forecasts of unparalleled success for the firms involved and for the public in general. For a decade, they claimed that the merger would permit considerable benefits of consolidation and would yield annual cost savings in excess of $80 million. A forecasting error of this magnitude suggests that a reasonable course in the future would dictate an appropriate discounting of the alleged benefits of mergers. The lesson is clear since these optimistic assessments have turned out to be nonsense and there was a classic and costly *merger failure* in the process.

The Penn Central merger is by no means the only recent rail consolida-tion that did not live up to expectations. In a recent study by Robert Gallamore of nine post-World War II railroad mergers, only one seems to have lived up to its promise, and this merger represented a special situation since the two roads were under common ownership prior to the merger.[6] Of the other eight, one may have come close to expectations; for another, the statistical evidence was inconclusive; and the remaining six did *not* realize the anticipated cost savings. The six mergers that failed involved a variety of different kinds of combinations including mergers among two or three large carriers, mergers of small carriers into large carriers, and mergers which represented only acquisition of control of one carrier by another. Railroads which were parallel to each other and which were supposed to offer economies of density or routing did not appear to do better than those which were not primarily parallel. There also was no evidence to indicate that end-to-end mergers would be satisfactory either. What did appear to be significant was that regardless of the type of merger, there were usually serious unanticipated difficulties, a universal situation which is also readily apparent in many industrial and banking combinations.

One observer of combination activities among the rail firms, Stanley C. Vance, observed the problem, particularly as it related to the Penn Central, as follows:

> As subsequent Penn Central events have shown, there certainly was no magic in this merger. The expectations of synergy never materialized. The "green" (for the color of its box cars) New York Central team seemed to be treated as an acquisition rather than a full-fledged merger partner of the dominant Pennsy "red team." Alfred E. Perlman, who became New York Central's chief executive officer in 1954 and reconstituted that near-bankrupt Vanderbilt possession, is quoted as being less than enthusiastic over the merger. "This wasn't a merger—it was a takeover," Mr. Perlman conceded to friends after the two roads joined. This attitude was reflected in the flight of many top executives from the newly merged railroad. "And if they didn't quit, they were often relegated to positions where they didn't get responsibility commensurate with ability, knowledgeable observers say." Mr. Perlman himself was shunted into an out-of-the-way corporate corner as vice-chairman.[7]

A look at the summary tabulation presented in Table 10.1 reveals that mergers involving or creating large rail systems rather consistently failed to live up to their promoters' representations. The union of the B&O and the C&O, resulting in a rail firm with revenues of over $700 million, did not even yield the modest $13 million in expected annual savings. Rather, the combination resulted in added costs. The second largest merger in the study—that of the Norfolk and Western with the Nickel Plate and the Wabash—produced even worse results. Mergers of the smaller railroads, by contrast, have occasionally produced a better showing, although even here the evidence is such as to warrant a meticulous examination of projected cost savings and facile representations as to overall operational improvements in the public interest.

After years of hearings, which have resulted in numerous rail mergers approved by the Interstate Commerce Commission, the industry is a mess. The prices of rail services have continued to increase, while service has deteriorated to new lows. The lack of maintenance of track and equipment has caused a serious safety problem, as roadbeds across the nation are strewn with the debris resulting from thousands of derailments occurring annually. Shortages of freight cars are common as the remaining carriers divert their investments into nonrail activities.

The final blow to the public (as taxpayers) was the abandonment of passenger service by the carriers and the resulting bail-out of the railroads by the government, while freight operations remained in private hands. The costs to the American public have been staggering and will continue into the future. Mergers and regulation have not solved the problems of the

Table 10.1 Qualitative Summary of Performance of Recent Railroad Mergers

Merger case	Operating revenues, year of merger (millions)	Annual anticipated savings (millions)	Actual performance	Performance relative to expectations
L&N–NC&St.L*	$212 + $36 = $248	$ 3.2	Large-medium savings	Good—savings estimates probably met
N&W–VGN	204 + 50 = 254	10.3	Medium-small savings	Fair—savings estimates may have been met
Erie-Lackawanna	154 + 72 = 226	11.5	Small savings	Fair—savings estimates probably not met
CNW–M&StL	213 + 21 = 234	3.0	Small-medium extra costs	Poor—extra costs rather than savings
SOO Line*	40 + 32 + 7 = 79	1.2	Small extra costs	Poor—extra costs
C&O–B&O	339 + 366 = 705	13.4	Medium-large extra costs	Poor—extra costs
Sou–C of Ga.	271 + 44 = 315	5.9	Small extra costs	Poor—extra costs
DT&I–AA	21 + 7 = 28	0.2	No significant savings	Poor
N&W–NKP–Wabash	267 + 133 + 124 = 524	27.0	Medium extra costs	Poor—extra costs

*Common ownership or related management prior to merger.
Source: Interstate Commerce Commission Reports.

167

American railroads; rather, they have multiplied the costs to the public in what has become a national economic tragedy.

As stated previously, America has a discouraging propensity for neglecting the lessons of history. Despite the sad and discouraging record of the rail mergers, the newer and more glamorous airlines appear to be rushing head-on into the same economic madness in the search of elusive solutions to problems which could be better solved by other means. The remainder of this chapter will be devoted to this phenomenon.

THE AIRLINES—MERGERS, REGULATION, AND ALTERNATIVES

The domestic trunk airlines have displayed an increasing propensity to seek approval for merging as a means of correcting performance patterns. This development has occurred despite the dismal experiences in the rail and other industries. The rationale for this movement, which began in the early 1970s, is familiar to observers of the business scene—the persistent optimism that somehow mergers will solve basic problems and permit firms to realize certain scale economies, particularly those of the horizontal or geographical market-extension variety. All this is happening in the wake of the Penn Central debacle.

Actually, airline merger activity has been on the scene for a number of years; however, it has appeared to be random and rather gradual in its development. In the 33 years of regulation by the Civil Aeronautics Board, the number of domestic trunk airlines has declined from 38 to the current low of 10 carriers.

In the current period, the impetus for combination appears to center on the declining profits (or substantial losses) recorded by some carriers during the 1969–70 and 1974–75 recession periods. While there obviously are alternate solutions, the traditional merger alternative has generated some managerial support, which has been reinforced by the approval of the Department of Transportation.[8] Thus, the learning curve of this government agency appears to take an odd shape.

In order to determine if there is an empirical and logical basis for support of airline combinations and to examine the size-profitability hypothesis in this regulated industry, an empirical study was conducted.[9]

The size-profitability hypothesis received primary focus since approved mergers would instantly add increased size dimensions to the surviving airline firm. The suggestion that mere *size* influences profitability has long intrigued economists, as noted and discussed in Chapter 4. Most previous studies of the hypothesis have been concerned with the industrial firms and industries. Thus, an examination of the size-profitability hypothesis in the domestic trunk airlines industry has the advantage of data accessibility and homogenity, and the results should be more germane than those of the generalized industrial studies.

A Test of the Size-Profitability Hypothesis as Applied to the Airlines

As noted previously, the domestic trunk airlines industry is highly concentrated, with the four largest firms controlling about 70 percent of the assets. This study examines these four firms plus the remaining seven carriers for an 11-year period (1960–1970).[10] For purposes of analysis, these latter firms are divided into two groups, the medium four and the small three.[11] Statistics were compiled using data published by the Civil Aeronautics Board and *Moody's Handbook of Common Stocks.*

In order to obtain a measure by which profit, revenue, and expenses could be evaluated as a function of size, the operational parameters are expressed on a per unit basis—the unit being the *revenue-ton-mile.*[12] This unit is preferable to *available ton-miles* because it measures actual rather than potential airline performance. In order to determine the effect of size on each parameter, regression equations were computed which are mathematical models of the relationship between size and each parameter.[13] These regression equations describe the relationship of size to a parameter (see Table 10.2), and size is measured as either operating revenue or total assets. Both size parameters reveal similar trends, therefore the graphs and the table utilize operating revenue; however, the results are the same with either variable.

Size and Profitability

An examination of the data presented in Table 10.2 and Charts 10.1 and 10.2 reveals that increasing the size of an airline firm beyond the point of minimum unit operating expense will not result in increased profitability. If the firm's size is already at or beyond the point of maximum unit profit, reductions in unit operating expense will not result in increased unit profit because unit revenue resulting from growth decreases at a greater rate than unit expenses.

Total profitability will also decrease with any substantial growth beyond the point of maximum unit profit, because unit operating profit decreases faster than *size* increases, whether measured by operating revenue, revenue-ton-miles, or total assets.

Size and Cost

Ideally, one would expect the unit operating expense curve to decrease with size if benefits due to large scale exist in the industry. Unit costs

Table 10-2 Regression coefficients (B's) with respective t ratios and correlation coefficients (R^2) for first- and second-order equations. First-order equations are in the form of $Y = B_0 + B_1\ln(X)$, and second-order equations are in the form of $Y = B_0 + B_1\ln(X) + B_2[\ln(X)]^2$, where Y is an operational or profitability parameter and X is airline size (operating revenue)

	Second-order equations				First-order equations		
	B_0 (t ratio)	B_1 (t ratio)	B_2 (t ratio)	R^2	B_0 (t ratio)	B_1 (t ratio)	R^2
Operational parameters							
Operating profit/rtm*	-10.3 (-5.46)	1.06 (5.44)	-2.73×10^{-2} (-5.40)	.202	-1.32×10^{-1} (-1.26)	8.78×10^{-3} (1.64)	.014
Operating revenue/rtm	6.79 (2.73)	$-.598$ (-2.32)	1.42×10^{-2} (2.13)	.349	1.51 (12.08)	-5.02×10^{-2} (-7.76)	.330
First class/rtm	2.65×10^{-4} (13.57)	-2.65×10^{-5} (-13.10)	6.63×10^{-7} (12.65)	.802	1.82×10^{-5} (12.32)	-9.05×10^{-7} (-11.84)	.537
Coach/rtm	2.225×10^{-4} (13.57)	-2.21×10^{-5} (-12.86)	5.44×10^{-7} (12.20)	.876	2.30×10^{-5} (18.63)	-1.13×10^{-6} (-17.29)	.723
Freight and other/rtm	2.28×10^{-5} (8.55)	-2.18×10^{-6} (-7.91)	5.24×10^{-8} (7.34)	.830	3.24×10^{-6} (20.38)	-1.58×10^{-7} (-19.25)	.755
Operating expense/rtm	17.1 (5.11)	-1.66 (-4.79)	4.15×10^{-2} (4.62)	.357	1.64 (9.15)	-5.89×10^{-2} (-6.35)	.247
Flying operation/rtm	4.99 (4.14)	-4.86×10^{-1} (-3.89)	1.21×10^{-2} (3.75)	.264	4.77×10^{-1} (7.57)	$-^{1}$ (-5.29)	.183
Maintenance/rtm	3.84 (4.97)	-3.76×10^{-1} (-4.69)	9.39×10^{-3} (4.53)	.339	3.42×10^{-1} (8.27)	-1.30×10^{-2} (-6.07)	.230

			R^2			R^2
Aircraft and traffic servicing/rtm	2.85 (4.26)	-2.79×10^{-1} (−4.01)	7.01×10^{-3} (3.89)	.238	2.46×10^{-1} (6.99)	-8.46×10^{-3} (−4.66)	.147
Passenger service/rtm	1.59 (3.81)	-1.55×10^{-1} (−3.59)	3.88×10^{-3} (3.48)	.205	1.40×10^{-1} (6.49)	-4.88×10^{-3} (−4.37)	.131
Promotion and sales/rtm	2.14 (4.25)	-2.08×10^{-1} (−3.98)	5.18×10^{-3} (3.84)	.282	2.09×10^{-1} (7.91)	-7.55×10^{-3} (−5.54)	.199
General and admin./rtm	6.64×10^{-1} (2.76)	-6.43×10^{-2} (−2.58)	1.60×10^{-3} (2.48)	.138	6.80×10^{-2} (5.57)	-2.40×10^{-3} (−3.80)	.101
Depreciation and amortization/rtm	9.69×10^{-1} (1.19)	-8.93×10^{-2} (−.06)	2.18×10^{-3} (1.00)	.044	1.59×10^{-1} (3.94)	-5.31×10^{-3} (−2.55)	.044
Load factor	−518. (−2.78)	57.6 (2.98)	−1.46 (−2.92)	.087	26.0 (2.72)	1.06 (2.16)	.029
Profitability parameters							
Operating profit/total assets	−24.1 (−5.82)	2.47 (5.77)	-6.33×10^{-2} (−5.71)	.242	-5.13×10^{-1} (−2.22)	2.93×10^{-2} (2.46)	.040
Net income/total assets	−25.0 (−5.63)	2.54 (5.53)	-6.46×10^{-2} (−5.44)	.268	-8.85×10^{-1} (−3.61)	4.61×10^{-2} (3.64)	.092
Operating profit/operating revenue	−18.8 (−5.46)	1.94 (5.44)	-4.99×10^{-2} (−5.39)	.204	-2.54×10^{-1} (−1.34)	1.71×10^{-2} (1.74)	.016
Net income/operating revenue	−15.6 (−6.02)	1.60 (5.95)	-4.08×10^{-2} (−5.86)	.277	-4.50×10^{-1} (−3.09)	2.46×10^{-2} (3.27)	.075
Earnings per share	−285. (−3.98)	28.8 (3.87)	-7.21×10^{-1} (−3.75)	.231	−16.75 (−4.47)	9.02×10^{-1} (4.66)	.147

*Revenue-ton-mile.

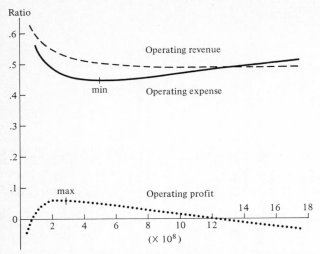

Chart 10.1 Operating revenue per revenue ton mile (RTM), operating expense per RTM, and operating profit per RTM versus size (operating revenue).

should move downward if stage length (length of flight from takeoff to landing) increases, as is the case for the large airlines.[14] However, this phenomenon has *not* been revealed in this study. The data underlying Chart 10.1 illustrate that unit operating expense is lowest for a range between the 1960–1970 mean size of the medium group of carriers and the four largest airline firms. In relation to current firm size, this minimum point is slightly above the 1969–1970 mean size of the medium four airlines.[15]

A breakdown of unit operating expenses reveals that six of the seven individual unit-expense curves have the same shape as the unit-operating-expense curve.[16] Only the depreciation and amortization curve goes down as size increases. Therefore, no one individual expense controls the shape of the overall unit-operating-expense curve.

The analysis indicates that the large airlines do *not* operate as efficiently as the smaller airlines and that the expected benefits of size were not attained in the domestic trunk airline industry in the 1960–1970 decade.

FURTHER ANALYSIS

Load factor (percentage of capacity utilized) is critical to the profitability and unit-cost measures of airline performance. The increased costs incurred in handling a higher load factor are almost negligible because fixed costs per flight far exceed variable costs; however, an increased load factor

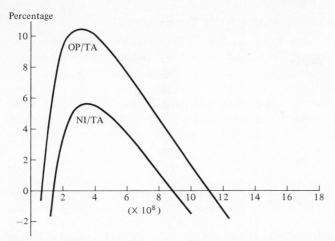

Chart 10.2 Operating profit per total assets and net income per total assets versus size (operating revenue).

causes unit operating revenue to increase faster than unit costs, contributing to increased profitability. During this study period, load factor and profitability *(NI/TA)* reach maximum values at the same airline size, demonstrating that the larger airlines are unable to fill their flights as well as the medium-sized airlines. Thus, the size-load factor relationship is a partial explanation for the existence of diseconomies of scale of the large airlines.

Another way of evaluating a firm's relative success is from the point of view of the stockholders, particularly those who invest for long-term gain. Earnings per share of the airlines follow curves similar to that of profitability (see Chart 10.2). Both curves attain a maximum point well below the current mean size of the largest airlines. This finding strongly suggests that proposed mergers involving any of the large airlines do not appear to be in the best interests of the public or the airlines and their shareholders.

Regulatory Implications

The public policy implications are straightforward and rather clearly indicate that the merger alternative is a suboptimal solution to the problems confronting the domestic trunk airlines industry. There are other alternatives which should be explored and encouraged such as *price* competition designed to increase load factors for the industry (as well as for the individual firms). In addition, consideration should also be given to deconcentration policies which would reduce the largest firms to a more efficient and profitable scale of operations.

The Load Factor and Price and Nonprice Competition

In addition to entry and mergers, the CAB regulates prices and even services to some extent.[17] This regulatory agency apparently favors target-return pricing, which contributes to a reduction in load factors in periods of declining business. As noted by *Fortune,* "CAB decisions have encouraged airline executives in a mistaken policy of seeking higher fares when business falls off in order to keep returns up—instead of cutting fares to attract new customers."[18] Richard E. Caves recognized this regulatory problem when he stated:

> . . . regulation that aims at normal profits implies a movement of prices counter to the business cycle and counter to most other prices in the economy. Meaningless shifts of relative prices would occur—shifts that might draw too many resources into the regulated industry in time of prosperity only to force the regulatory authority to raise prices to guarantee a normal reward in time of recession.[19]

As load factors declined during the 1969–70 and 1974–75 recessions, and profits along with them, the airlines clamored for higher fares. Starting in early 1969, the CAB granted several increases. Since then, air fares have increased considerably and load factors have generally declined. The fare increases were in part a consequence of underutilized capacity and at the same time a cause of lower utilization. *Fortune* has noted that "After so many years of anticompetitive regulation, not many airline executives tend to think in terms of trying to attract additional customers with lower fares."[20]

In the absence of price competition, most of the firm rivalry has been of the nonprice variety, as noted by Alfred E. Kahn:

> In part because the doors to price competition are closed, airline companies compete very strenuously among themselves in the quality of service they offer—most notably in adopting the most modern and attractive equipment and in the frequency with which they schedule flights, but also in providing comfort, attractive hostesses, in-flight entertainment, food and drink.[21]

In conclusion, it appears that increased pricing freedom coupled with a restrictive merger policy by the Civil Aeronautics Board would be the most beneficial course for both private and public interests. Target rates of return should be abolished in pricing and service decisions in the interests of all concerned. Richard E. Caves, in a prophetic and perceptive observation, stated:

The variety of services offered to travelers can be improved somewhat if the Board allows the carriers more freedom to experiment, but the Board's ultimate fear of subnormal profits will remain. The number of carriers may continue to shrink, even if profits for the industry as a whole average better than normal, unless the Board sees the long-run danger in mergers.[22]

The evidence rather strongly suggests that the regulatory course in this industry should be a strict policy regarding merger activity and a more relaxed policy on pricing practices designed to increase the load factor.

Airline Deconcentration

Rather than encouraging higher levels of concentration in the domestic airlines industry, a program of periodic and orderly spinoffs of components of the larger firms would appear to be in the interests of the airlines, as well as the public. Proposals of this type generally are greeted with minimum enthusiasm, yet the fact remains that diseconomies of scale are as real and as possible to attain as economies of scale.[23] This factor appears to have become obscured in the rhetoric surrounding the discussions of relative firm size in all segments of the economy. The situation has been summed up quite well by the chief executive officer of a large airline, Najeeb Haloby, who observed that "Running a huge corporation is not pure, unmitigated joy."[24] It is possible to return some joy to the executive suite through a program of corporate shrinkage, designed to restore balance and efficiency in airline and other industries.

THE REGULATORY AFTERMATH

America is mired in a transportation mess created by a complexity of forces, not the least of which is the massive dose of inept management aided and abetted by the transportation regulatory agencies. The situation has received attention but no solutions, with the public paying while the carriers struggle to keep afloat. For example, in 1970, the 50 largest transportation firms, taken as a group, lost money despite widespread rate increases. Only one of the largest six firms turned a profit during 1970—the Southern Pacific, and the return was less than 5 percent on equity. While the profit picture improved somewhat in the early 1970s, the outlook remains dim for many large firms in the important transportation sector.

Until bold new steps are initiated related to structure and pricing, there is scant reason to be optimistic that the mess will evaporate. Crisis follows crisis, and the solutions usually revolve around either a merger or some form of government subsidy from the taxpayers' pockets. A new economic

America needs, and must encourage, imaginative alternatives in the decade ahead if the transportation mess is to be solved. Meanwhile, the airlines, led by the international carriers and closely followed by the large domestic carriers, are rapidly approaching the fate of the rail industry in the new industrial order.

NOTES

1 For the period 1925–1968, more than 1,000 railroads lost their identity, the majority due to mergers.
2 For those who might be unaware of the synergy concept, it is usually referred to as the so-called 2 + 2 = 5 effect. See H. Igor Ansoff and J. Fred Weston, "Merger Objectives and Organization Structure," *The Quarterly Review of Economics and Business,* vol. 2, no. 3, pp. 49–58, August 1962.
3 See Staff Report of the House Committee on Banking and Currency, *The Penn Central Failure and the Role of Financial Institutions,* part V, "Trading in Penn Central Stock: Financial Institutions and Privileged Information," Washington, D.C., March 29, 1971.
4 Ibid., see letter of transmittal by Hon. Wright Patman, Chairman of the Committee, on pp. III–IV.
5 See J. Fred Weston, "The Industrial Economics Background of the Penn Central Bankruptcy," *Journal of Finance,* vol. 26, no. 2, pp. 311–322, May 1971.
6 Robert Gallamore, "Railroad Mergers: Cost, Competition and the Future Organization of the American Railroad Industry," unpublished thesis, Harvard University, 1970.
7 Stanley C. Vance, *Managers in the Conglomerate Era,* New York: Wiley-Interscience, 1971, p. 218.
8 The Department of Transportation approved the pending application of American Airlines and Western Airlines to merge. The Department of Justice expressed opposition to the merger on anticompetitive grounds, and the CAB rejected the merger.
9 This study was conducted in collaboration with James W. Mohrfeld, a graduate student at the University of New Hampshire and currently a doctoral candidate at the University of Texas at Austin.
10 The domestic trunk airlines, listed according to size, are: United, American, TWA, Eastern, Delta, Northwest, National, Western, Braniff, Continental, and Northeast.
11 Based on 1960–1970 operating revenue the large airlines (1–4) hold 68.2 percent of the market, while the medium-sized firms (5–8) hold 22.2 percent, and the smaller firms (9–11) have the remaining 9.6 percent.
12 A revenue-ton-mile is a ton of cargo carried a mile.
13 Two regression equations were computed for each parameter, first-order and second-order logarithms. First-order equations are of the form $Y - B8 + B_1$ (ln

X) where Y is the magnitude of the specific parameter and X is airline size. Second-order equations are in the form $Y - B8 + B_1(\ln X) + B_2(\ln X)^2$. The coefficient of determination (R^2) for each equation is used to determine if the equation is a good fit of the data. If the R^2 values of both first- and second-order equations for a parameter are significant, the t ratio of the coefficient of the $(\ln X)^2$ factor is examined. If the $(\ln X)^2$ value significantly improves the fit of the equation to the data, the t ratio for this value is significant, and hence the second-order equation is taken as a better mathematical model.

14 The mean stage length of the four airlines is 536 miles, the mean for the medium four airlines is 402 miles, and for the small three airlines it is 385 miles (during the 1960–1970 period).

15 The mean size (operating revenue) for the three airlines groups during the 1960–1970 period was: large four, -7.0×10^8; medium four, -2.3×10^8; and small three, -1.3×10^8. During the 1969–1970 period the mean size was: large four, -11.5×10^8; medium four, -3.8×10^8; and small three, -2.4×10^8.

16 The seven individual unit operating expenses are: flying operations, maintenance, passenger service, aircraft and traffic servicing, promotion and sales, general and administrative, and amortization and depreciation.

17 In approving a fare increase, the Board for the first time in 1972 established a standard for equipment utilization. Major airlines are now expected to fill at least 55 percent of their seats on an *industrywide* average. Thus, a new regulatory twist has been instituted *sans* competitive pricing and appears to be an economic paradox.

18 "A Case for Grounding the CAB," *Fortune,* vol. 84, no. 1, p. 146, July 1971. It is worth noting that international fares, which have displayed a downward movement (and increased load factors), are not under the CAB's control.

19 Richard E. Caves, "Performance, Structure, and the Goals of Civil Aeronautics Board Regulation," in Paul W. MacAvoy (ed.), *The Crisis of the Regulatory Commission,* New York: W. W. Norton & Co., Inc., 1970, p. 148. For a more complete discussion of the problems of airline regulation see Caves' book, *Air Transport and Its Regulators; An Industry Study,* Cambridge: Harvard University Press, 1962.

20 "A Case for Grounding the CAB," op. cit., p. 146.

21 Alfred E. Kahn, *The Economics of Regulation: Principles and Institutions,* vol. II, *Institutional Issues,* New York: John Wiley & Sons, Inc., 1971, p. 211. As noted by Kahn, the expenses in the latter catagory alone are not negligible, since it is reported that an airline spends more than $30 for food and drink for each transatlantic first-class passenger.

22 Caves, "Performance, Structure, and the Goals of Civil Aeronautics Board Regulation," op. cit., p. 149.

23 Some belated recognition of this factor is evident in the announcement by United Airlines, the largest firm in the industry, that it is drastically decentralizing decision-making and operating responsibility. Three operating divisions have been established—each of which by itself would rank in size among the top half dozen or so airlines. The president of the firm listed the following advantages of the decentralization: shorter lines of authority, greater field autonomy, increased stress on the profit center concept and cost control. See *The Wall Street Journal,* October 1, 1971, p. 6. Deconcentration is a step beyond decentralization since independence is also achieved in addition to the other benefits.

24 See "Pan American: Carrier in Crisis," *Time,* October 25, 1971, p. 84.

Bank Holding Companies
and the Regulators

Another dimension of the lopsided economy is the structure of the commercial banking business in the United States. Despite the fact that there are over 14,000 commercial banks, the 100 largest banking firms control 70 percent of all bank deposits. In addition, bank holding companies have multiplied in recent years and have become a potent economic force in national, regional, and local markets. The deposits controlled by multiple-bank holding companies increased over 1,500 percent between 1960 and 1973 and amounted to 35 percent of all deposits, while the newer one-bank holding companies held 30 percent of the total deposits by 1973. Combined, the holding companies control almost two-thirds of the nation's commercial bank deposits in what has been an explosive development.

Bank mergers and holding company formations, which must be approved by a regulatory agency (unlike the industrials), continued at a high level during the 1960s and early 1970s, despite congressional concern and statutory mandates. Congress has long sought to protect the banking system against overconcentration and monopoly practices. In the Clayton Act of

1914, the Federal Reserve System was charged with the responsibility for enforcing prohibitions against bank stock acquisitions whenever the effect might substantially lessen competition or tend to create a monopoly. Needless to say, the agency did not carry out this mandate, nor have the bank regulators followed the newer congressional mandates of the last two decades. Banking provides a prime example of regulatory breakdown on the economic scene, as well as a powerful illustration of the role of vested interests in the imbalanced economy.

This chapter is concerned with the multiple-bank holding company development since passage of legislation in 1956 designed to curb activities in this area. The following chapter will examine bank merger developments since passage of the Bank Merger Act of 1960.

MULTIPLE-BANK HOLDING COMPANIES

Multiple-bank holding companies, firms that own or control two or more banks, have been a part of the American banking structure since the turn of the century. As with other types of holding companies, these firms did not become significant until the late 1920s, at the peak of a period of combination activity when a number of the leading firms were formed.[1] This flurry of activity brought bank holding companies under federal regulation and supervision for the first time by the Banking Act of 1933.[2] Since the coverage of the act was limited and did not regulate the growth of these firms, Congress passed the Bank Holding Company Act of 1956 to strengthen public control over holding company formation, expansion, and other activities.

Congressional Intent

The executive, legislative, and bank-regulatory agencies expressed concern over the potential dangers inherent in bank holding company activity prior to the signing of Public Law 511 on May 9, 1956, by President Eisenhower. As early as 1938, President Roosevelt made recommendations to stop further expansion of bank holding companies and to order their gradual liquidation as part of his program to strengthen and enforce the antitrust laws.

During the late 1920s, the Federal Reserve Board requested Congress to grant the Board authority to gather data on bank holding companies. Following the stock market collapse in 1929, the Board became concerned with the manner in which holding companies combined banking and non-banking activities. Congressional hearings in the early 1930s revealed the abuses of investment banking operations during the speculative whirl which culminated in the 1929 financial collapse. These operations were conducted mainly through securities affiliates controlled by banks or by holding companies which owned stock in the banks. The result of these hearings was the Banking Act of 1933, which included a provision designed to curb the abuses resulting from the association of banking (including holding companies) with the securities business.

Again in 1943, the Board of Governors of the Federal Reserve System went on record recommending new bank holding company legislation. The Board requested immediate enactment of legislation to restrict the formation and expansion of holding companies. Specific bills were proposed by the Board in 1945, 1949, 1952, and 1955. The Federal Deposit Insurance Corporation advocated the same measures (suggested by President Roosevelt in 1938) as late as 1945 because of concern about the monopolistic tendencies of bank holding companies and the difficulty of proper supervision.

In 1947, the Senate Banking and Currency Committee felt the need for legislation to be pressing and clear. Numerous bills and committee hearings, whose record spreads across volumes of printed pages, reveal the attention and concern of Congress on the problem of regulating multibank holding companies. All this activity culminated in the passage of the Bank Holding Company Act of 1956 by an overwhelming margin almost a decade later.[3]

The original act was amended on July 1, 1966, and congressional intent concerning this legislation can be summarized. Broadly speaking, the major objectives of the 1956 act, as amended, are (1) to preserve competition in banking markets; (2) to protect the rights of states to determine the type of banking structure within their borders; and (3) to prevent undue concentration of economic power.

The prolonged and obvious concern of numerous public officials and agencies concerning the need for regulation of multibank holding companies, in order to prevent growing concentration and to protect the public interest, is a matter of record and mandate. In order to determine the alignment of congressional intent and objectives with regulatory performance, the pattern of bank holding company activity since the passage of the legislation is worthy of review.

The Pattern and Intensity of Multiple-Bank Holding Company Activity

Following passage of the Bank Holding Company Act, the growth of group banking firms came to a halt and actually declined during the period 1957 to 1962. At least two major contributing factors reversed this pattern midway through the 1960s. It became evident to bankers that the policies of the Board of Governors concerning holding company activity were not especially restrictive, coupled with a substantial increase in combination activity by industrial firms and commercial banking firms. In other words, there was a favorable regulatory and economic environment which contributed to an increased tempo of group banking activity.

The data for the period 1957–1973 are presented in Table 11.1 and reveal that there are two rather distinct periods, one of relative stability from 1957 to 1965, and another of rapid and accelerating growth from 1966 to 1973. A closer look at these distinct time periods and the relative change of the various measures of magnitude is available in Table 11.2. During the initial 1957–1965 period, the number of registered multiple-bank holding companies increased by only 6 percent, during the 1966–1970 and 1970–1973 periods, the increase almost doubled in each period.[4] In each of the categories, the increase was higher during the early 1970s and in some cases the increase was substantial, reflecting the intensity of activity. This is an economic development of substantial magnitude in a relatively brief period of time and suggests a need for more examination of the regulatory record.

SEVEN PEOPLE AND REGULATORY BEHAVIOR

The Record

The relative role of multiple-bank holding companies in the structure of commercial banking is basically determined by a single bank-regulatory agency—the Board of Governors of the Federal Reserve System. Responsibility for the formation of these firms and any expansion of activities and/or mergers rests with this single agency as provided in the Bank Holding Company Act of 1956.[5]

One primary objective of the legislation was to prevent undue concentration of ownership of banking activities through the holding company device. The Board of Governors of the Federal Reserve System, composed of seven people, was provided with the authority to approve or disapprove mergers and acquisitions of additional banks by registered firms. Amendments to the act in 1966 were more specific, since the Board was charged with disapproving any merger by a bank holding company "Whose effect in any section of the country may be to substantially lessen competition, or to tend to create a monopoly, or which in any manner could be in restraint of trade, unless it finds that the anticompetitive effects are clearly outweighed in the public interest by the probable effect of the transaction in meeting the convenience and needs of the community."

The "anticompetitive" and "convenience and needs" tests appear to be the direct result of the efforts by the Antitrust Division of the Department of Justice to challenge some approved mergers in the courts for antitrust violations.[6] This amendment appears to have weakened the origi-

Table 11.1 Comparison of Offices and Deposits of Banks Affiliated with Registered Multiple-Bank Holding Companies from December 31, 1957, to December 31, 1973

Year	1957	1958	1959	1960	1961	1962	1963	1964	1965	1966	1967	1968	1969	1970	1973*
Number of companies	50	49	48	47	46	49	52	54	53	65	74	80	97	121	251
Banks	417	418	413	427	427	442	454	460	468	561	603	629	723	895	1,815
Total offices	851	848	967	1,107	1,107	1,215	1,278	1,379	1,486	1,802	2,085	2,262	2,674	3,260	9,328
Offices as a percentage of commercial bank offices:															
In holding co. states	7.7	7.9	8.7	9.1	9.3	9.6	9.4	9.5	9.6	10.4	11.5	12.2	14.8	15.9	
In United States	5.6	5.7	6.0	6.2	6.3	6.5	6.5	6.5	6.7	7.8	8.6	8.9	10.1	11.8	
Deposits ($, millions)	15,139	15,998	17,311	18,274	19,836	21,203	24,528	24,959	27,560	41,081	49,827	57,634	62,574	78,064	239,148
Deposits as a percentage of all commercial bank deposits:															
In holding co. states	8.8	9.6	10.4	10.6	10.6	10.8	10.8	10.7	10.9	14.2	15.4	16.4	18.9	20.3	n.a.
In United States	6.8	7.4	7.9	8.0	8.0	8.1	8.2	8.1	8.3	11.6	12.6	13.2	14.3	16.2	35.1

*Separate data for multibank holding companies were not published by the Federal Reserve for the years 1971 and 1972.

Source: Federal Reserve Bulletins.

Table 11.2 Multibank Holding Company Statistics for the 1957–1973, 1957–1965, 1965–1970, and 1970–1973 Periods

	1957	1973	Percentage change	1957	1965	Percentage change	1965	1970	Percentage change	1970	1973	Percentage change
Number of companies	50	251	402.0	50	53	6.0	53	121	128.3	121	251	107.4
Banks	417	1,815	335.3	417	468	12.2	468	895	91.2	895	1,815	102.8
Branches	851	7,513	782.8	851	1,486	74.6	1,486	3,260	119.4	3,260	7,513	130.5
Total offices	1,268	9,328	635.6	1,268	1,954	54.1	1,954	4,155	112.6	4,155	9,328	124.5
Offices as a percentage of bank offices												
In United States	5.6	*	—	5.6	6.7	19.6	6.7	11.8	76.1	11.8	*	—
Deposits ($, billions)	15.1	239.1	1,483.4	15.1	27.6	82.8	27.6	78.1	183.0	78.1	239.1	206.1
Deposits as a percentage of bank deposits												
In United States	6.8	35.1	616.2	6.8	8.3	22.1	8.3	16.2	95.2	16.2	35.1	116.7

*Not available for multibank holding companies separately since 1970.
Source: Federal Reserve Bulletins.

nal act of 1956 by providing the Board of Governors with a ready-made loophole, that is, falling back on the so-called convenience and needs criterion in approving bank mergers and applications for the formation of holding companies.

An examination of the approval rates of each member of the Board of Governors (as presented in Table 11.3) reveals a varied pattern of approval rates ranging from a low of 71 percent to a perfect 100 percent, with a median rate of 86 percent for the 1956–1970 period. When the approval rates are determined for separate time periods, that is, the 1956–1965 period and the 1966–1970 period, a different pattern results. The median approval rate in the initial period was 78 percent, with a low of 55 percent and a high of 100 percent. During the 1965–1970 period of increasing activity, the median rate was 89 percent, with a low of 76 percent and a high of 96 percent. These increased approval rates by the Board of Governors of the Federal Reserve System must be considered as a contributory cause for the increased activity in the bank holding company field in recent years.

Some Explanations

The regulatory record indicates a more liberal approach to bank holding company applications since the mid-1960s. There appear to be several factors which account for this development. The basic underlying factor is the lack of an adequate definition and identification of the public interest in these matters. This factor has persisted since the inception of the original act in 1956; however, the problem has intensified since the dispute between the bank regulatory agencies and the Antitrust Division of the Department of Justice following the judicial challenges of approved bank mergers during the 1960s.

Another factor is the "snowball" effect of the rapidly growing number of applications upon administrative procedures within the regulatory process. A recognized "lenient" policy encourages applications for new formations as well as expansion of existing groups. Each of these factors, as well as related factors, deserves additional brief comment.

The Definition of the "Public Interest"   In section 3c of the 1956 act, Congress listed several factors to be considered by the Board in determining whether to approve proposals by holding companies: these factors are:

(1) the financial history and condition of the company or companies and the banks concerned; (2) their prospects; (3) the character of their management; (4) the convenience, needs, and welfare of the communities and the area con-

Table 11.3 Number of Bank Holding Cases, Approvals, and Rates of Approval, 1956–1970, 1956–1965, and 1966–1970

Governor	1956–1970			1956–1965			1966–1970		
	Cases	Approved	Rate (%)	Cases	Approved	Rate (%)	Cases	Approved	Rate (%)
Martin	238	205	86.1	84	65	77.4	154	140	90.9
Balderstrom	95	73	76.8	90	70	77.8	5	3	60.0
Szymczak	32	24	75.0	32	24	75.0			
Mills	81	67	82.7	81	67	82.7			
Robertson	384	274	71.4	92	51	55.4	292	223	76.4
Shephardson	129	104	80.6	92	73	79.3	37	31	83.8
King	44	32	72.7	44	32	72.7			
Vardaman	3	3	100.0	3	3	100.0			
Mitchell	327	291	80.0	53	38	71.7	274	253	92.3
Daane	253	234	92.5	21	19	90.5	232	215	92.7
Maisel	299	264	88.3	9	8	88.9	290	256	88.3
Brimmer	266	231	86.8	—	—	—	266	231	86.8
Sherrill	237	227	95.8	—	—	—	237	227	95.8
Burns	96	90	93.8	—	—	—	96	90	93.8
Average			85.1			79.2			86.1
Median			86.5			77.4			89.6

Source: *Federal Reserve Bulletins*, January 1956–January 1971.

cerned; and (5) whether or not the effect of such acquisition or merger or consolidation would be to expand the size or extent of the bank holding company systems involved beyond limits consistent with adequate and sound banking, the public interest, and the preservation of competition in the field of banking.

Since no weights were assigned to these five factors by the legislation, a considerable amount of regulatory discretion resulted. The governor with the lowest approval rate, J. L. Robertson, has noted that "these factors do not constitute a standard to govern the Board's actions. The only requirement is that consideration be given to the factors named; the weight to be accorded to each is completely within the Board's discretion."[7]

In the absence of an identified and workable definition of "the public interest," it is reasonable to expect personal viewpoints to prevail in the decision-making process. Larry R. Mote, of the Federal Reserve Bank of Chicago, has noted the fact that the Board votes more from a position of varied personal judgment than from a detailed objective concerning bank structure, or from knowledge gained from research. Mote concludes:

> What the voting in these cases does indicate is that the evidence on which the Board relies in judging merger and holding company cases is something less than unequivocal. Given the major disagreements that still exist within the Board—and between the Board and the other agencies—regarding the delineation of the relevant geographic market and the proper focus of policy, it is clear that it will be a long time before tested and transferable knowledge displaces, to any appreciable extent, the large element of personal judgment in merger and holding company decisions.[8]

It is interesting to note that this position persists despite the fact that economists have generated a number of empirical research studies relating bank structure and performance. These various studies appear to have been largely ignored by the bank regulatory agencies in favor of the views of private and special interest groups. In other words, in the absence of a clear definition of the public interest in banking beyond the safety of deposits, private interests can influence the direction of regulatory discretion to a subset of goals with varying degrees of desirability for the general public. Thus, concern about banking structure and performance on pricing can be mitigated to concerns over the size of lending limits, the provision of data-processing services, the provision of trust services, bank credit cards, and other types of services. Since a segment of the public may have an interest in some of these services, it is presumed that the benefits flow to the general public.

The "Snowball Effect" and Administrative Procedure   A factor of increasing significance is the growing administrative burden upon the Board of Governors of the Federal Reserve System. This burden is substantial as imposed by law and is growing through self-imposition. That is, the more applications are approved for the formation of new companies, the more future applications can be expected for expansion purposes until there is a substantial regulatory or legislation change. This pattern is apparent during the 1966–1970 period, and the problem becomes compounded since each case takes time and the demands on the Board are increasing in all areas. Dissent is even costlier to the individual governor since it usually involves a written opinion.[9]

In addition to the growing caseload of multiple-bank holding company applications and merger cases which must be decided under the provisions of the Bank Merger Act of 1960, Congress amended the Bank Holding Company Act of 1956 to include the activities of one-bank holding companies.[10] This regulatory burden seems incomprehensible to the outside observer and suggests the need for a comprehensive examination of the bank regulatory processes if congressional intent and the public interest are to be served adequately in the years ahead. The outcome of the recent permissiveness in regulatory behavior illustrates the point and is presented in the next section.

The Outcome

In order to determine if the increased permissiveness of the Board of Governors (as reflected by their voting records concerning bank holding company applications and the resulting surge in activity) has been aligned with the original congressional mandate, an examination of changes in levels of concentration is in order. The data in Table 11.4 separate the various states by the intensity of approved applications of bank holding companies for the period 1957–1970. In addition to this dichotomy based upon activity, the changes in concentration during the period are listed.

An examination of the data reveals that concentration has increased substantially in most of the "active" states. Some of the notable increases by percentage points were in Virginia (2,638 percent), Colorado (1,038 percent), Florida (323 percent), Maine (818 percent), New York (343 percent), and Ohio (248 percent). The average increase for the active group was 578 percent. The only state which registered a decline was Minnesota, which was also the only state among the active group which had a decline in the percentage of banking offices controlled by holding companies.

Eight of the 11 "moderate" states had relatively small increases in concentration with an average increase of 40 percent. The remaining states with bank holding companies which were *not* involved in any approved

Table 11.4 Approved Multiple-Bank Holding Company Orders and Changes in Concentration of Deposits by States, 1957–1970

States	Number of approved orders, 1957–1970	Percentage of deposits controlled by holding companies		Percentage change
		1957	1970	
Active group				
(10+ approvals)				
Florida (U)*	88	11.5	48.6	322.6
Wisconsin (B)	56	20.9	43.4	107.7
Virginia (B)	41	1.6	43.8	2,637.5
Ohio (B)	30	6.0	20.9	248.3
New York (B)	23	5.4	23.9	342.6
Missouri (U)	23	8.7	27.7	218.4
Colorado (U)	19	4.5	51.2	1,037.8
Iowa (U)	13	7.6	10.8	42.1
Maine (B)	12	5.0	45.9	818.0
Minnesota (B)	12	61.7	59.7	(−3.2)
Average	31.7	13.3	37.6	577.2
Moderate group				
(1–9 approvals)				
Massachusetts (B)	8	20.2	22.3	10.4
Tennessee (B)	7	3.5	8.3	137.1
California (B)	6	7.0	9.7	38.6
New Mexico (B)	5	13.5	19.4	43.7
Montana (B)	5	53.4	52.4	(−1.9)
Texas (U)	5	3.0	7.1	136.7
Utah (B)	4	52.7	45.7	(−13.3)
Washington (B)	3	13.6	18.6	36.8
New Hampshire (B)	3	9.5	13.1	37.9
Georgia (B)	2	34.7	33.0	(−4.9)
South Dakota (B)	2	32.9	43.2	31.3
Wyoming (U)	1	17.1	21.7	26.9
Average	4.3	21.8	24.5	39.7
No-approval states (9)				
North Dakota (B)	0	37.8	39.7	5.0
Indiana (B)	0	2.2	1.0	(−54.5)
Kentucky (B)	0	7.9	9.4	19.0
Idaho (B)	0	40.4	40.6	.5
Illinois (U)	0	.9	.2	(−77.8)
Nebraska (B)	0	10.2	9.1	(−10.8)
Oregon (B)	0	44.5	42.2	(−5.2)
Arizona (B)	0	38.2	32.9	(−13.9)
Nevada (B)	0	74.9	62.5	(−16.6)
Average	0	33.0	26.4	(−17.1)

*The (U) or (B) following the name of the state indicates either a unit or branching state law in 1970.

Source: Federal Reserve Bulletins.

Table 11.5   Results of Analysis of Variance Tests Related to Changes in Control Ratios Concerning Percentage of Commercial Bank Deposits Held by Multiple-Bank Holding Companies, 1957–1970

	Active states (10)	Moderate states (12)	states (9)	F ratio
Average percentage change in ratio of deposits controlled	577.2	39.7	(−17.1)	$5.25^{(0.025)}$

Source: The data as presented by state and group in Table 11.5 were tested for significant differences in group means through use of a one-way analysis of various tests. The significance level is shown in parentheses as a superscript to the *F* ratio and indicates that the probability is 0.025 that the observed differences in group means could be the result of chance.

applications generally exhibited a decline in concentration over the period, with an average decline of minus 17 percent during the period. This is an indication that if there were no approved bank holding company applications, there may well be a trend toward gradual deconcentration of multiple-bank holding company control of assets and deposits in many sections of the country.

Another method of determining whether the applications approved by the Board of Governors of the Federal Reserve System have significantly altered the banking structure (as it relates to holding companies) is to make an analysis of the variance of the group means. The results of these tests are presented in Table 11.5. The average change in the percentage of deposits controlled by the bank holding companies from 1957 to 1970 in the 10 *active* states was plus 577 percent; for the *moderate* states, the gain was 40 percent; and for the states with *no* activity, the percentage declined an average of minus 17 percent. The results are statistically significant at the 0.025 level, which indicates that the evidence strongly suggests that regulatory permissiveness has contributed to structural changes.

EFFECT OF STATE BRANCHING LAWS

It has been a rather common belief in banking circles that bank holding company activity is related to the type of branching regulation which exists in particular states, in other words, that the holding company form of organization has been utilized as a method of avoiding restrictive branching legislation, particularly in unit banking states. It appears that this belief is at least partially correct in some states, since four of the ten "active" states have unit banking. Thus, further tests were developed to examine this hypothesis, and the results are presented in Table 11.6

Table 11.6 Results of Analysis of Variance Tests Related to Changes in Deposits, the Percentage of Deposits Controlled in Various States, Banking Offices, and the Percentage of Offices in the States, 1957–1970

Variables	Unit states	Limited-branching states	Statewide-branching states	F ratio*	No-approval states	Moderate-approval states	Active-approval states	F ratio*
Deposits ($)	594.7	336.1	1,087.2	0.75	122.3	249.8	1,641.9	$4.43^{(0.025)}$
Percentage of deposits controlled	169.9	80.4	351.4	0.74	(−17.1)	39.7	577.2	$5.25^{(0.025)}$
Banking offices	318.2	218.3	795.3	0.78	52.7	130.0	1,150.2	$3.60^{(0.05)}$
Percentage of banking offices	180.3	88.9	355.7	0.63	(−4.7)	26.9	605.7	$5.18^{(0.025)}$

*The F ratios shown for each variable are based on one-way analysis of variance tests of the significance of the observed differences in group means for that variable. The italicized F ratios are those for which the probability is 0.05 or less that the observed differences in group means could be the result of chance; in these cases, the significance levels are shown in parentheses as superscripts to the F ratios.
Source: Federal Reserve Bulletins.

Four dependent variables were included in the analysis of variance tests: deposits (in dollars) controlled by bank holding companies; percentage of deposits (in the state) controlled; the number of banking offices; and the number of offices controlled. The analysis of variance tests of the group means, utilizing the type of state branching law as the independent variable, indicates that there was no significant difference between the groups. By contrast, each of the variables was statistically significant when the groups are separated according to the amount of holding company activity approved by the Board of Governors of the Federal Reserve System. The differences are extreme and indicate that *regulatory behavior* is more significant than the type of state regulation. Despite the fact that regulatory discretion appears in conflict with the original statutory mandate, the Bank Holding Company Act was amended to include the one-bank holding companies in late 1970.

THE 1970 AMENDMENTS

On the last day of 1970, Congress expanded the coverage of the Bank Holding Company Act to include one-bank holding companies (Public Law 91–607). There was also a revision of section 4(c) (8) under which bank holding companies may acquire interests in nonbanking activities subject to certain restrictions and upon certain conditions. The sole regulatory agency in these matters remains the Board of Governors of the Federal Reserve System, despite the permissive record outlined above.

The changes in bank holding company control (as defined under the amendments) of banks, branches, deposits, and assets have been spectacular. The data are presented in Table 11.7 and are awesome indeed. For example, the number of bank holding companies, including the one-bank variety, has increased from 50 in 1957 to 1,677 in 1973, a spectacular gain. Deposits increased from about $15 billion in 1957 to close to $450 billion in 1973. Holding companies now hold a majority, 65 percent, of the nation's bank deposits compared to a mere 7 percent in 1957, the year after the legislation was passed. Of the 200 largest banking firms in 1973, a total of 172 are holding companies.

In 1970, there were four states where holding companies controlled the majority of the bank deposits. These states and the percentage controlled in 1970 are: Colorado (51 percent), Minnesota (60 percent), Montana (52 percent), and Nevada (63 percent). As the data in Table 11.8 indicate, there are now 32 states where the majority of the deposits are held by holding company groups. The vast majority of these states permit branch banking (25 of the 32 states), and the structural changes resulting from holding company activities, mergers, and branching have been profound.

Table 11.7 Bank Holding Company Statistics for the 1957–1973 Period

	1957	1965	Percentage increase	1965	1970	Percentage increase	1957	1973	Percentage increase
Holding companies	50	53	6.0	53	121	128.3	50	1,677	3,254.2
Banks	417	468	12.2	468	895	91.2	417	3,097	642.7
Branches	851	1,482	74.6	1,482	3,260	119.4	851	15,374	1,706.5
Total offices	1,268	1,954	54.1	1,954	4,155	112.6	1,268	18,471	1,556.7
Deposits (billions)	$15.1	$27.6	82.8	$27.6	$78.1	183.0	$15.1	$446.6	2,857.6
Deposits as a percentage of United States bank deposits	6.8	8.3	22.1	8.3	16.2	95.2	6.8	65.4	861.8

Source: Federal Reserve Bulletins.

193

Table 11.8 States where Bank Holding Companies Control the Majority of Deposits, 1973

States (32)	Bank holding company deposits as a percentage of total deposits		
	1957	1970	1973
Alabama (B)*	—	—	54.0
Arizona (B)	38.2	32.9	56.1
California (B)	7.0	9.7	93.3
Colorado (U)	4.5	52.1	78.1
Connecticut (B)	—	3.5	71.5
Florida (U)	11.5	48.6	78.5
Georgia (B)	34.7	33.0	54.1
Illinois (U)	0.9	0.2	59.4
Maine (B)	5.0	45.9	72.0
Maryland (B)	—	7.5	61.2
Massachusetts (B)	20.2	22.3	84.7
Michigan (B)	—	—	67.8
Minnesota (B)	61.7	59.7	68.3
Missouri (U)	8.7	27.7	63.4
Montana (B)	53.4	52.4	68.2
Nebraska (U)	10.2	9.1	54.1
Nevada (B)	74.9	62.5	66.6
New Jersey (B)	—	16.8	50.4
New Mexico (B)	13.5	19.4	69.2
New York (B)	5.4	23.9	90.3
North Carolina (B)	—	2.3	68.2
Oregon (B)	44.5	42.2	81.1
Pennsylvania (B)	—	—	54.0
Rhode Island (B)	—	—	95.4
South Carolina (B)	—	—	53.5
South Dakota (B)	32.9	43.2	60.6
Tennessee (B)	3.5	8.3	62.2
Texas (U)	2.9	7.1	51.9
Utah (B)	52.7	45.7	80.8
Virginia (B)	1.6	43.8	77.4
Wisconsin (B)	20.9	43.4	50.6
Wyoming (U)	17.1	21.7	57.1
Median percentage	6.2	22.0	66.6

*The (U) or (B) following the name of the state indicates either a unit or branching state law in 1970.
Source: Federal Reserve Bulletins.

A CONCLUDING NOTE

There were relatively few bank holding companies in 1956 when Congress passed legislation designed to curtail their expansion and activities. Now there are over 1,600 of these firms engaging in a "laundry list" of activities with the approval of the Board of Governors of the Federal Reserve System. The administrative burden, as it relates to these microeconomic activities, is substantial. This is particularly true for an agency with major macroeconomic responsibilities and suggests the need for an extensive review of the bank regulatory process and structure. It almost appears as an understatement to brand the massive regulated bank holding company movement as another example of regulatory collapse.[11] The next chapter examines a related dimension of this collage of regulatory failure.

NOTES

1 Most of the early growth took place in the 1927–1930 period. The booming stock market was a factor in this development during the late 1920s. Bank holding company shares were largely sought by investors as a means of participating in this growing field. The willingness to buy shares in holding companies or to accept holding company shares in exchange as part of a combination made the formation of these firms relatively easy.

2 See section 19, amended slightly in 1935, Pub. L. No. 66, 12 U.S.C. §§61, 121,221. This legislation was in response to some of the abuses which had taken place in the late 1920s. Of the 90 holding companies combining 300 more banks at the end of 1931, 24 had become insolvent by 1934.

3 The House vote was 371 in favor to 24 opposed. (Congressional Record, CI[1955], 6977.)

4 Data were not published by the Federal Reserve System as related to multiple-bank holding companies for 1971 and 1972 in the *Federal Reserve Bulletin*.

5 Due to a loophole in the original act, one-bank holding companies were excluded from regulation by the Board of Governors until new legislation was passed and became law late in 1970.

6 Governor Mitchell discussed these developments as follows: " . . . the Justice Department continued to challenge bank mergers as violations of the antitrust laws, with the result that the antagonism between bankers, Federal regulatory agencies, and the Justice Department grew commensurably. By 1965 the Justice Department and the Comptroller of the Currency faced each other as court litigants in key merger cases, an unprecedented situation. Moreover, notwithstanding the aggressive activity of the Justice Department, the three federal bank-regulatory agencies together approved nearly 800 mergers during the 5-year period 1960–1965, while denying only 31. Thus, a continued high rate of merger activity among banks, an outraged banking community, and an unparalleled antagonism between the Justice Department and federal bank-

regulatory agencies, all combined to pressure Congress into once again tackling the knotty problem of bank mergers. The result was the Bank Merger Act of 1966, a confusing compromise at best."

7 *Federal Reserve Bulletin,* vol. 48, no. 12, p. 1618, December 1962.

8 Larry Mote, "Review of Federal Reserve Board Split Merger and Holding Company Decisions," in *Bank Structure and Competition,* Chicago: Federal Reserve Bank of Chicago, 1968, p. 54.

9 It is interesting to note that the approval rate of Governor J. L. Robertson increased from 55.4 percent during the 1956–1965 period to 76.4 percent since 1966 when he was named Vice Chairman of the Board, a position he held until his retirement in 1973. Whether the additional administrative responsibilities have contributed to this development is speculative, yet entirely possible in the organizational milieu of a bureaucracy.

10 As of April 1, 1970, there were 1,116 of these holding companies, with total deposits of $138.8 billion, or 32.6 percent of total deposits of all banks.

11 The candid remarks of George J. Stigler are especially appropriate; he has stated that "Oil and water are much closer friends than regulation and competition." See "Discussion," *The Journal of Finance,* vol. 27, no. 2, p. 341, May 1972.

Chapter 12

Bank Mergers, the Public Interest, and the Regulators

During the past decade and a half there was a kaleidoscope of legislative, regulatory, trade association, antitrust, academic, and other concerns related to the bank merger problem, which surfaced and clashed over these economic events. The initial legislation was passed in 1960 and was followed by antitrust action, which resulted in a Supreme Court decision in the early 1960s. The *Philadelphia National Bank* case triggered a barrage of activity by bankers and their regulatory agencies resulting in important amendments to the original act in 1966.

This chapter will focus on the background of the events leading to the initial legislation; the intervention of the Antitrust Division in an attempt to prevent some basically horizontal mergers; the regulatory record before and after the legislative efforts of Congress during the eventful 1960s; and the relative performance characteristics of a sample of merging and non-merging banks.

THE BANK MERGER ACT OF 1960

There were less than 100 bank mergers per year from 1940 through 1951; however, the pace quickened from that date forward. During the entire decade of the 1950s the Comptroller of the Currency approved 904 mergers involving national banks and 735 mergers were approved by the various state regulators. In the latter half of that decade there were 883 approved mergers involving resources amounting to $16.6 billion.

The chief avenue of review during this period by the federal agencies was through their authority to regulate branches, which was an indirect approach at best. Even this merger control through regulations on branching was thrown out by the Federal Court in the *Old Kent* case in 1960.[1] Congressional concern was mounting prior to this case, however, and the *Report on the Bank Merger Bill* of the House Committee on Banking and Currency summarized the situation prior to 1960 as follows:

> Controls over bank mergers are incomplete and confusing particularly with respect to the competitive factors involved. There are gaps in the controls exercised by the Federal banking agencies under banking statutes, and even where Federal approval is required before a merger may be completed, the standards are not clearly spelled out. . . . The Federal antitrust laws are also inadequate to the task of regulating bank mergers. . . .[2]

The growing discontent with increased bank merger activity during the 1950s (along with increased concentration in some banking markets) provided the impetus for congressional enactment of the Bank Merger Act of 1960. The record, as displayed over volumes of printed pages, clearly indicates an interest in banking concentration and competition in commercial banking. While the act reflected this interest as related to the competitive effects of bank mergers, it did *not* indicate the relative *weight* which the regulators should assign to *competition* in passing on merger applications. Instead, it merely listed competition among a number of factors to be considered. Continued approval of a vast majority of horizontal merger applications came to the attention of the Antitrust Division of the Justice Department.

Entry by the Department of Justice

During 1961, the first full year following the enactment of the original Bank Merger Act, almost $6 billion of bank resources were involved in agency-approved mergers. This development, in addition to the almost complete disregard of the competitive factor by the regulatory agencies when examining merger applications, seemed to be reason enough for the Antitrust

Division to initiate court proceedings to correct this deficiency of regulatory discretion.[3] The opinions of the agencies appeared to concede little relevance to oligopoly theory in these matters; rather, the focus was on the traditional banking factors and the assumed efficiency and other benefits of large banking institutions.

The result was that the 1960 Act had little effect in curbing mergers and increased concentration in the banking markets involved. The agencies approved a substantial majority of the merger applications which came before them; more significantly, they continued to approve horizontal mergers between large banks in major metropolitan areas such as Philadelphia, Chicago, and New York in the early 1960s.

The result of this permissive approach by the bank regulatory agencies was the initiation of the first suit challenging a proposed and approved merger involving the Philadelphia National Bank and the Girard Trust Corn Exchange Bank during 1961. The Supreme Court's decision in 1963 in this case not only confirmed the applicability of section 7 of the Clayton Act to bank mergers, but it also expressly adopted simple standards based on market shares of the merging firms as the touchstone of section 7 legality. The Court grounded its decision on the failure of the Merger Act to expressly provide antitrust immunity. This decision was soon followed by the *Lexington* case in 1964, in which the Supreme Court removed any doubt that the Sherman Act applied to bank mergers; the "competitive impact" of the mergers was held to be the overriding factor. These developments caused a furious response by some commercial bankers, the American Bankers Association, and even the regulators themselves.

The Bankers' and Regulators' Backlash

The regulatory agencies and a segment of the commercial banking community were dismayed by these actions brought by the Antitrust Division of the Department of Justice and the decisions of the Supreme Court. The prevailing view was that commercial banking had antitrust immunity, and further, that regulatory approval should be binding. Thus, the powerful banking lobbyists and the regulatory agencies went to Congress to attempt to change the law. The basic objective was to gain immunity from the antitrust laws for banking and, in the process, to overturn the judicial verdicts of the highest court in the land. B. J. Klebaner articulated the situation as follows:

> Stirred into action by a series of Antitrust Division victories, the American Bankers Association sponsored legislation introduced by Senator Robertson within a month after the Manufacturers Hanover decision was announced. Bankers (other than those sponsoring the Independent Bankers Association)

were convinced that under the 1960 law, competition was not intended to be the controlling factor in bank merger cases, and the Attorney General was assigned only as advisory role, but the courts had decided otherwise.[4]

The negative reaction of a large segment of the banking community to law enforcement activities and unfavorable judicial opinions of this type is of particular interest. The powerful bankers and their major trade association were generally supported by the bank regulatory agencies. The situation was described by Governor Mitchell in the following statement:

> Bankers were outraged. They argued that if bank mergers which had the approval of a Federal banking regulatory agency were also subject to antitrust laws, the resulting overlap of jurisdiction would cause unnecessary confusion and uncertainty. In addition, since banking is a very specialized and highly regulated industry, there is no reason to further regulate it by applying the antitrust laws. To demand a standard of competition in banking similar to that in other industries would jeopardize the soundness of our banking system, they argued, since many banks would be driven into bankruptcy by intensive competition . . . By 1965 the Justice Department and the Comptroller of the Currency faced each other as court litigants in key merger cases, an unprecedented situation.[5]

It is apparent that the reason for the confusion and outrage was the successful attempt by the Antitrust Division to enforce the antitrust laws in the banking community. The fact that antitrust actions appeared necessary in order to enforce the congressional mandate concerning banking structure and competition was a definite implication that the regulatory agencies were *failing* in their responsibility in these matters during this period.

Overlooked in the discussion of the application of the antitrust laws to commercial banking is the fact that a congressional subcommittee, chaired by Representative Celler of New York, recommended action as early as 1955, prior to passage of the Bank Merger Act. The report of the Antitrust Subcommittee of the House Judiciary Committee stated:

> Pending congressional consideration of this bank bill, the Department of Justice should avail itself of the remedy at hand, namely, the Sherman Act. The subcommittee recommends that the Department invoke the Sherman Act wherever possible, not only to block the consummation of bank mergers but to prosecute those that have already taken place, where a substantial lessening of competition has resulted. Until a few months ago, the subcommittee believes, the Department of Justice brushed the Sherman Act aside as a remedy in this area; indeed, it scarcely seemed aware of the act's possible utility in connection with a number of bank-merger transactions that took place, particularly

the Chase-Bank of Manhattan merger. Had the Department denied merger clearance to the Chase-Manhattan transaction (as it was in a position to do), the merger probably would not have taken place at all.[6]

The Regulatory Record, 1960–1965

One predictable outcome of increased antitrust law enforcement would be an expected deterrent effect upon bank merger activity. Yet an examination of approved bank merger activity during this period fails to reveal this type of discernible pattern. The data presented in Table 12.1 reveal that despite the filing of the suit in the *Philadelphia National Bank* case in February 1961, this was a year of extensive activity with 135 approved mergers involving close to $6 billion of bank resources. The following year there were over 190 approved mergers, which was the largest number of approvals during the period. For the entire time span from May 13, 1960 (when the Bank Merger Act became law) through 1965, the regulatory agencies approved 859 mergers and denied 28, for an approval rate of 97 percent. The Antitrust Division found *adverse* anticompetitive effects in 494 of the approved mergers, or 58 percent, which is a substantial difference of opinion and ample justification for intensified law enforcement activity. Even here, less than 1 percent of the mergers were challenged.

It appears clear to an outside observer that neither the initiation of legal action by the Antitrust Division nor the rendering of adverse opinions concerning potential or actual anticompetitive consequences of particular bank mergers served as much of a deterrent to continued high levels of activity. As Governor Mitchell observed:

> Thus, a continued high level of merger activity among banks, an outraged banking community, and an unparalleled antagonism between the Justice Department and Federal bank regulatory agencies, all combined to pressure Congress into once again tackling the knotty problem of bank mergers. The result was the Bank Merger Act of 1966, a confusing compromise at best.[7]

THE 1966 AMENDMENT TO THE BANK MERGER ACT

Legislative compromise is seldom more apparent than in the 1966 amendment to the Bank Merger Act. The American Bankers Association (with the help of the bank regulatory agencies) attempted to gain immunity for commercial banking from the antitrust laws, and while this objective was not attained, the new law immunized all mergers unchallenged before February 21, 1966, from subsequent litigation. In addition, the American Bankers Association and its associates attempted to gain a "gateway" provision forgiving each of the litigated mergers that the court had declared

Table 12.1 Bank Merger Decision by Federal Regulatory Agencies, 1960–1972

Bank mergers	1960	1961	1962	1963	1964	1965	1966	1967	1968	1969	1970	1971	1972	Total
Comptroller of the Currency														
Approvals	56*	72	110	91	90	81	85	88	88	88	79	65	54	1047
Denials	0	0	7	0	0	1	3	1	0	0	0	0	0	12
Federal Deposit Insurance Corp.														
Approvals	21	31	44	31	29	47	37	38	68	79	59	45	39	568
Denials	0	0	0	2	0	0	0	2	3	1	4	5	4	17
Federal Reserve Board of Governors														
Approvals	17*	32	37	31	16	23	21	13	14	22	30	13	7	274
Denials	3	5	5	3	2	0	1	2	1	1	1	2	1	27
Resources involved ($, billions)	$1.73	$5.99	$2.21	$3.52	$2.24	$2.10	$1.65	$2.89	$2.18	$3.99	$5.13	$4.26	$3.04	$40.94
Comptroller of the Currency	$1.14	$1.99	$1.17	$2.02	$1.39	$1.04	$0.79	$2.34	$1.09	$1.86	$2.70	$2.77	$1.76	$22.06 (54%)
Federal Deposit Insurance Corp.	$0.14	$0.71	$0.73	$0.99	$0.56	$0.54	$0.25	$0.41	$0.91	$1.75	$1.68	$1.31	$1.15	$11.13 (27%)
Federal Reserve Board of Gov.	$0.46	$3.29	$0.31	$0.50	$0.29	$0.52	$0.61	$0.14	$0.18	$0.39	$0.75	$0.18	$0.13	$ 7.75 (19%)

*From passage of Bank Merger Act, May 13, 1960–December 31, 1960.

Sources: Board of Governors of the Federal Reserve System, Federal Reserve Bulletin, (December 1961 to January 1973); Annual Reports of the Comptroller of the Currency, 1950–1972; and Annual Reports of the Federal Deposit Insurance Corporation, 1960–1972. Supplementary information was obtained by direct inquiries to the federal regulatory agencies.

to be in violation of the antitrust laws, as well as the court cases then pending. This display of a lack of respect for law enforcement and judicial decision was partially successful, since the "forgiveness" provision concerning the three pre-Philadelphia mergers was included in the 1966 amendment.

Despite the above provisions, the final version of the 1966 amendment indicated that Congress had retained its traditional interest concerning the possible anticompetitive consequences resulting from bank mergers.[8] A merger violating the antitrust laws is forbidden under the 1966 act, unless the regulatory agency finds "the anticompetitive effects of the proposed merger are clearly outweighed in the public interest by the probable effect of the merger in meeting the convenience and needs of the community to be served." This imposed dichotomy between the concept of competition and convenience and needs is a curious development. Most economists have long held that competitive conditions will satisfy convenience and needs and provide a measure of *price* competition in the process. Since bank regulators have consistently ignored the *price* competition aspect of banking (as it relates to important and unique services such as checking accounts), the dichotomy is understandable but regrettable.

BANK MERGER ACTIVITY SINCE PASSAGE OF THE 1966 AMENDMENT

While the 1966 amendment altered the Bank Merger Act of 1960 in a variety of ways, Congress continued to display concern about competition and concentration in banking. The amendment adopted the Supreme Court's approach and brought banking directly under the Sherman and Clayton Antitrust Acts. Despite this congressional interest in the bank merger problem, the bank regulatory agencies appear to have behaved in a "business as usual" approach since the new statutory mandate.

The data for the activity in the post-1965 period are presented in Table 12.1. In the 4 years 1966–1969, there were 641 approved mergers, involving $11 billion of resources. This is a larger amount of activity than in the 4-year period (1962–1965) prior to enactment of the amendment, when there were 630 approved mergers involving $10 billion of bank resources.

The approval rate in the 1966–1969 period is also higher, 98 percent, compared with 97 percent in the 1962–1965 period. The number of approved mergers considered to have anticompetitive effects by the Antitrust Division declined from 62 percent in the 1962–1965 period to 48 percent in the 1966–1969 period. This is a rather small decline considering the fact that Congress had again mandated its concern about bank competition in the 1966 Amendment and close to a majority of those approved have some adverse competitive effects.

A PROFILE OF REGULATORY BEHAVIOR

An analysis of the voting records of the federal banking regulators in merger cases since the passage of the Bank Merger Act of 1960 reveals an interesting pattern (see Table 12.2). Members of the Board of Governors of the Federal Reserve System have the lowest approval rates of the three responsible agencies. Governors who have approved over 90 percent of the merger cases in which they were involved are ex-Chairman Martin (95 percent); Chairman Burns (91 percent); Governor King (94 percent); Shepardson (94 percent); Balderstron (94 percent); Sherrill (95 percent); and Daane (92 percent). Governors who have approved over 80 percent of the merger applications are Mills (89 percent); Maisel (83 percent); Mitchell (84 percent); and Brimmer (81 percent). The lowest approval rate of all the regulators belongs to Governor J. L. Robertson (65 percent), a man whose dissents in many merger cases are worthy of note and who has since resigned from the Board of Governors.

The various Comptrollers of the Currency have each recorded substantial approval rates, with Comptroller W. B. Camp approving 459 of the 460 applications submitted since he assumed office in 1966. A record of this type (99.8 percent) is even purer than the famous soap that floats. History appears to be repeating itself since the House Antitrust Subcommittee made the following observation in a report on corporate and bank mergers published in 1955, several years prior to passage of the original Bank Merger Act:

> The Comptroller of the Currency also has responsibility for blocking bank mergers inimical to competition by virtue of statutory provisions requiring his approval for all mergers between National and State banks into national banks. The Comptroller's Office has indicated that its policy is not to approve any bank merger which is violative of the policy of the Celler-Kefauver Act. Since 1950, however, the Comptroller and his predecessors have approved 376 bank mergers and consolidations involving total resources of $7,464 million. And in no case has the Comptroller's Office disapproved a merger application on the ground that it might substantially lessen competition.[9]

It appears that some problems and concerns are continually recycled through the economic and political system despite periodic legislative and judicial mandates. At times it appears that regulatory behavior is impervious to conditions and influences beyond the realm of the industry which is regulated or quasi-regulated, presumably in the public interest.

The fact that 97 percent of bank merger applications have been approved by the regulators suggests a potential conflict relative to the public interest. In the opinion of the Department of Justice, a majority of

Table 12.2 Voting Records of Federal Banking Regulators in Merger Cases Since Enactment of the Bank Merger Act of 1960, through 1972

Board of Governors of the Federal Reserve System:*	Number of cases	Percent favoring merger
A. F. Burns, Chairman	37	91.9
W. M. Martin, Jr., Chairman	168	95.2
G. H. King, Jr.	35	94.3
C. N. Shepardson	140	93.6
C. C. Balderston	123	93.5
J. D. Daane	138	91.3
W. W. Sherrill	78	94.9
A. L. Mills, Jr.	93	89.2
G. W. Mitchell	190	83.7
S. J. Maisel	126	83.3
A. F. Brimmer	102	81.3
J. F. Robertson	220	64.5
J. E. Sheehan	6	100.0

Comptroller of the Currency	Number of cases	Percent favoring merger
R. M. Sidney	123	100.0
J. J. Saxon	145	97.6
W. B. Camp	459	99.8

Federal Deposit Insurance Corporation (chairperson)†	Number of cases	Percent favoring merger
J. P. Wolcott	22	100.0
Erle Cocke, Jr.	97	98.0
J. J. Saxon (Acting Chairman)	12	100.0
J. W. Barr	38	100.0
K. A. Randall	341	98.2
F. Wille	119	90.8

*As published in the Federal Reserve Bulletin, 1962–1972.

†In the absence of information on the voting records of the individuals comprising the three-man Board of Directors of the FDIC, the approval rates in this table reflect decisions made during the tenure of the various chairpersons, and do not necessarily indicate their personal records.

Sources: Board of Governors of the Federal Reserve System, Federal Reserve Bulletin, December 1961 to December, 1972; Annual Reports of the Comptroller of the Currency, 1960–1970; and Annual Reports of the Federal Deposit Insurance Corporation, 1960–1972. Supplementary information was obtained by direct inquiries to the Federal regulatory agencies.

Table 12.3 Number of Bank Mergers Approved and Denied by the Bank Regulatory Agencies and the Department of Justice Opinions on Competitive Impact, 1960–1972

	1960	1961	1962	1963	1964	1965	1966	1967	1968	1969	1970	1971	1972	Total	Rate
Federal Reserve Board															
Merger approvals	17	32	37	31	16	23	21	13	14	22	24	13	7	270	90.6%
Merger denials	3	5	5	3	2	0	1	2	1	1	2	2	1	28	9.4%
Merger anticompetitive (Department of Justice opinion)*	8	16	14	23	13	16	8	7	5	10	15	9	5	149	50.0%
Comptroller of the Currency															
Merger approvals	56	72	110	91	90	81	85	88	88	88	82	65	54	1,050	98.9%
Merger denials	0	0	7	0	0	1	3	1	0	0	0	0	0	12	1.1%
Merger anticompetitive (Department of Justice opinion)*	20	39	67	65	72	51	36	53	48	50	41	35	30	607	57.2%
Federal Deposit Insurance Corporation															
Merger approvals	21	31	44	31	29	47	37	38	68	79	48	45	39	557	96.4%
Merger denials	0	0	0	2	0	0	0	2	3	1	4	5	4	21	3.6%
Merger anticompetitive (Department of Justice opinion)*	9	13	17	21	15	15	9	23	32	26	24	24	28	256	50.5%
Total—all agencies															
Merger approvals	94	135	191	153	135	151	143	139	170	189	154	123	100	1,877	97.0%
Merger denials	3	5	12	5	2	1	4	5	4	2	6	7	5	61	3.0%
Merger anticompetitive (Department of Justice opinion)*	37	68	98	109	100	82	53	83	85	86	80	68	63	1012	52.2%

*Some opinions were not rendered in emergency situations.

Source: Annual reports of the Board of Governors of the Federal Reserve System, 1960–1972; Comptroller of the Currency, 1960–1972; and the Federal Deposit Insurance Corporation, 1960–1972.

the applications involved a situation where there would be an adverse competitive impact (as noted in Table 12.3). Only about 3 percent of the applications were denied, while a majority would have been denied if a stricter policy had been followed concerning the competitive impact (however slight) of the mergers. This permissive approach to regulation has meant significant changes in numerous banking markets.

STRUCTURAL CHANGES SINCE PASSAGE OF THE BANK MERGER ACT OF 1960

There have been several significant developments in the banking structure in the United States since passage of the original Bank Merger Act in 1960.[10] The number of commercial banks increased slightly, mainly due to two factors: an increase in entry in unit banking states and relatively few approved mergers in these same states. Thus, the 15 states with unit banking had a net gain of 727 banks (11 percent). The 20 states that permit statewide branching had a decline of 137 banks (minus 9 percent) in the 1961–1969 period. The 16 states in the limited branching group experienced a decline of 250 banks (minus 5 percent) during this interval of time.[11]

The relationship between bank mergers and branching activity is a rather widely accepted fact and becomes quite apparent in the data presented in Table 12.4. The overwhelming majority of the bank mergers were consummated in states which permit branching (94 percent). This is the major factor explaining the decline in the number of banks in branching states during the period. New entry in these states did not keep pace with the absorption of banks through approved mergers. Thus, a high level of combination activity in an industry (or line of commerce where entry is restricted) inevitably leads to a decline in the number of competitors, with a resulting effect on structure in particular areas or markets.

THE EFFECTS OF APPROVED MERGERS ON BANKING STRUCTURE IN THE LEADING STATES

The impact of approved bank mergers upon the structure of banking is evident in an examination of the leading states (i.e., those with the most activity) during the 1960s. The data are presented in Table 12.5 and list the 10 most active states and also the change in the number of commercial banks during the decade. Nine of these states had a decline in the number of banks during the period, and the group displayed a net loss of 672 banks, or a negative change of minus 16 percent. The remaining 40 states registered a net gain of 860 banks for an increase of 9 percent during the period.

The vast majority of approved bank mergers occurred in a relatively few states; that is, over two-thirds of the mergers were consummated in

Table 12.4 Number of Approved Bank Mergers in Branching and Unit Banking States, 1960–1972

	1960	1961	1962	1963	1964	1965	1966	1967	1968	1969	1970	1971	1972	Total	Percentage of mergers
Comptroller of the Currency															
Branching states	53	67	104	88	87	76	81	82	82	83	81	64	54	1002	95.4
Unit states	3	5	6	3	3	5	4	6	6	5	1	1	0	48	4.6
Federal Deposit Insurance Corporation															
Branching states	18	26	38	29	27	40	31	35	63	72	44	44	38	505	90.6
Unit states	3	5	6	2	2	7	6	3	5	7	4	1	1	52	9.4
Board of Governors, Federal Reserve System															
Branching states	15	32	36	31	14	23	19	12	14	20	22	13	7	258	95.6
Unit states	2	0	1	0	2	0	2	1	0	2	2	0	0	12	4.4
Branching states, total	86	125	178	148	128	139	131	129	159	169	147	121	99	1765	94.0
Unit states, total	8	10	13	5	7	12	12	10	11	14	7	2	1	112	6.0

Source: Annual reports of the Board of Governors of the Federal Reserve System, 1960–1972; the Comptroller of the Currency, 1960–1972; and the Federal Deposit Insurance Corporation, 1960–1972.

Table 12.5 Ten States Leading in Approved Bank Merger Activity and Change in the Number of Banking Institutions in these States during the 1960s

Leading states	Number of approved mergers, 1960–1969	Number of commercial banks			
		January 1, 1960	December 31, 1969	Net change	Percentage change
Pennsylvania	243	722	492	(−230)	(−31.9)
New York	148	415	320	(−95)	(−22.9)
Virginia	125	309	233	(−76)	(−24.6)
California	93	115	155	+40	+34.8
Ohio	87	588	521	(−67)	(−11.4)
North Carolina	86	192	109	(−83)	(−43.2)
New Jersey	85	258	228	(−30)	(−11.6)
Michigan	66	383	332	(−51)	(−13.3)
South Carolina	49	145	105	(−40)	(−27.6)
Indiana	48	450	410	(−40)	(−8.9)
Total, leading states	1,030	3,577	2,905	(−672)	(−16.1)
Remaining 40 states and the District of Columbia	464	9,897	10,757	+860	+8.7

Sources: Merger data from annual reports of the Board of Governors of the Federal Reserve System, the Comptroller of the Currency, and the Federal Deposit Insurance Corporation. The number of commercial banks from the *Federal Reserve Bulletin*, p. 441, April 1960, and *Federal Reserve Bulletin*, p. A94, April 1970.

one-fifth of the states during the period. All 10 of the most active states permit branching, which provides further evidence of the close link between mergers and branching activity.

While the number of banks is one important variable in any analysis of banking structure, it is also worth examining the changes in concentration of deposits held in these states to determine if the approved bank mergers have had any effect in this basically oligopolistic industry. The data on these changes are presented in Table 12.6, for the period 1961–1969. It is obvious that the states with the most approved bank mergers had an increase in concentration during the period as measured by both the mean and median ratio. The remaining 40 states (as a group) actually experienced a decline during the period.

Since all the leading states permit branching, another breakdown was made comparing the 10 leading states with the other 25 branching states that experienced less merger activity and with the 15 unit banking states. Again, it is apparent that there is a relationship between branching, merger, and changes in concentration, since the 10 leading states (all branching) registered the largest increases in concentration, followed by the other branching states that were less active in mergers. The unit banking states had relatively few mergers (as noted above) and concentration declined in this group. Thus, as a group, the active states have experienced a decline in commercial banking organizations accompanied by an increase in the concentration of deposits resulting from regulatory agency–approved bank mergers.

Further statistical evidence of this development is presented in Table 12.6. Analysis of variance tests was conducted and indicates that there was a 16 percent gain in the number of banks in the unit banking states, while the concentration ratio in these states declined minus 10 percent. The limited branching states had a slight decline, minus 2 percent, while the concentration ratio also declined minus 6 percent. The statewide branching states had the largest decline in the number of banks, minus 4 percent, and the largest increase in concentration, 8 percent. Each of the variables is statistically significant, indicating that these developments were highly unlikely to be the result of change.

The merger intensity test presented in Table 12.6 reveals that the most active states experienced an average decline of minus 16 percent in the number of banks and an increase of 8 percent in concentration. The reverse pattern is apparent in the remaining states, that is, an average increase in the number of banks of 7 percent, and a decrease in concentration of minus 4 percent. Again, each variable in this test was highly significant statistically.

Table 12.6 Analysis of Variance Tests of Mean Changes in the Number of Commercial Banks (1960–1969) and State Concentration Ratios (June 1961–June 1969) as Measured by State Branching Laws and Approved Merger Intensity

Variable	Unit banking states (15)	Limited branch states (16)	Statewide branch states (20)*	F ratio	10 most active merging states	Remaining states (41)	F ratio	10 most active merging states	Moderate merging states (15)	Little or no merger states (22)	F ratio
Change in the number of banks (%)	15.6	(−2.3)	(−4.0)	4.75 (0.025)	(16.1)	6.8	10.97 (0.005)	(−16.1)	(−3.2)	12.6	9.63 (0.0010)
Change in state concentration ratio (%)	(−9.6)	(−6.1)	7.5	7.32 (0.005)	7.5	(−4.1)	4.64 (0.05)	7.5	0.6	(−6.8)	3.50 (0.05)

*Includes the District of Columbia.

Sources: Concentration data from "Recent Changes in the Structure of Commercial Banking," *Federal Reserve Bulletin*, March 1970, pp. 195–210; the number of commercial banks from the *Federal Reserve Bulletin*, April 1960, p. 441, and *Federal Reserve Bulletin*, April 1970, p. A94. Merger data from the annual reports of the bank regulatory agencies.

Table 12.7 Effects of Mergers on Growth of Large Banks, 1962–1971

Variable	Simple dichotomy			Merger intensity				
	No merger	Merger	F ratio*	No merger	1 merger	2 + 3 mergers	4 + mergers	F ratio*
Management interest								
(y^1) assets	107.7	149.5	*14.80*(.001)	107.7	109.1	155.3	205.0	*15.49*(.001)
(y^2) deposits	94.2	141.5	*22.83*(.001)	94.2	107.7	144.1	191.5	*17.46*(.001)
(y^3) loans	127.8	182.5	*18.97*(.001)	127.8	148.0	185.5	232.9	*12.12*(.001)
(y^4) employees	46.7	100.1	*15.06*(.001)	46.7	59.4	108.5	152.1	*10.87*(.001)
Stockholder interest								
(y^5) earnings per share	11.8	7.5	0.21	11.8	3.1	4.0	19.8	0.47
(y^6) market price	39.6	38.1	0.01	39.6	49.4	32.3	28.7	0.37
Number of banks	80	90		80	35	33	22	

*The F ratios shown for each variable are based on one-way analysis of variance tests of the significance of the observed differences in group means for that variable. The F ratios which are italicized are those for which the probability is less than 0.10 that the observed differences in group means could be the result of chance; in these cases, the significance levels are shown in parentheses as superscripts to the F ratios.

THE PERFORMANCE PATTERN OF MERGING AND
NONMERGING BANKS

Another aspect of the public interest relates to the relative performance of merging and nonmerging banks. A number of the studies addressing this problem were discussed previously in Chapter 7. One of the early empirical tests related to the performance patterns of banks consisted of a nationwide sample of 165 large commercial banks for the 1952–1961 period and for another smaller sample of New York and Virginia banks.[12]

Since a considerable amount of approved merger activity has taken place since these original studies, an update of the large bank study was undertaken to determine if the performance pattern had changed during this period. The original tests were designed to reveal if there were different performance characteristics between merging and nonmerging banks, and further if the interests of shareholders and managers of merging banks were complementary, independent, or conflicting. Since it is reasonable to assume that approved mergers add to the size of the existing banking firm, four size-related variables (the change in assets, deposits, loans, and employees) were utilized. Two stockholder variables were identified, the change in earnings per share and the market price of the common stock. The original study also included three "public interest" variables which added the values of assets, deposits, and loans acquired to the base figures of the merging banks in an attempt to measure whether merging banks were growing more from the attraction of new business or from the merger effect. These "public interest" variables were omitted in the update study because of the extensive additional research necessary to trace the numerous banks which have been acquired (well over a thousand banks).

The sample consisted of 170 large commercial banks, including all those for which data were available for the 1962–1971 period. The initial list of banks consisted of the 300 largest banks in 1962.[13] This list was chosen to eliminate the potential bias which might be present if the current list was used, since presumably banks engaging in mergers may be on the newer list, due to their merger activity in recent years.

The results of these update tests for the 1962–1971 period are presented in Table 12.7. An examination of these results reveals a similar pattern to the earlier studies. Each of the size-related (management interest) variables favors the merging firms and is statistically significant at a high level. In contrast, neither of the stockholder variables is significant, indicating the independence of interests between the two groups. This is another striking confirmation of the fact that mergers matter in the growth of the banking firm. Further, this updated study confirms the previous finding concerning the apparent lack of alignment between the interests of shareholders and the managers of merging banks. An appropriate question looms and remains, Bank mergers for whom?

The next chapter examines the important question of the public interest in commercial banking and the regulatory process, since there appears to be an economic gap.

NOTES

1 *Old Kent Bank and Trust Co. v. Martin et al.,* 281 F.2d 61 (Cir., D.C., April 28, 1960, rehearing denied, September 9, 1960).
2 U.S. Congress, House Committee on Banking and Currency, *Regulation of Bank Mergers,* Report No. 1416, 86th Cong. 2d Sess., Washington, 1959, p. 5.
3 See George R. Hall and C. F. Phillips, Jr., *Bank Mergers and the Regulatory Agencies—Application of the Bank Merger Act of 1960,* Washington: Board of Governors of the Federal Reserve System, 1964.
4 Benjamin J. Klebaner, "The Bank Merger Act: Background of the 1966 Version," *Southern Economic Journal,* vol. 34, no. 2, p. 250, October 1967.
5 George W. Mitchell, "Getting the Most Out of the Banking System in the '70's," *The Economic and Business Bulletin,* vol. 21, no. 1, pp. 2–3, Winter 1969.
6 U.S. Congress, House Subcommittee on Antitrust and Monopoly, *Corporate and Bank Mergers,* 84th Congress, 1st Session, Washington, 1955, p. 41.
7 Mitchell, op. cit., p. 2.
8 Congress has consistently expressed concern about the degree of competitiveness in banking markets over the years as indicated in the legislation.
9 U.S. Congress, House Subcommittee on Antitrust and Monopoly, *Corporate and Bank Mergers,* op. cit., p. 41.
10 See "Recent Changes in the Structure of Commercial Banking," *Federal Reserve Bulletin,* March 1970, pp. 195–210.
11 Ibid., p. 210.
12 See Kalman J. Cohen and Samuel Richardson Reid, "The Benefits and Costs of Bank Mergers," *Journal of Financial and Quantitative Analysis,* vol. 1, no. 4, pp. 15–57, December 1966, and "Effects of Regulation, Branching, and Mergers on Banking Structure and Performance," *Southern Economic Journal,* vol. 34, no. 2, pp. 231–249, September 1967.
13 This list is published in *Moody's Bank and Finance* manual, 1963.
14 While the number of banks in the United States has not varied greatly, the number of banks which are independent of bank holding company control has declined substantially. This distinction is important in assessing the independence of the decisions and policy making of the firms.

Chapter 13

The Public Interest and Banking—An Economic Gap

The American public should have a vital interest in the commercial banking business, since the activities in this important segment of the economy touch the lives of most citizens in numerous and sundry ways. Over the years Congress has attempted to provide an array of safeguards as well as a superstructure of regulatory institutions with the avowed intention of protecting the public interest. Despite this legislative interest, it appears that the public has been shortchanged on a consistent and persistent basis by a segment of the banking establishment, with the aid and consent of the various bank regulatory agencies. Some evidence has been introduced in the two previous chapters to support this proposition. An examination of other evidence will be presented in this chapter in order to attempt to isolate the sometimes elusive concept of just what "the public interest" is in relation to banking.

After all the years of commercial banking regulation, it may appear strange to be attempting to delineate "the public interest" in banking at the present time. Yet, this is precisely the problem as related to the regulation of banking and other fields of economic activity. Historically, the bank regulation problem has revolved around a traditional concern for deposit safety. This is a continuing problem and an important aspect of the public interest. While deposit insurance has helped to mitigate this problem, it appears that bank regulation is complicating the problem of deposit safety. In addition, there are other areas of the public interest which should receive special attention through an appropriate awareness on the part of the banking regulators.

One fundamental approach to the proper and relevant determination of the public interest is to identify which of the services provided by commercial banks are most in demand. Related to this determination is the quality, prices, and costs of these services and the effect of the industry structure upon their provision. The needed information on relevant services is readily available from various studies of different banking markets conducted by the research department of the Federal Reserve Bank of Chicago.[1] These studies clearly indicate that the most widely used services by households and business firms are checking accounts (demand deposits) and loans. Logic dictates that the appropriate definition of the public interest should revolve around the price and quality of these particular services for which there are either no or few substitutes.

Fortunately, economists have produced an extensive array of empirical research evidence concerning the relationship of concentrated banking markets and the pricing of these fundamental services. Additional studies have also been conducted on the relationship between approved bank mergers and the subsequent pricing practices of the banks involved.

In the area of concentration and pricing, George G. Kaufman found poorer performance on the pricing of checking accounts and loans associated with increased concentration; that is, higher levels of concentration generally mean higher prices.[2] Franklin R. Edwards found that there is a positive relationship between the degree of banking concentration and interest rates charged on short-term loans; again higher concentration is translated into generally higher prices.[3] A study by Theodore G. Flechsig of the Federal Reserve System found no significant differences in interest rates charged.[4] Frederick W. Bell and Neil B. Murphy determined that service charges on checking accounts are higher in concentrated markets.[5] Steven Weiss also found a relationship between levels of concentration and the introduction of "free" checking accounts.[6] The probabilities increased as concentration decreased. Irving Schweiger and John McGee found that interest rates in small towns are a function of the number of banks, that is, lower rates with more competitors.[7] Paul A. Meyer found that the number of banks is insignificant in his study of metropolitan areas and that loan-rate variations due to banking structure, or even bank size alone, were larger than cyclical variations.[8] Almarin Phillips found significant associations between concentration and interest rates on business loans charged by banks in 19 metropolitan areas.[9]

In a major study concerning the relative performance of bank holding companies, Robert J. Lawrence found that the supply of loanable funds would increase in a bank holding company bank, but that " . . . customers of the subsidiary banks would probably be paying higher service charges on their demand deposit accounts but would not be receiving significantly higher interest payments on their time deposits."[10] Lawrence also found that " . . . there would probably be no significant change in interest rates on loans at the subsidiary banks . . . it is also likely that the acquired bank would lose autonomy as the holding company took over some of the decision-making."[11] On the subject of a potential increase in postmerger operating efficiency, Lawrence concluded that "In terms of the operating ratio (operating expenses to operating revenues) the answer is 'No.' "[12] All holding companies (by definition) support an additional tier of administration, which adds to operating costs.

George J. Benston found that the expenses of total demand deposit operations (checking accounts) would be higher if five unit banks were to merge to form a bank with four branches than if each bank remained independent.[13] Paul Horvitz and Bernard Shull studied the changes in policy in regard to checking account charges following approved bank mergers.[14] They reported that "in 12 of these cases the changes resulted in a net reduction in monthly service charges, while in 26 there were net increases."[15] They further stated that in only two out of 16 was there a net decrease in the cost of maintaining a special checking account at the office of the acquired bank.[16] A study by the New York State Banking Department also found that increases in service charges on checking accounts greatly exceeded reductions. The New York study, in discussing bank mergers, stated: "The major detrimental effects would be higher service charges in special and regular checking accounts of individuals and small businesses."[17]

New evidence continues to be reported which verifies these earlier findings in this important aspect of the public interest. Frederick W. Bell and Neil B. Murphy made a statistical study from a sample survey of banks in the First Federal Reserve District concerning the impact of market structure on the price of demand deposit services.[18] The study revealed that "the results of our tests indicate that concentration does have a positive and significant effect on price . . . merger will also bring about increased concentration and higher prices."[19] Bell and Murphy further stated " . . . the most important findings of this article are the effects of concentration on prices. A *consistent, positive, statistically significant* (at the 0.05 level) relationship was found between the market share of the largest three banks, however measured, and the prices charged. A ten per cent increase in the concentration ratio results in a two per cent increase in price."[20]

Another study by Bell and Murphy was concerned with the impact of regulation on inter- and intraregional variation in commercial bank costs. The purpose was to expand knowledge concerning the existing cost structure within and between market areas. They found that " . . . a branch organization was shown to be more costly than a unit bank . . . that high cost banks (or areas) tend to have higher service charges."[21] They stated that high cost areas " . . . are characterized by relatively large banks having many branches and operating in high wage areas."[22] They also found that expansion by branching acts as an offset to economies of scale, a finding which has been demonstrated by George Benston in his previous work.[23] Another interesting finding was that " . . . new bank entry may increase competition, but not at the expense of greater probability of bank failure."[24] Bell and Murphy concluded that " . . . the recent trend in branch systems acquiring unit banks is not so much to gain efficiency, but probably to achieve monopoly power and/or maximize the firm's rate of growth. This is consistent with the findings of Cohen and Reid."[25]

Bell and Murphy have also revealed some of the increased cost factors related to merger activity and demand deposits. In a study of returns to scale for banking products, they stated:

> The cost of demand deposits for a main office and one branch would be on the average 6.1 percent higher than for a unit bank handling the same total volume at one office. Therefore, total direct cost of demand deposits would rise by 97.1 percent due to the merger. Costs would rise further if the bank added more offices to share the fixed output. Hence, expansion via merger and branching may substantially offset any scale economies which might accrue.[26]

David L. Smith also found significant differences in the expense and pricing performance of merging and nonmerging banks.[27] According to Smith, "merging banks incurred significantly higher increases in total current operating expenses than nonmerging banks . . ."[28] Smith found that "wage and salary expense at merging banks rose relative to nonmerging banks."[29] In addition, service charges on demand deposits (checking accounts) declined five times more among the nonmerging banks than for the merging banks. Other studies of the performance of merging banks were discussed previously in Chapter 7.

Most of these statistical studies reveal significant effects of concentration on commercial-loan interest rates to smaller businesses, as well as higher service charges on checking accounts.

The consistency of the results with industrial organization predictions concerning behavior in concentrated markets is impressive and should receive the attention of the regulators (and others), since these studies have been more comprehensive than those in any other single industry. The studies cover various time periods with varying money market conditions and include an array of observations—from large metropolitan banks to country banks—in different regions of the nation and utilize various statistical techniques.

The behavior of the bank regulators indicates that they are more concerned with the so-called banking factors and that they generally tend to fall back on the so-called convenience and needs factor rather than cope with *price* competition and concentration levels. Economists associate competitive markets with the satisfaction of convenience and needs, while the regulators appear to have separated these functions.

In summary, a substantial body of research findings indicates that concentrated markets do *not* serve the public interest on the services which are most widely utilized by individuals, households, and small businesses. As demonstrated in the preceding chapters, concentration has increased in numerous markets due to the approval policies of the various regulatory agencies. The picture reveals a high propensity of permissiveness concerning merger applications coupled with a restrictive policy on new *entry* in the industry. The relationship among concentration, entry, and mergers deserves more attention and recognition if a competitive banking structure is to be realized.

NEW BANK ENTRY AND STRUCTURE

A major reason why the number of independent decision-making banking units has remained relatively constant in recent years while population, bank deposits, gross national product, and all the other important indices (related to growth) have expanded, is due to not only the permissive attitude of banking regulators in approving mergers, but also to the regulators' restrictive bank *entry* policies.

An interesting and important study by Sam Peltzman concerning the effect of regulation on new banking entry is worth examining.[30] Certainly there would be more banking entry if there were not restrictions imposed by the regulators; however, Peltzman provides a measure of magnitude of this loss to the American public:

> The legal restrictions on entry in banking enacted into the Banking Act of 1935 have significantly reduced the entry rate into banking compared to what it would have been without these restrictions. In the period since 1935 the number of new banks formed each year has averaged .6 per cent of the existing

number of banks. Had the legal restrictions been absent, we estimate that this annual average could have been twice as high—about 1.2 per cent of the existing number of banks. At a minimum, it would have been .9 per cent, still 50 per cent higher than the rate we have observed. Put simply in terms of the number of new banks, a total of 2,272 new banks have formed in the years 1936 through 1962—an average of 84 banks per year. Had there been no legal restrictions on entry in this period, we estimate that about twice that number— approximately 4,500 new banks—would have been formed. Regulation has thus caused there to be 2,200 fewer banks than there would otherwise have been.[31]

During the same period used in the Peltzman study (1936–1962), there were 3,344 bank mergers—an annual average of 124 mergers—or close to half again *more* mergers than *new entry* with regulation. According to Peltzman, the existence of regulation has resulted in an estimated loss of 2,200 potential banks, and the rubber-stamp philosophy of the regulators concerning bank mergers among existing banks has contributed another 3,344 casualties to the list of potential competitors and independent decision-making units. The loss of acquired banks as independent firms is particularly harmful since established banks are generally in stronger competitive positions than newly organized banks.

Protecting the public interest involves providing not only adequate safeguards for deposits but also safeguards in the important and unique services such as checking accounts and loans. Ideally, this should be accomplished through the provision of more independent alternatives, which means increased bank entry and a severely restrictive merger policy rather than price controls. Elimination of the prohibition on interest payments for checking accounts also should be promoted by the regulators and Congress, particularly since the payment gap between time deposits and demand deposits is so wide. Several years ago an attempt was made to promote this concept, as follows:

> Competition of this type (price) would benefit the public more than nonprice competition waged between a few large banks in terms of advertising expenditures, marketing gimmicks, credit card plans, and so on. It appears reasonable to believe that many segments of the public (given the choice) would prefer lower or no service charges to fancy banking establishments, elaborate advertisements, esoteric dining facilities (available in some large banks), or a deluge of bank credit cards. The opportunity for this trade-off seldom presents itself in concentrated markets.[32]

The American public is paying hundreds of millions of dollars each year to the banking community for checking account services at the same time that bankers are paying substantial amounts for other types of deposits and commercial paper. The individual citizen and taxpayer is being squeezed on all sides with the cooperation and approval of government officials. For example, the federal government keeps billions of dollars of the taxpayer's money in banks across the nation without receiving interest on these funds. A similar situation prevails at the state and local levels of government.

Political considerations also enter this deposit game, as noted by the Washington watchdog, Jack Anderson, who notes that this golden gravy is concentrated in the big "Republican" banks. For example, Chase Manhattan, which is controlled by the Rockefeller family, had over $200 million in federal deposits in recent years. One of the directors of the bank happened to be the GOP national finance committee chairman. The pattern is repeated at other large banks, as noted by Anderson, who cites the case of Charls Walker, an Undersecretary of the Treasury and active worker for the special interests of bankers. In 1955, Walker became an executive of Republic National Bank in Dallas. After he joined the Eisenhower administration as an assistant to the Secretary of Treasury in 1959, the bank suddenly started receiving large, interest-free federal deposits. Walker returned to Washington again to the Treasury Department during the Nixon administration, and coincidentally Republic National Bank's balances that year grew to a whopping $56 million in federal deposits. Thus, the public is being shortchanged on both their personal *and* public demand deposit accounts. Growing numbers of people are also paying millions and millions of dollars of interest on bank credit card accounts at rates which are close to usurious to say the least. Despite these huge payments at interest rates of up to 18 percent or more on an annual basis, losses on these operations have outweighed gains to the bankers, and the net result has been a diversion of much-needed funds to this marginal activity by the bankers.

It is important to realize that no one has yet produced any substantial empirical evidence demonstrating that the *public* benefits in a significant manner from a concentrated banking structure for the appropriate services. Thus, the costs at the micro level of the household and firm far outdistance the elusive benefits. The situation is just as dismal at the macro level of the national economy. In the important area of monetary policy transmission, Sam Peltzman has found that a less concentrated structure in banking is more responsive to policy developments.[33] In a significant research study, Peltzman found " . . . that rapid response to monetary policy impulses is facilitated by small bank size, where open market operations are used extensively."[34]

The generally unnoticed paradox is that the Board of Governors of the Federal Reserve System has contributed to the formation of a banking structure which is *adverse* to its important functions concerning money supply operations conducted (for the most part) through open market operations. It appears that the Federal Reserve is bogged down in a microeconomic swamp at a time when its role in the macroeconomic area is of considerable importance. This paradox is another dismal example of misplaced regulatory policy and effort.

THE NATIONWIDE BRANCH BANKING MOVEMENT

It appears reasonable to predict that a future course of banking will be toward nationwide and regional branching. Some bankers have moved into multinational banking activities, and with the vast structural changes resulting from domestic bank holding company formations, pressure will grow for intensive development of national and regional banking networks. Big bankers, like their industrial and commercial counterparts, seem to have the same unrelenting bent for diversification of all types, including the spatial (geographical) variety. Some major banks have already opened regional loan-generating offices. The important public policy question is whether a development of this type (nationwide and regional branching) is in the broad "public interest"—as well as the interest of the shareholders of participating banks.

Since there has been no attempt to date to distinguish between the performance of banks engaged in spatial diversification, a number of statistical tests were conducted on a sample of large banks.[35] Available evidence does suggest that branching banks have higher operating costs than unit banks, but there has been no previous attempt to isolate the performance differences based on the range of the branching operations.

In this study, the extent of the spatial diversification of a banking firm was determined by the location of the branches and then the average distance from home base. The project was extensive, involving the need to determine the location of each bank and the branches (totaling close to 4,800 separate locations). An examination of the data revealed two distinct groups of spatially diversified banks, those which branched close to home (0–20 miles average) and those branching distant (over 20 miles average). Variables related to size, profitability to shareholders, and "public interest" were utilized.[36] The results of an analysis of variance test are presented in Table 13.1. The time period covered in the study was 1952–1961, a period of rapid expansion in bank branching similar to the past decade. The preliminary results of a subsequent study of the 1962–1971 period support the observed performance pattern.

It is obvious that branching contributes in a significant manner to the addition of increments of size to the banking firm. Each of the size-related

Table 13.1 Means of the Variables by Simple Dichotomy and Spatial Diversification

Variables	Simple dichotomy			Spatial diversification				Branching banks		
	Unit banks	Branching banks	F-ratio*	Unit banks	Branch close	Branch distant	F-ratio*	Branch close	Branch distant	F-ratio*
Size-related variables										
Assets Y^1	0.58	0.93	$4.75^{(0.05)}$	0.58	0.86	1.16	$3.79^{(0.05)}$	0.86	1.16	2.30
Deposits Y^2	0.54	0.93	$4.81^{(0.05)}$	0.54	0.89	1.09	$2.96^{(0.10)}$	0.89	1.09	0.91
Loans Y^3	1.21	1.91	$5.27^{(0.05)}$	1.21	1.91	1.90	$2.61^{(0.10)}$	1.91	1.90	0.00
Stockholder interest										
Employees Y^4	0.56	1.03	$5.48^{(0.05)}$	0.56	0.96	1.24	$3.56^{(0.05)}$			
Earnings per share Y^5	1.09	0.65	$10.07^{(0.01)}$	1.09	0.70	0.51	$5.91^{(0.01)}$	0.70	0.51	2.57
Market price Y^6	2.04	1.68	2.42	2.04	1.63	1.85	1.57	1.63	1.85	0.79
Public interest										
Assets Y^7	0.40	0.49	1.44	0.40	0.46	0.58	1.68	0.46	0.58	1.70
Deposits Y^8	0.36	0.45	1.52	0.36	0.43	0.54	1.65	0.43	0.54	1.60
Loans Y^9	0.98	1.20	1.98	0.98	1.25	1.02	1.90	1.25	1.02	1.61
Number of banks	35	130		35	100	30		100	30	

*The F-ratios shown for each variable are based on one-way analysis of variance tests of the significance of the observed differences in group means for that variable. The F-ratios which are italicized are those for which the probability is less than 0.10 that the observed differences in group means could be the result of chance; in these cases, the significance levels are shown in parentheses as superscripts to the F-ratios.

variables favored the branching banks when compared with unit banks, and each was statistically significant. The results for the two variables representing stockholder interests indicate that both favor the unit banks; however, only net operating earnings per share is statistically significant. None of the "public interest" variables were statistically significant in this test. Thus, the results cast doubt upon the assumption that banks operating geographically diverse systems have distinct economic advantages over unit banks and those that branch closer to home.[37] In fact, the advantages of unit banking appear to deserve more attention in the banking sector. This is especially true in view of the development of customer-bank communication terminals (CBCTs) which can reach the people at a considerably lower cost than the construction of a branching network. The question of whether CBCTs are considered branches will depend upon the decision of the courts since litigation is pending on this matter.

BANK GROWTH AND DEPOSIT SAFETY

The recession of 1974–75 has contributed to the plight of many of the aggressive banks which were undercapitalized and overloaned, overborrowed, and overdiversified. Taken as a whole, the banking system was in more trouble then than at any time since the 1930s. A long-time observer of banks, Paul Nadler, observed that, "Between 1964 and 1974 the banks went from local institutions that did only banking to multinational financial conglomerates."[38] In the process, some large aggressive banks collapsed, such as Franklin National of New York (which was the nation's twentieth largest bank at one time), despite the massive infusion of funds (over $1 billion) by the Federal Reserve. Other large banks have failed and more would have been on the rocks were it not for the Federal Reserve and the FDIC, which offered banks credit lines to bail them out of their problems.

All of these developments have prompted the treasurer of a New York City bank to observe that "After this is over, I think we'll see some of the regional banks culled. The small banks will remain, but concentration of banking will end up in the hands of 25 or 30 banks."[39] The policies and decisions of the bank regulators have basically shaped the existing structure, as noted in these chapters on banking. It is interesting to note that the Director of Research of the FDIC and another former bank regulator have defended the regulatory record on bank mergers during the 1960s and have defended the bank diversification movement, in terms of both geographical movements and entry into nonbanking activities.[40] Both of these developments, particularly as related to bank holding company activities, have contributed to rapid increases in concentration and deposit safety problems. A belated recognition of the role of merger in banking concentration is apparent in the statement of a Federal Reserve economist, Stephen A. Rhoades, who observed that "since banking organizations today are diversifying by merger into more geographical markets . . . and into an increasing number of product and geographic markets under section 4(c) (8) of the Bank Holding Company Act, it appears that the banking authorities will be faced with the question of aggregate concentration."[41]

In the area of deposit safety, bank regulators have focused on the capital adequacy ratio of banking firms following the large bank failures in 1974 and the growing list of "problem" banks. This policy seems erroneous since bank failure appears to be related more to asset management than liability management. In other words, failures occur when firms do not generate sufficient cash flows to cover expenses. The only area of bank asset management where the regulators can make a significant contribution originates in their statutory responsibilities as related to bank expansion and diversification. That is, many banks moved into the "problem bank" status following the whirl of regulatory-approved expansion activities discussed above.

Attempts to move America toward widespread interstate banking before the numerous complexities of this development are determined and demonstrated to be in the public interest would be premature and foolhardy. Developments in the bank merger and bank holding company areas should serve as prime examples of regulatory permissiveness and Congress should examine the regulatory discretion in this vital sector of the economy. Regulatory charades appear so pervasive that one doubts if existing regulatory systems can or should be retained. Perhaps the public interest would best be served by dismantling the structure and beginning anew with more public input in the process.

THE PUBLIC INTEREST AND THE VOICE OF THE PEOPLE

Seldom have the people had a direct voice in determining important matters related to banking generally and especially state and local banking structures. Either a few regulators or a handful of legislators are the decision makers in the overwhelming majority of the cases. Yet these matters are so basic that a case should be made for a direct popular vote on matters pertaining to bank structure changes.

The few times that the public has had the opportunity to vote on branch banking laws, they have consistently *rejected* the proposals. For example, in the November 1958 election in Missouri, over 70 percent (of close to a million voters) *opposed* the change in the law and every city and county in the state voted against the referendum. The same question was on the Illinois ballot in the November 1968 election and the voters rejected the branching proposal. A few years ago, voters in Missouri and Illinois again rejected the branching proposition at the ballot box. It is clear that the people view these matters quite differently than the *appointed* bank regulators.

The public has had even less of a voice in the area of local bank merger applications. Economic events of this type are handled by government agencies generally far removed from the local scene. A classic example involved banks located in Mississippi. The local opposition was substantial. The merger was opposed by the City Council, the Adams County Board of Supervisors and a petition in opposition was signed by over 3,000 citizens of the community. Despite this strong negative local reaction, the bank regulators in Washington approved the merger despite the finding by the Justice Department that the combination would have a significantly adverse effect on potential competition.[42] The people rarely have a chance to speak in these matters and when they do their voice is seldom heard.

A CONCLUDING NOTE

The national trend toward comprehensive concentration is clearly evident in this important basic regulated industry. Approved bank mergers and holding company activity have been directly responsible for the growth in the share of the 100 largest banking organizations from 48 percent of the total deposits in 1969 to 70 percent in 1974.[43] While there are over 14,000 banks in the United States, the *five* largest organizations hold 25 percent of all deposits and 22 percent of all bank loans in another lopsided segment of the economy. There is some evidence that Congress will attempt to correct some basic problems as related to the public and financial institutions; however, the task is substantial and needs a massive dose of attention.[44]

NOTES

1   See George G. Kaufman, *Business Firms and Households View Commercial Banks: A Survey of Appleton, Wisconsin,* Federal Reserve Bank of Chicago, 1967, and *Customers View Bank Markets and Services: A Survey of Elkhart, Indiana,* Federal Reserve Bank of Chicago, 1967.

2   George G. Kaufman, "Bank Market Structure and Performance," *Southern Economic Journal,* vol. 32, no. 4, pp. 429–439, April 1966.

3   Franklin R. Edwards, "Concentration in Banking and Its Effect on Business Loan Rates," *The Review of Economics and Statistics,* vol. 46, no. 3, pp. 294–300, August 1964.

4   Theodore G. Flechsig, *Banking Market Structure and Performance in Metropolitan Areas: A Statistical Study of Factors Affecting Rates on Bank Loans,* Washington: Board of Governors of the Federal Reserve System, 1965.

5 Frederick W. Bell and Neil B. Murphy, "Impact of Market Structure on the Price of Commercial Banking Service," *The Review of Economics and Statistics,* vol. 51, no. 2, pp. 210–213, May 1969.

6 Steven J. Weiss, "Commercial Bank Price Competition: The Case of 'Free' Checking Accounts," *New England Economic Review,* pp. 3–22, October 1969.

7 Irving Schweiger and John McGee, "Chicago Banking," *Journal of Business,* vol. 34, no. 3, pp. 203–366, July 1961.

8 Paul A. Meyer, "Price Discrimination, Regional Loan Rates, and the Structure of the Banking Industry," *Journal of Finance,* vol. 21, no. 1, pp. 37–48, March 1967.

9 Almarin Phillips, "Evidence on Concentration in Banking Markets and Interest Rates," *Federal Reserve Bulletin,* pp. 916–926, June 1967.

10 Robert J. Lawrence, *The Performance of Bank Holding Companies,* Washington, D.C.: Board of Governors of The Federal Reserve System, June 1967.

11 Ibid.

12 Ibid. A recent study of the profitability of approved bank mergers involving multibank holding companies by Thomas R. Piper, *The Economics of Bank Acquisitions by Registered Bank Holding Companies,* Boston: Federal Reserve Bank of Boston, 1971, found that the majority of the mergers (53 percent) were " . . . in fact unprofitable and their incidence was spread across a majority of the holding companies." This lack of success was not the result of acquiring weak banking institutions since Piper found that "acquisition activities centered on banks that seemed successful in their operations . . ." Piper also discovered that "Service charges on checking accounts tended to rise subsequent to bank mergers and to bank affiliation with holding companies."

13 George J. Benston, "Branch Banking and Economies of Scale," *The Journal of Finance,* vol. 20, no. 2, pp. 312–331, May 1965.

14 Paul M. Horvitz and Bernard Shull, "The Impact of Branch Banking on Bank Performance." *National Banking Review,* vol. 2, no. 2, pp. 143–188, December 1964.

15 Ibid., p. 160.

16 Ibid.

17 *Branch Banking, Bank Mergers, and the Public Interest; A Summary Report,* New York State Banking Department, p. 34, January 1964.

18 Bell and Murphy, "Impact of Market Structure on the Price of a Commercial Banking Service," op. cit.

19 Ibid., p. 213.

20 Ibid.

21 Frederick W. Bell and Neil B. Murphy, *Costs in Commercial Banking: A Quantitative Analysis of Bank Behavior and Its Relation to Bank Regulation,* Research Report No. 41, Federal Reserve Bank of Boston, April 1968.

22 Ibid., pp. 203–208.

23 Benston, op. cit.

24 Bell and Murphy, *Costs in Commercial Banking,* op. cit., p. 215.

25   Ibid.

26   Ibid.

27   David L. Smith, "The Performance of Merging Banks," op. cit.

28   Ibid.. p. 189.

29   Ibid., p. 190.

30   Sam Peltzman, "Entry in Commercial Banking," *The Journal of Law and Economics,* vol. 8, pp. 11–50, October 1965.

31   Ibid., p. 48.

32   Samuel R. Reid, *Mergers, Managers, and the Economy,* New York: McGraw-Hill, 1968, p. 283.

33   Sam Peltzman, "The Banking Structure and the Transmission of Monetary Policy," *The Journal of Finance,* vol. 24, no. 3, pp. 387–411, June 1969.

34   Ibid., p. 409.

35   See Kalman J. Cohen and Samuel R. Reid, "The Benefits and Costs of Bank Mergers," *Journal of Financial and Quantitative Analysis,* vol. 1, no. 4, pp. 15–57, December 1966 and Kalman J. Cohen and Samuel R. Reid, "Effects of Regulation, Branching, and Mergers on Banking Structure and Performance," *Southern Economic Journal,* vol. 34, no. 2, pp. 231–249, October 1967.

36   For a description of these variables, see the articles referred to above in the previous footnote. The data reported relative changes which, if multiplied by 100, would become percentage changes.

37   A number of other tests were conducted utilizing a variety of independent variables such as state branching laws, branching intensity, merger intensity and concentration levels. While the results varied, the basic pattern reported emerged. Of all the independent variables, merger activity proved again to be the most robust in explaining various performance patterns.

38   See "Are the Banks Overextended?" *Business Week,* no. 2349, pp. 52–56, September 21, 1974.

39   Ibid., p. 56.

40   A contrary position concerning bank regulation since passage of the Bank Merger Act of 1960 has been expressed by the Director of Research of the Federal Deposit Insurance Corporation and a former staff member of the Comptroller of the Currency in the Treasury Department. See Paul M. Horvitz and Bernard Shull, "The Bank Merger Act of 1960: A Decade After," *The Antitrust Bulletin,* vol. 16, no. 4, pp. 859–889, Winter 1971. Additional related material is contained in Samuel Richardson Reid, "The Bank Merger Act of 1960: A Decade After: Comment," *The Antitrust Bulletin,* vol. 18, no. 3, pp. 449–462, Fall 1973.

41   Stephen A. Rhoades, "Diversification, Competition, and Aggregate Concentration," *Bank Structure and Competition,* Chicago: Federal Reserve Bank of Chicago, 1974, p. 184. Rhoades indicates that the share of the 100 largest banking firms was decreasing in the 1961–1971 period. However, his analysis has been overshadowed by recent developments, as noted in the previous chapters.

42   The Mississippi cases also illustrate the application of political pressure and chicanery discussed previously, as noted by Mark Green, *The Closed Enter-*

prise System, New York: Grossman Publishers, 1972, p. 35: "Senator James Eastland (D.—Miss.) also made a blatantly self-interested pitch to Attorney General Ramsey Clark, in 1968, when three Mississippi banks planned to merge. The merger seemed illegal, as the memorandum from Assistant Attorney General Turner to Clark explained: 'The present Mississippi mergers represent the clearest examples of . . . anticompetitive market extension mergers which have come to our attention to date.' Nevertheless, Eastland tried to get the case killed, both because Mississippi banks were involved and because his wife had financial interests in one of them."

43 Rhoades, op. cit., p. 180. Rhoades estimated the share of the 100 largest banking firms at 45.7 percent in 1971, indicating the vast changes presided over by the bank regulators in a few years.

44 Senator Thomas J. McIntyre of New Hampshire, the Chairman of the Senate Subcommittee on Financial Institutions, held field hearings in early September 1975 on the impact of the NOW (negative order of withdrawal) account. These are checking accounts on which interest is paid and have been limited by federal law to banks in New Hampshire and Massachusetts. I was invited to testify on behalf of the consumer and urged that the antiquated prohibition of the payment of interest on checking accounts of all types be abolished. This prohibition is an accident of history which has cost consumers, business firms, and government units billions of dollars annually. I related an incident which involved one of my fellow students at the Yale Law School, who was offered a free frisbee for opening a checking account in New Haven. It is clear that even devoted "frisbee freaks" would prefer cash, yet the prohibition prevents this alternative and causes the frisbee effect or, as christened by George Oldfield at Dartmouth, the "Wham-o effect." The Senate Banking Committee amended the Financial Institution Act in early October 1975 to permit the payment of interest on demand deposits, a positive move which may benefit the public someday.

Part Four

Economic Power, Public Policy, and the Quality of Life

The previous parts presented the pattern of economic power; the role of mergers in the power process plus the relative microeconomic performance profile; and the antitrust and regulatory phenomena as they relate to the public interest. The final part of this book consists of three chapters which bring together the previous parts into a discussion of the impact of these developments and a public policy program designed to reach the problem.

Chapter 14 examines the relationship between various aspects of the economic power collage and their impact upon the quality of life. Chapter 15 relates the various policy alternatives, both short-run and long-run, to cope with an economic power dilemma in the political economy. Chapter 16, the concluding chapter, addresses the public policy question and suggests a variety of alternatives at the federal, state, and local levels designed to give shape to a new economic America.

Chapter 14

The Economic Power Collage and the Quality of Life

The gravitation of capital, control, and other manifestations of economic power toward large firms and away from the small- and medium-sized units contributes to an imbalanced economy. The purpose of this chapter is to examines how these developments have had an effect upon the quality of life in relation to a variety of public and private interests.

Quality of life consists of many facets including the condition of the various environments, the amount of control that people have over their own destinies, and the style of living which is affected by the condition of the urban and rural scene. Each of these qualitative aspects of life will be examined in the context of the various microeconomic developments and movements which contributed to the economic collage presented in Chapter 2.

THE ECONOMIC AND LEGAL ENVIRONMENT

The quality of life of the American public, composed of millions of citizens and taxpayers, is obviously affected by the condition of the economic environment. The public's standard of living is determined in a large part by how well the nation (and in particular the major areas where people live and work) attains its economic goals. It has already been demonstrated that the lopsided structure contributes to the growth and concentration of economic and political power and (with the help of mergers) to geographical shifts in power. A closer view of the havoc wrought by these special economic events upon the economic environment should help to further emphasize the need for more attention to these developments.

MERGERS AND ECONOMIC GROWTH, STABILITY, AND DECLINE

The quantitative and qualitative aspects of economic growth, stability, and decline are important to every society. Both aspects deserve consideration if we are to assess the impact of economic conditions and practices on the quality of life. Those individuals and groups that are critical of a primary emphasis on economic growth usually reach this position because of a breakdown in the *qualitative* aspects of the growth and the resulting misallocation of the additional increments of expansion.

A historian, Sir John Clapham,[1] has put this situation in proper perspective when he stated "how a man lives with his family, his tribe or his fellow-citizens; the songs he sings; what he feels and thinks when he looks at the sunset; the prayers he raises—all these are more important than the nature of his tools, his trick of swapping things with his neighbors, the way he holds and tills his fields, his inventions and their consequences, his money . . . his savings and what he does with them." The historian went on to say that "economic activity, with its tools, fields, trade, inventions and investment has in course of ages, provided, first for a privileged few and then for more, chances to practice high arts, organize great states, design splendid temples, or think at leisure about the meaning of the world."

Certainly, the capacity to produce goods and services is a necessary prerequisite in providing a standard of living. In addition, growth and increased productivity of the capacity are necessary if expanding populations are to survive and improve their standards of living. Economic growth is measured by the output of *new* goods and services including the plant and equipment necessary to produce the output. Both the quantitative and qualitative aspects of the capacity are important in producing increased levels of standards of living and increased employment opportunities.

When assessing the role of mergers in the economic growth process, it is important to realize that these economic combinations produce absolutely *nothing* to the attainment of the economic growth objective. A merger is nothing more than an exchange of title to *existing* assets, which, in the process, enlarges the acquiring firm but *not* industry capacity or national productive capacity. Thus, the quantitative advantages of mergers are nonexistent for society in general, yet they add capacity and power to the individual firm. Since the assets acquired are existing assets in various stages of obsolescence, they more than likely continue to contribute to the existing levels of pollution of the environment. A prime example is the steel industry, where the older mills and equipment generally produce the most smoke and the wastes which pollute lakes, rivers, and streams; thus, combinations of these older firms would have little if any positive contribution to improving living standards and would have a negative impact on the quality of air and water in areas where these firms are located.

MERGERS AND PRICE STABILITY

The frustrated attempts to curb inflation during the past few years have contributed to the "greening" of economic policy and to new levels of consciousness concerning the problem. As noted previously, the battle has been fought on a note of discord, with both monetary and fiscal policy coming up short in the process. Sole emphasis on either of these tools as a policy guide has proved to be ineffective in curbing inflation. Certainly, the war in Vietnam was a contributing factor to this ineffectiveness; however, another factor has been the blatant neglect of structure and power by the monetary and fiscal theorists and by government policymakers.

Some industrial organization economists have attempted to correct this situation; for example, during the summer of 1966 the following statement was written:

> The contribution of merger activity to the accomplishment of the reasonable price stability objective is, of course, difficult to measure. Prices generally tend to rise when capacity utilization rates are high and/or when market structures become highly concentrated. Since mergers do not add new capacity to an industry, it is likely that during periods of strong aggregate demand the capacity constraints will eventually become a factor causing prices to rise. Since horizontal mergers add capacity to the firm (although not to the industry), the pressure to raise prices may be postponed until the impact of rising demand manifests itself on an industry-wide basis. Since a merger results in the acquisition of existing capacity (which is in various states of obsolescence), the relative costs of operation may also be higher than if a similar expenditure had been made on new, modern capacity with the increased probabilities of realizing productivity gains. Increased productivity gains are particularly important during periods of rising labor costs, and the most logical method of achieving these benefits is through replacement and expansion investments in *new* plant and equipment.[2]

Both consumer and wholesale price increases have occurred during the recent merger wave and especially in its wake. The escalation of military spending and the expansion of domestic programs have contributed to increased government and consumer spending. The resulting strain on capacity has contributed to sharp price increases since 1965. During this same period expenditures by business people on *new* industrial plant and equipment capacity declined in actual—and especially in *real*—terms. The investment figure for 1966 was $26.99 billion; in 1967, $26.69 billion; and in 1968, a record year for merger expenditures, the figure was $26.44 billion. Obviously a substantial portion of these expenditures were for *replacement* of existing aged capacity rather than *new* additional capacity. The amount of replacement should increase as the industrial base becomes larger, if living standards are to be improved or even maintained.

It is not surprising that inflation is a major current problem, since American industrial capacity has not been expanding sufficiently to cope with the rising aggregate demand stimulated by increased consumer and government expenditures. History will record that it has been a grave error to focus primarily on monetary and fiscal policy (in varied mixes) as a remedy for persistent and increasing inflation and ignoring the industrial structure and capacity in the imbalanced economy.

Further pressures have been put on prices due to strong and increasing demands for higher wages at a time when productivity growth (output per worker-hour) will be the smallest since 1956, when it was 0.2 percent. It is *new* plant and equipment expenditures rather than business combinations, which provide an important part of the conditions necessary for productivity gains. If the public is to enjoy the fruits of production, then emphasis must be shifted to the core of the problem. In the meantime, the quality of life will continue to deteriorate in yet another manner through the eroding effects of inflation and periodic governmental attempts at control of wages and prices outside of the distorted marketplace.

THE EMPLOYMENT OBJECTIVE

A national economic goal of particular importance to individuals and families across the land in the urban ghettos, in suburban areas, and in rural places is the full employment objective. The President of the United States has the responsibility by law (the Employment Act of 1946) to strive to achieve full employment, or conversely, relatively low unemployment. Mergers have a definite impact on employment patterns; this relationship was also discussed in *Mergers, Managers, and the Economy* as follows:

The act of merger does not contribute to the full employment objective in the economy since the employees involved remain with the same firm or with the new owners. In other words, new jobs are not created by the merger act *per se*. Actually, the much-stated efficiency objective of merger suggests that some jobs will be eliminated in the process.

The ultimate effect of a merger upon employment creation depends upon the relative success and the eventual internal expansion of the combination. The fact that the number of employees in merging firms generally increases faster than that in nonmerging firms does not indicate that more jobs have been created by merging firms. An acquiring firm instantly adds size dimensions, including the employees of the acquired firm, and does not change aggregate employment with the merger.[3]

Since this statement concerning mergers and employment was published, a study of the effect of acquisitions on employment was contained in the "Wisconsin report" requested by the governor of that state.[4] The findings of this study reveal the following pattern:

. . . 55 percent of the merged corporations saw their employment growth rates decline after their acquisition. This finding tends to discredit the hypothesis (and frequently cited reason for being acquired) that a merger will accelerate the growth of the acquired firm because of the advantages of large scale and the financial strength, management skills, and research and development programs of the acquiring company. The evidence against this hypothesis is even stronger than the 55/45 decline-advance ratio suggests, because employment changes in the state as a whole were substantially smaller in the first half of the 1960–1968 period than in the latter half. In other words, the movement of Wisconsin's economy in recent years would have produced more advances than declines had the mergers had no effect on employment growth.[5]

In order to determine if there is a difference in the postmerger performance of firms acquired by out-of-state owners and in-state mergers, other tests were conducted and reported as follows:

The average pre-merger Wisconsin employment growth rate of out-of-state acquired firms was 6.02 percent. Following the mergers, their employment growth rate declined to −.48 percent. In other words, *the growth of aggregate Wisconsin employment among the out-of-state acquired companies has declined 108 percent since their mergers.*[6]

Similar results on employment and payrolls were evident in the Nebraska study. Stanley L. Brue found that in both cases, postmerger rates were substantially lower than premerger rates. The firms in the sample were growing at an average annual premerger employment rate of slightly over 1 percent. The average postmerger rate declined considerably to minus 8 percent. The mean annual premerger payroll rates for the acquired firms was nearly 7 percent, while the postmerger rate was minus 2 percent. The results were the same in all the subgroups; for example, firms acquired in product extension (circular) mergers were growing at a premerger rate of 7 percent, while their postmerger growth declined to an average of minus 10 percent.[7] Brue presents further evidence as follows:

> Manufacturing firms were particularly adversely affected by the mergers. The hypothetical average firm engaged in manufacturing had an average annual payroll growth rate of 5.609 percent during the post-merger years. The acquired manufacturing firms, however, had a negative post-merger rate of −5.248.[8]

Large and small firms were affected alike, with each group displaying average employment and payroll declines in the period following mergers. Thus, these economic events actually have a negative impact on the people, firms, and areas involved. For example, in Nebraska, Brue estimates that the 1970 loss to the Nebraska economy for 51 mergers was approximately $23,673,872.[9] This is a substantial impact in a state the size of Nebraska.

Another study of postmerger employment patterns in the state of Maine confirms the pattern noted above:

> There are rarely any employment benefits from absentee ownership in a small community. Some studies show that the immediate direct effect of a merger on jobs is negative, and there is evidence that outside ownership has a deadening effect upon growth. For example, between 1958 and 1969, firms headquartered in Maine with over 500 employees expanded employment by over 82 percent while firms owned outside the state grew only eight percent.[10]

CONCENTRATION OF ASSETS AND RISKS AND THE QUALITY OF LIFE

A major cost of the imbalanced economy has been an increase in *concentration* in the industrial structure, which is already quite concentrated in numerous important industries and markets. In addition, another major cost is the increased *risks* resulting from the creation of larger economic units. When any of these giant firms experiences financial difficulty, the repercussions are widespread in the economy. Let us not deceive ourselves about the dangers of bigness in a financial sense, as well as the costs to the public in higher prices, poorer service, and less quality which may be associated with many of these firms. Many large firms have become big with the help of the *merger* route (and other anticompetitive practices) rather than having a better product or service at a lower price in a competitive market consisting of numerous alternatives and/or rivals. A new economic America should be built on more sensible values, with special attention focused on the role of bigness for the sake of bigness. Scale diseconomies need to be recognized and treated when they are found to exist in the years ahead in both the public and private sectors.

THE RELATIVE MAGNITUDE OF THE COST OF CONCENTRATION TO THE PUBLIC

Perhaps the least known fact in America today is the vast price that citizens are paying because of high levels of concentration in many industries. Senator William Proxmire requested the Federal Trade Commission to make an investigation of the oligopoly industries. In this request he stated:

> The social case for such an investigation ought to be abundantly clear at this point in our national life. The complaints of our young and disadvantaged are not directed to the workings of small-scale enterprise in our atomistic industries but to the country's industrial heartland, to the several hundred firms that hold leading positions in our major oligopolies and that, by virtue of those positions, exercise a significant amount of power—both economic and political—over vast numbers of other human beings in our society. While some of our more alienated young may believe they have grievances against the "system" as a whole, the examples they point to are generally the workings of firms with substantial degrees of monopoly power, not of competitive businesses in unconcentrated industries. To be sure, there are social problems that have to be taken care of by extra-market institutions. These are by no means insoluble, however, and are not at the heart of the current case against the so-called "establishment." The social indictment currently presented, in short, runs against monopoly (or oligopoly), not against the market system, as such.[11]

The reason for the Senator's concern is that "the economic costs—and the social costs that go hand in hand with it—of maintaining the industrial status quo in this country have now reached intolerable proportions."[12]

In order to put the problem in its proper perspective, an examination of the relative costs can add the necessary dimension. Various estimates have been made concerning the annual cost of monopoly and consumer deception to the American consumer.[13] Senator Philip A. Hart recently estimated that "easily 30 percent of all consumer spending is wasted. . . . In other words, $174 to $231 billion consumers spend each year may buy no product value."[14] The bulk of this loss is the result of pricing policies in highly concentrated industries, particularly price-fixing conspiracies and other forms of collusion. The magnitude of this "transfer" from consumers to the sellers is best appreciated by examining other comparative figures as provided in a professional law and economic journal: "The country's total *crime bill,* according to the FBI, came to $32 billion last year;—the *Vietnam War's total price tag,* according to the Defense Department, was $27 billion last year;—*Eliminating poverty* in the United States ($3,000 minimum income for all families) would cost $11 billion per year."[15]

If the cost of each of these areas of national concern is added together, including the estimated annual cost of abating the major sources of pollution ($15 billion), the total is considerably less than the cost to the American consumer of tolerating concentrated industries, according to these figures.

As noted previously, *Business Week* has estimated the costs of economic regulation to be as high as $60 billion a year. Thus, there is a pressing need to develop an appropriate cost-benefit analysis of both concentration and regulation.

THE RELATIVE CONTRIBUTION OF MERGER TO THE QUALITY OF LIFE

Since business combinations contribute to the imbalanced economy, it is worth examining other effects that these economic events have upon the quality of life. Admittedly, these effects are difficult to measure, yet some facets of the problem have begun to emerge and will be discussed briefly in this section.

Rural–Small City–Urban Shifts of Economic Power—The "Main Street to Wall Street" Development

Another factor contributing to the deterioration of the quality of life is the "Main Street to Wall Street" movement. The transfer of control (by either ownership and/or management) and the movement of corporate headquarters from small- and/or medium-sized towns and cities to larger urban financial centers may have a serious negative effect upon numerous individuals and communities. The collective decline in the opportunities to live in smaller communities and the exodus to larger metropolitan areas complicate many existing problems. While production facilities may remain in smaller communities, many of the executives (and those associated with their paperwork) usually are transferred to larger urban centers containing huge multiple-office complexes. The resulting strain on facilities, including transportation, education, housing, medical, etc., adds to the costs (physical, mental, and monetary) and has a very discernible effect upon living conditions, as observed in New York City, the municipal conglomerate that has experienced financial problems of substantial magnitude.

Table 14.1   Population of Headquarters City of Acquired Firms of over $25 Million in Asset Size, 1948–1968

1960 population of headquarters city	Number of firms acquired
Over 1 million	88
500,000–1 million	67
100,000–500,000	66
25,000–100,000	47
Under 25,000	50
Total*	318

*Of the 354 acquired firms, the location city was known for 318.

Source: Bureau of Economics, Federal Trade Commission.

It was previously noted that firms headquartering in New York have become a "merger machine" which gobbles up numerous independent firms from all sections of the country. These New York firms acquired 153 of the 354 larger firms (those with assets of over $25 million) during the recent merger wave. It is worth noting that, although large firms tend to be located in major urban centers, a significant number of the "larger" *acquired* firms were headquartered in smaller cities and towns, as noted in Table 14.1. The 50 acquired firms headquartered in towns of less than 25,000 population were clearly of major importance to these communities, as were the 47 firms located in cities ranging from 21,000 to 100,000 people. This development is at the heart of the "Main Street to Wall Street" movement which is adding another lopsided dimension to the concentration and dispersion aspects of economic power in the new industrial order.

The Local Fight to Save Control

The headquarters question is important to communities, and there have been some examples of local cooperation to fend off outside raiders. Some notable examples are in New York State and Ohio, both states which have shown a net gain in merger activity during the recent merger wave. A business weekly reports on the situation as follows:

> Shareholders of two Rochester (N.Y.) companies, Taylor Instruments Co. and Ritter Pfaudler Corp., will hold separate meetings in their home city next month to decide whether they should merge.

The answer on this hometown get-together will probably be "yes." Earlier this year, a company from outside Rochester tried to take over Taylor via a tender offer for its shares. Taylor's quick riposte was to reach terms with Ritter Pfaudler.

The affair is one more example of an increasingly common phenomenon in these frenetic merger days: intervention by the entire business establishment in some cities—industries, law firms, advertising and public relations agencies—when outsiders try to take over a local company. More and more, managements are fighting off bids by outsiders by making deals—often only temporary—with their neighbors and golf partners.

Ritter Pfaudler doesn't deny that this is the present case. "Rochester people have decided," says an executive, "that they want its companies to remain based here."[16]

Business people in Cleveland openly boast of their efforts to fight off outsiders attempting to merge firms in their city. One investment banking executive stated that " . . . we fight to keep companies in Cleveland. Cities that lose corporate headquarters lose important men who could contribute to the local scene. This is extremely vital for the rebuilding of Cleveland."[17] *Business Week* listed the reasons why Cleveland can pull off the rescues: "First, its Establishment is closely knit, with members lunching together daily at the Union Club, where all SOS signals originally go up. Secondly, Cleveland has, for its size, a disproportionate number of large banks and investment banking companies, all of which have helped greatly in the saves. Finally, Clevelanders are unusually suspicious of outsiders . . . as a Cleveland blueblood observes: 'You can beat our Browns and our Indians. But it's tough to beat our Union Club.' "[18]

It is interesting to note that these communities recognize the value of retaining headquarters; however, they oppose merger activity by becoming involved themselves, which is a defensive position and not a solution of any substance. The local bankers and professional groups retain customers and depositors and yet they are contributing to increased local control, since the local acquiring firm is gaining in power. In addition, the ethical question is also in the picture, as *Business Week* observes: " . . . the money men in most cities are reluctant to talk about their 'arrangements' because of a gnawing point of ethics: Is such maneuvering in the interests of the stockholders? Do top managers run to their neighbors only to save their own jobs? When the money of shareholders is involved, who cares about the good of the city?"[19]

In addition to the intervention of private interests, in some Ohio merger attempts which would have caused the loss of a firm's headquarters public officials have also intervened. The classic case here is involvement of the Commissioner of Securities for the state of Ohio in the attempt by Northwest Industries, the rail-based holding company, to take over B. F. Goodrich Co. of Ohio during 1969. In another case, the Insurance Commissioner in Connecticut delayed the merger between IT&T and Hartford Fire Insurance Co. during 1969 in an effort to protect some of the numerous interested parties involved. However, except for the rather rare case, little has been done concerning the merger problem at the state and local level.

FINANCIAL POLLUTION

The recent merger movement has also contributed to the pollution of the financial scene by providing an impetus to a speculative whirl in the securities markets. This development inevitably brings back memories of the late 1920s. The increased use of the takeover bid has led to economic warfare, which has propelled the market price of some *acquired* firms to ranges which would be difficult to justify in any reasonable manner.[20]

The utilization of a myriad of securities, including convertible preferred stock, convertible debentures, and warrants (plus vague financial accounting and reporting), has caused a number of problems for investors who have been attracted to, yet bewildered by, the financial footwork of some of these firms. Many of these securities have been termed "funny money" by financial analysts, yet the holders of these securities have found little humor during the recent securities market plunge.

Another development in the recent merger wave which is reminiscent of the "roaring 20s" is the special promotional practices of a segment of investment bankers. Some of these firms launched their own "conglomo-rockets" in recent years with the objective of riding the curve up and hopefully backing out prior to the almost inevitable sharp decline experienced by these firms. The "insiders" are usually the gainers in these transactions, while the relative success of the smaller investor is generally serendipitous and usually nonexistent.

The point of this discussion concerning financial speculation is that when "insiders" and/or special groups are in preferred positions to realize gains not available to others, or to minimize losses at the expense of others, then the quality of life is affected. Obviously, merger is not the sole cause of this development, yet it is a *major* contributing factor, as it was in 1929. These happenings tend to corrupt the resource-allocation mechanism, since portfolio objectives can be attained by individual stockholders at a lower cost than through the efforts of the managers of conglomerates or other large firms. Joel Segall has also reached much the same conclusion; for example, Segall states:

. . . there is absolutely no reason why the firm should perform such a diversification function for its stockholders. First, not all stockholders may want the stability that a merger for diversification implies; some may prefer the possibility of a very large gain even at the risk of exposure to a very large loss. Second and more important, stockholders can get all the diversification they want at a relatively low cost through adjustments of their personal portfolios without the intervention of the firm. Nothing prevents a Litton stockholder from selling some of his Litton shares and putting the proceeds in another or several other firms; or in a mutual fund for that matter. In short, each stockholder may achieve exactly the degree of diversification suitable for his own preferences and his own portfolio all by himself. Diversification through merger seems unwieldy and inefficient.[21]

Thus, mergers play a very special role in the financial pollution of the capital and money markets and consequently affect the quality of life in a special manner in the imbalanced economy through their emphasis on financial speculation rather than productivity.

DETERIORATION OF PRODUCT AND SERVICE QUALITY

We have been told by numerous advocates of merger activity about all the benefits which can be expected from combination. For some unexplained reason, the sum of the parts is supposed to add up to more than the components—the so-called synergy effect.[22] Empirical research reveals quite a different pattern concerning synergy, and even casual observation reveals postmerger disappointments and a deterioration of quality. Perhaps the prime example of this is the Penn Central combination discussed previously, the ICC approved merger that was to result in vast savings and improved services to the public. In the years following the merger, it has become increasingly difficult to ride a train as a passenger, or to obtain the services of a freight car as a shipper. Obviously, the stockholders and creditors would also be curious to find out what ever happened to the synergistic benefits expected in this merger. It appears that the more active firms in the merger race are prone to be more financially oriented rather than production-minded, another factor contributing to the deterioration of the quality of goods and services.

In summary, major waves of merger activity make a generally negative contribution to the quality of life for most individuals and communities. Merger waves have provided a substantial impetus to the "Main Street to Wall Street" movement; they have provided the opportunity for ambitious promoters to issue securities of dubious value and endanger the equity holdings of many investors through the creation of excess debt in the capital structure of numerous merging firms, thus causing a special variety of financial pollution. Further, these events have diminished the amount of control that many individuals and communities have over their own destiny and, in addition, have contributed to a deterioration of quality in goods and services.

CONTROL OVER ONE'S DESTINY

The individual is faced with a constant challenge, during this period of relatively high concentration of political and economic power, to maintain some control over his or her own destiny. In a similar fashion, the same situation holds for local communities, individual states, and regions of the country. This is a practical problem which affects not only the youth of the country, but parents, executives, mayors, legislators, governors, and others—in short, everyone is affected to some degree.

The growth of power centers of any type—business, government, educational, military, religious, racial, ethnic, etc.—can be considered a threat to the individual. The large institutions and establishments in all these areas have had a profound impact on the lives of many citizens. The net effect is of considerable concern, since the problems are becoming increasingly evident as times, customs, values, traditions, and life-styles change while many of the entrenched establishments and institutions generally resist the changes. The problem of individual opportunity will receive increasing attention in the years ahead. It is reasonable to speculate on the role of the relative size of institutions and how this dimension affects the opportunities of the individual.

Sheer size can cause a number of problems, particularly when the gain in scale is accomplished through the combination of assets. When a formerly independent firm becomes a division of a division of International Everything, Inc., it is reasonable to expect numerous changes to occur. The changes will most likely be varied, the net effect depending upon prior conditions in the acquired firm and the management of the acquiring firm. One rather universal fact of life related to combinations is the creation of additional hierarchical tiers in the organization which, in most cases, further separate many individuals from the power elite and diminish personal control over their destinies. Most of us who have been associated with large power centers (of any type) know the frustrations and inefficiencies, injustices, and other problems which result from large bureaucracies, whether they are public or private.

There is also a marked difference in the amount of "red tape" and regimentation in many organizations, and *size* is the critical variable. In one large, well-known conglomerate, it appears that the executive suite is being supplemented by the "executive community," as a business weekly reports:

> In what amounts to a merger of Jeffersonian architecture with Army post planning, conglomerate "Automatic" Sprinkler Corp. of America has announced plans for a new 106-acre headquarters complex.
>
> Three separate "Virginia estate type buildings" will be connected by arcades, in the manner of Jefferson's design for the University of Virginia, covering 50 acres. The remaining acreage will be subdivided into five-acre plots for executive residences.[23]

This is a novel fabrication of the old company-town concept, since the executives are the "class" in this case rather than the working people. It is further interesting to note that members of the executive group are each allocated 5 acres rather than living in the look-alike row houses which were assigned to the blue-collar tenants in the older version of the company town. Perhaps the ex–high-ranking military officer group of executives could adjust quite well to this type of living and thinking, yet it appears alien to the youth culture and many other Americans in these times. Granted, it is an alternative life-style which would appeal to a segment of the population, however bizarre or unique it may be.

THE LAWYER'S DILEMMA

The Canons of Professional Ethics of the American Bar Assocation frown upon representation of conflicting interests, that is, situations where, in behalf of one client, it is the lawyer's duty to "contend for that which duty to another client requires him to oppose." In light of this caveat, as well as potential financial loss, can and will lawyers, law firms, and bar associations fight for more strict legislation which would curtail mergers and a resulting loss of substantial revenue from clients engaged in these types of economic events? The problem, as it affects the quality of life, is broader than this important issue. Can the public expect these individuals and groups practicing law to fight for increased automobile safety requirements while representing automobile manufacturers and distributors, to seek greater code enforcement in housing while representing major owners of real estate, or engage in tax reform efforts which, if successful, would adversely affect corporate clients?

In my opinion, the legal profession (as well as the economics profession) has been silent for too long on all these issues, and particularly the merger problem and the resulting power created from these events. Again, the only ray of hope appears to be in the emerging attitudes and expressions of some of the younger lawyers and some law students who have challenged the legal establishment for not undertaking work involving major controversial legal causes such as welfare reform, code enforcement, voting rights, or consumer protection. The almost solitary example of a Ralph Nader has served to open the consciences of some in the profession, particularly the young members of the profession who are not as yet in established and secure positions in the legal establishment.

The lawyer, like the accountant, is in a difficult position, since the immediate financial gain resulting from working on a merger contract, or an application for merger to be presented to regulatory agencies, is seldom viewed as a long-run problem, and the consequences are ignored, since allegiance to the client is paramount. It is only when the cumulative effect of various actions has a direct effect upon the lawyer that the problem becomes slightly important. For example, a leading partner in a large law firm in Chicago suggested to me that something has to be done about the merger movement in this country. The reason—he had previously sat on the boards of directors of seven major firms, and because of mergers, the number had been reduced to three boards. Some commercial and investment bankers have expressed similar complaints, yet they hesitate to take a stand for fear of offending an existing client or depositor and the resultant loss of an account.

Actually, the long-run interests of financial and legal institutions would be to find alternatives to mergers as solutions to business problems. Both the Wisconsin and Nebraska studies demonstrate that out-of-state acquirers of local firms generally transfer their financial, accounting, and legal services to their headquarters city. In reference to the bankers, Stanley I. Brue observed that " . . . nearly 75 percent of the Nebraska firms apparently abandoned the services of some or all of their local financial institutions. The biggest local loss was probably in the banking area."[24] The Wisconsin study found that in 70 percent of the cases the acquired firms had shifted in whole or in part to the financial institutions of the acquiring companies.[25]

The same pattern is found concerning legal services. In the Nebraska study, nearly 75 percent of the acquired companies utilized the legal services provided by the parent corporation, to the detriment of the local lawyers.[26] Once again the Nebraska experience is in conformity with the results of the Wisconsin study. In 75 percent of the Wisconsin cases, the acquiring firms' legal services were used in whole or in part.

While lawyers, law firms, bar associations, and others related to the legal profession have spent a considerable amount of time and effort fighting and lobbying against "no-fault" automobile insurance in recent years, they appear to have missed the significance of a different type of "menace" to local law business with much broader ramifications—the corporate merger.

Local communities and regions are at a distinct disadvantage without the interest and support of their leading local citizens such as the lawyers, accountants, bankers, and others who are usually involved and aware of combination and other activities which have an impact upon the quality of life in their areas. Admittedly, they do have conflicts which are real and immediate, yet some personal concern for the public interest should be programmed into the decision-making process. As an example, which certainly is not an isolated one, the Attorney General of the state of Vermont recently stated that "Lawyers in Vermont should pay more attention to public service and less to their pocketbooks. . . ." One of the reasons for this statement was a charge by a conservationist that there wasn't a lawyer in Southern Vermont that a private citizen could hire for protection against the rapid land development in the area, since they all were on the payrolls of the developers. In other words, entry is restricted in the legal profession on the supposition that the public interest is served better than if anyone could enter.[27] Yet, it appears that in this instance the Vermont public did not receive the legal support necessary to protect the quality of life in the imbalanced economy, even in the beautiful state of Vermont.

NOTES

1   See Sir John Clapham, *A Concise Economic History of Britain to Seventeen Fifty,* vol. 1, New York: Cambridge University Press, 1949.
2   Samuel Richardson Reid, *Mergers, Managers, and the Economy,* New York: McGraw-Hill, 1968, p. 108.
3   Ibid., p. 109.
4   Jon G. Udell, *Social and Economic Consequences of the Merger Movement in Wisconsin,* Wisconsin Economy Studies Number 3, Madison: Bureau of Business Research and Service, May 1969, pp. 5–27.
5   Ibid., pp. 39–40.
6   Ibid., p. 44.
7   Stanley L. Brue, *Local Economic Impacts of Corporate Mergers: The Nebraska Experience,* New Series no. 43, Lincoln University of Nebraska, May 1972, p. 49.
8   Ibid., p. 51.
9   Ibid., p. 56.
10 Geoffrey Faux, "Colonial New England," *The New Republic,* vol. 167, no. 20, Nov. 25, 1972, p. 17.
11 See "Oligopoly Investigation," *Antitrust Law and Economic Review,* vol. 3, no. 1, Fall 1969, pp. 11–12.

12 Ibid., p. 12.
13 Ralph Nader has estimated consumer costs at more than $100 billion a year, which is reasonably consistent with some of the work done by economists. See, for example, David R. Kamerschen, *An Estimate of the "Welfare Losses" from Monopoly in the American Economy,* Michigan State University, 1964 (doctoral dissertation), and W. G. Shepherd, "Conglomerate Mergers in Perspective," *Antitrust Law and Economics Review,* vol. 2, no. 1, pp. 15–32, Fall 1968.
14 Philip A. Hart, "Congressional Consumer Investigations: What Do They Tell Us?" speech before New York Consumer Assembly, Commodore Hotel, New York City, March 7, 1970, p. 1.
15 See "Foreword," *Antitrust Law and Economic Review,* vol. 4, no. 2, p. 1, Summer 1969.
16 "Hometown Companies Fight Off Invaders," *Business Week,* August 17, 1968, p. 78.
17 Ibid., p. 80.
18 Ibid., p. 83.
19 Ibid., p. 78.
20 One of the reasons for the rather high "failure" rate among merging firms is the large "premium" paid by acquiring firms which either dilutes the equity position or adds debt magnitudes which are difficult to service.
21 Joel Segall, "Merging for Fun and Profit," *Industrial Management Review,* vol. 9, no. 2, pp. 17–29, Winter 1968.
22 See H. Igor Ansoff and J. Fred Weston, "Merger Objectives and Organizational Structure," *The Quarterly Review of Economics and Business,* vol. 2, no. 3, pp. 49–58, August 1962.
23 See "'Automatic' Sprinkler Plans Headquarters with Executive Residences on the 'Post,'" (Management Briefs) *Business Week,* October 26, 1968, p. 92. The new name of the firm is A-T-O Corporation.
24 Stanley L. Brue, op. cit., p. 74.
25 Jon G. Udell, op. cit., p. 26.
26 Stanley L. Brue, op. cit., p. 75.
27 State and local bar associations and the judiciary have effectively restricted entry into the business of providing legal services through a variety of barriers mostly related to requiring attendance at a bar association–approved school. In the 1950s, 35 states permitted "law readers" to take bar examinations; now only five—California, Mississippi, Vermont, Virginia, and Washington—allow this alternative. Perhaps the situation will improve in the future in Vermont as the number of law readers has increased from 2 in 1969 to 58 in 1975. Legal entry problems may well be settled in the courts during the 1970s. Pricing policies, such as minimum fee schedules, have been struck down by the Supreme Court, which held that some legal services are subject to the antitrust laws and entry restrictions may be next in line. See "Do-It-Yourself Lawyers," *Newsweek,* p. 40, June 16, 1975.

Chapter 15

The Political Economy, Microeconomics, and Public Policy

The microeconomic field of "industrial organization" has traditionally been devoted to the study and analysis of the structure of the economy, and the resulting behavior and performance of firms and industries. Over the years, this special branch of economics has produced a variety of insights related to various economic phenomena which deserve special attention in the battle to improve the quality of life in America.

Many economists and public officials appear to continually concentrate on the traditional macroeconomic solutions when attempting to control pressing national problems. Monetary and fiscal policy tend to receive an inordinate amount of attention to the detriment of microeconomic alternatives and supplements to public policy. The underlying purpose of this treatise has been to call attention to important basic microeconomic developments which have had a significant impact upon the economy and that deserve the renewed attention of those concerned with economic matters. The basic nature of the performance of the economy demands new and different approaches in public policy. A surprising number of alternatives exist in the generally ignored microeconomic area. Some of these alternatives are short-run in nature, while others can contribute important long-run benefits to the economy. This chapter will spell out some of the more pertinent policy alternatives following a brief examination of the so-called inflation and stagflation problems which have emerged in recent years and which provide a convenient case study.

THE INFLATION AND STAGFLATION PROBLEMS

Inflation is a rise in the general level of prices in an economy, and is usually measured through a *price* index—a weighted average of a whole range of prices. The two most widely used indexes are the Wholesale Price Index and the Consumer Price Index.[1] When a general price index goes up significantly, as in the 1972–1974 period, it is clear that inflation is in process (see Table 15.1). A graphic illustration of each price index is presented in Chart 15.1. Following the relatively stable years of the early 1960s, prices began to move upward with more intensity and suddenly exploded in 1973 and 1974. This almost unprecedented surge in peacetime price levels prompted President Ford to term inflation as "public enemy number one" in the early stage of his administration.

"Stagflation" is a newly coined word which describes the economic phenomenon of inflation occurring simultaneously with a stagnant or declining economy (recession or depression). This anomaly runs counter to

Table 15.1   Wholesale and Consumer Price Indexes, 1960–1974
Annual Average (1967 = 100)

Year	Wholesale prices	Consumer prices
1960	94.9	88.7
1961	94.5	89.6
1962	94.8	90.6
1963	94.5	91.7
1964	94.7	92.9
1965	96.6	94.5
1966	99.8	97.2
1967	100.0	100.0
1968	102.5	104.2
1969	106.5	109.8
1970	110.4	116.3
1971	113.9	121.3
1972	119.1	125.3
1973	134.7	133.1
1974	160.1	147.7

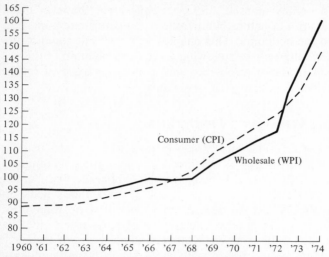

Chart 15.1   Wholesale and Consumer Price Indexes, 1960–1974.

traditional economic theory, where widespread declines in demand and/or production are expected to result in downward pressures on the levels of prices. The stagflation problem focuses attention on the microeconomic area of price behavior as it relates to industry structure. While the word is new, the phenomenon is not. Industrial organization economists have had a serious interest in differing patterns of price behavior among industries of differing structures since the 1930s; more specifically, the basic interest can be traced to the administered price controversy initiated by Gardiner C. Means. The argument of Means was that prices of concentrated industries[2] registered smaller depression decreases than those of unconcentrated industries and this finding dovetailed nicely into the theories of "imperfect" and "monopolistic competition" which emerged about the same time.[3] Thus pricing behavior and the structural characteristics of an economy have been recognized by industrial organization economists for some time.[4]

Stagflation in the Post-World War II Recessions

In the recessions since the Second World War, there has developed a new form of price behavior counter to that of the Great Depression. In the 1930s the direction of change in the prices of concentrated industries was downward, although the decreases were much more limited in extent than the declines of the competitive industries. In the postwar and recent recessions, the price change direction of concentrated industries has been *upward;* thus the stagflation situation.

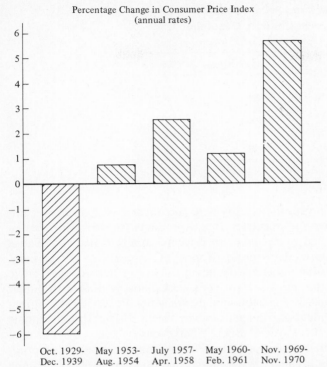

Percentage Change in Consumer Price Index
(annual rates)

| | Oct. 1929-
Dec. 1939 | May 1953-
Aug. 1954 | July 1957-
Apr. 1958 | May 1960-
Feb. 1961 | Nov. 1969-
Nov. 1970 |

Chart 15.2 Percentage Change in Consumer Price Index during
the Depression and Post–World War II Recessions.

Stagflation first appeared during the postwar 1954 and 1958 recessions
(see Chart 15.2). In both periods, a number of indirect measures appeared
to show the general decline in demand to be accompanied by a tendency for
oligopolistic industrial prices to rise.[5] A continuation of this development
was also evident in the 1969–70 and 1974–75 recessions in the United
States.

The 1969–1970 Recession

A further manifestation of stagflation developed in the 1969–1970 period.
This was a recession which was ostensibly brought about to cure the inflation
which had developed during the relative economic boom of the late 1960s.
Economist John M. Blair conducted an extensive study of perverse price
behavior in the December 1969–December 1970 recession period.[6] The
study examined the weighted average price change for 296 industrial and
farm products divided into concentration catagories. The average *increase*

**Table 15.2   Industrial and Farm Products:
Weighted-average Price Change, December 1969–
December 1970, by Concentration Category**

Concentration ratio	Number of products	Change
Concentrated (50 percent and over)	137	5.9%
Intermediate (25–49 percent)	110	−1.0%
Unconcentrated (Under 25 percent)	49	−6.1%

Source: John M. Blair, *Journal of Economic Issues,* vol. 8, no. 2, p. 458, June 1974.

for products with concentration ratios of 50 percent and over was 6 percent, while the competitive (or unconcentrated) products (those with ratios of under 25 percent) had a *decrease* in price of minus 6 percent. Those products in the intermediate group (ratios of from 25 to 49 percent) recorded an intermediate change, declining a minus 1 percent (see Table 15.2). A variety of other price comparisons were made by Blair with similar results, indicating that during economic downswings (recession) the prices of concentrated products no longer remain "rigid." They have become flexible *upward.* In the words of Blair, "This form of behavior, accompanied by the traditional downward flexibility of the unconcentrated products, has created a bifurcated price structure whose average change in time of recession is merely a happenstance composite of the opposing movements of its components. Moreover, the recession behavior of concentrated products implies a Phillips curve, in reverse."[7] Thus, stagflation is a special case in the inflationary process which is beyond the scope of the traditional analyses of demand-pull and cost-push forms of inflation.[8] Preliminary observation of the 1974–75 recession period again indicates that stagflation is the economic problem. From a microeconomic perspective, stagflation implies a "structural" inflation related to both the concentrated nature of markets and the manifestation of economic power related to firms of a grand scale.

The same general pattern of administered prices inflation has been apparent in Canada in the post-World War II period. A study by Willy Sellekaerts and Richard Lesage indicates the need for an evaluation of classic *anti*-inflationary policies. They state:

> Monetary and fiscal policy, designed to eliminate inflation by reducing aggregate demand below potential output will be relatively unsuccessful if, *in concentrated industries, prices continue to rise in the face of a 10 to 20% fall in*

all manufacturing capacity utilization. The major consequence of a traditional *anti*-inflationary policy is an increase in the unemployment rate above what can be considered as socially and politically acceptable, rather than a fall in the rate of inflation.[9]

"Structural" Inflation and Public Policy Alternatives

While the basic focal point of structural inflation revolves around pricing behavior in concentrated economies, industries, and markets, the area of interest is broader than this narrow perspective. The absolute and relative size of firms is also important since economies or diseconomies of scale are worthy of examination in particular industries or sectors. Nonprice competitive factors, entry conditions, and the methods of growth (internal and merger) are important dimensions of the structure problem and public policies related to it.

Economic power, which is one characteristic of concentration and firm size, is not a new problem. A number of short-run public policies have been employed over the years, designed to curtail certain abuses of power. Some of these policies have been formal and others more informal, and their record in relation to inflation has been varied. Some examples of these short-run microeconomic policy alternatives are worth examining and assessing, since they appear periodically in the policy arena. It should be noted that each alternative (jawboning, guidelining. and wage-price controls) is basically a short-run response to either actual or potential abuses of economic power. Following a brief examination of these short-run policy alternatives, some long-run solutions to structural inflation will be presented.

SOME SHORT-RUN MICROECONOMIC POLICY ALTERNATIVES

Each of the three major short-run microeconomic policy alternatives designed to temporarily curb economic power has been utilized in varying degrees since 1960, and each has received some attention in recent inflation policy discussions. Each alternative is designed to correct the *effects* of economic power abuse rather than the basic *cause* of the problem.

Jawboning

The practice of "jawboning" generally takes the form of a presidential exhortation to labor and management for moderation in their wage and price actions. Every President since Harry S. Truman has used this policy alternative in efforts to check various forms of economic power and behavior.

The most significant utilization of jawboning was the 1962 confrontation of President John F. Kennedy with steel industry leaders. The background for the confrontation was the desire of the administration to attain reasonable price stability accompanied by an increase in the rate of economic growth and a lowering in the rate of unemployment. Secretary of Labor Arthur Goldberg (formerly general counsel for the United Steel Workers) had spent considerable time working out a noninflationary wage settlement—based on productivity. Following this agreement, Roger Blough, chairman of the board of U.S. Steel Company, visited the White House personally and announced a $6-per-ton across-the-board price increase. President Kennedy felt he had been knifed in the back by the leaders of this important industry and he was outraged in his reaction.

Similar reaction followed on a broad front. Members of the Cabinet denounced the price increase at press conferences. Congresspeople made numerous speeches attacking the price increase with demands for an investigation, and bills were introduced to break up excessive power in the industry. The Defense Department announced that henceforth contractors should buy their steel from producers who had not increased their prices. The Justice Department began to seek evidence of price collusion, and the Senate Antitrust Subcommittee called upon the major steel firms to produce their unit cost data—by product, by mill, and by type of expense. A few days after the jawboning had begun, Bethlehem Steel withdrew its price increase, and this was followed by a price rollback by U.S. Steel hours later.

Jawboning in this instance appeared to be effective in dealing with pricing behavior stemming from economic power. While some observers have argued that market conditions were more responsible for the price capitulation of the major firms, the fact remains that there were steel price increases by this industry during the recession years of 1954 and 1958 when demand was soft.

Under certain circumstances, jawboning can be effective as a short-run policy when used on a selective basis and buttressed by the force and weight of the office of the President of the United States. However, it is voluntary and does not carry the weight of law. Jawboning can be viewed as a short-run alternative which can be utilized quickly, without the usual delays associated with hearings, legal opinions, appeals, and so on. It is a microeconomic attempt to correct an abuse of economic power and does not aim at the underlying structural cause of the problem.

Guidelining

The 1962 Report of the Council of Economic Advisers formalized the wage-price guidelines, or guideposts, which had been utilized by the Kennedy administration in the attempt to stabilize prices and unit labor costs. The report stated that the general guide for noninflationary wage behavior was that the rate of increase in wage rates (including fringe benefits) in each industry be equal to the trend rate of overall productivity increase. The overall productivity increase for the economy as a whole during the preceding 5 years had averaged 3.2 percent. One weakness to this approach was that changes in wages were to be related to an overall productivity rate and not to that of individual industries or firms, which would have been a truly microeconomic guideline or guidepost. Simplicity was both the virtue and weakness of using an aggregate rate of change.

The general guide for noninflationary price behavior called for price reduction if an industry's rate of productivity increase exceeded the overall rate—since this would mean declining unit labor costs. If the opposite situation prevailed, then an appropriate increase in price would be justified. An obvious weakness in this approach is tying price changes to labor productivity to the exclusion of the other factors of production. The providers of capital should also be rewarded for their contributions to productivity through the provision of productive capital assets to a firm and to an industry.

Perhaps the most striking characteristic of the guidelining alternative was the almost universal opposition from labor and management. Among the objections to guidelining stressed by the AFL-CIO Executive Council in 1966 was that while wage increases could readily be compared with the 3.2 percent productivity yardstick, there was no comparable standard for profits and dividends. Management, particularly in concentrated areas of the economy, resented the government interference with their price-making prerogatives.

While guidelining is basically a selective short-run policy aimed at the abuses of power rather than an attack on the underlying cause of the problem, it has proved to be somewhat effective under certain circumstances. An examination of the remarkable price stability in the Wholesale Price Index for the early 1960s (see Table 15.1), when the guidelines were employed, is indicative of some relative success.[10] There are practical problems which limit the usefulness of this alternative; for example, productivity increases have averaged only about 2 percent per annum in recent years, and with inflation at record levels it would be difficult to restrict wage increases to minor increases of this magnitude since *real* income would decline drastically. Thus, under certain circumstances, guidelining may be a temporary expedient to correct the abuses of economic power, yet the basic structural problem remains intact. Perhaps it would be possible to devise guidelines tied to something other than productivity changes; however, few (if any) practical alternatives have been advanced.

Wage and Price Controls

The third short-run microeconomic policy alternative designed to curb inflation is control of wages and prices by the government. Policies of this type are usually employed only in periods of general inflation, when additional supplies, which are necessary to meet growing and high levels of demand, are needed in a wartime national emergency. A major shift in this policy occurred on August 15, 1971, when President Nixon announced a freeze order controlling a substantial array of prices and wages in what became Phase One of a new and different experiment by the administration to check inflation prior to an election year. The policy was relatively short term, with variations introduced during the limited life of controls.

While there are always proponents for this policy alternative, the opponents generally outnumber them, especially when the nation is not engaged in a declared war. Indeed, it is difficult to conceive how an attempt to freeze all, or many, prices and wages for any length of time in the face of changes in costs and demand can be considered a sensible policy. Any general order which freezes prices and wages at levels prevailing in a designated base period will inevitably favor some producers and employees and discriminate against others.

The administration of wage and price controls calls for the creation of a vast government bureaucracy to effectively enforce controls, since actual and potential variations of evasion are boundless. Alterations of quality and other forms of hidden price increases are difficult to detect, and buyers may be charged for "extras" and services formerly included in the price. Controls may also diminish incentives for more productivity, as the distribution of any resulting gains is uncertain. Selective price freezes may solve some of these problems, yet they generally add other economic and legal problems as well. In short, wage and price controls may be a necessary and temporary short-run policy, yet the costs will generally exceed any temporary benefits in a peacetime economy.

A separate but related case is that of statutory regulation of particular industries by special governmental regulatory agencies, such as the Interstate Commerce Commission, the Civil Aeronautics Board, the Federal Deposit Insurance Corporation, and so on. The record of these agencies as it relates to the structural characteristics of entry, merger, pricing, service, and other matters casts serious doubt that this special form of regulation can effectively serve public and private interests, except in unusual cases.

RESTORATION OF A COMPETITIVE, FREE ENTERPRISE MARKET SYSTEM—A LONG-RUN POLICY ALTERNATIVE

Up to this point, each of the short-run microeconomic policy alternatives presented—jawboning, guidelining, and controls—have been short-run and designed to correct abuses resulting from an economic structure which is less than competitive. In other words, the *effects* rather than the *causes* of the problem are treated. This is a natural and understandable situation since policymakers are interested in immediate solutions to inflationary and power problems. In addition, even if the basic cause of the problem is recognized, the political realities of attempting to reorganize the industrial, financial, and commercial organization and structure of the economy are staggering. It is precisely this situation which continually complicates the search for long-run solutions. Recognition of this serious drawback is acknowledged, yet the problem will not go away nor will it be solved by suboptimal solutions designed to mitigate the effects of, rather than correct, the basic structural dilemma. In this spirit, the need for a restoration of a competitive structure will be addressed briefly, followed by a long-run microeconomic policy alternative which merits adequate consideration and implementation.

The Need for a Comprehensive Competition Structure

It is almost embarrassing to treat this subject, even if only briefly, since market competition has long been hailed as the powerful and pervasive force depended upon to discipline private decision making and discretion in the greater part of the economy. Americans have traditionally held that effective market competition promotes efficient resource allocation, economic growth, price stability, and full employment.

It has also been held that a breakdown in market competition tends to distort efficient resource allocation by raising an industry's or firm's prices and lowering output. Without the spur of competition, industries and firms are generally slow to adopt innovations and the most efficient production processes.[11] If firms can readily pass on higher costs to customers, they will be less concerned with keeping costs to a minimum.

Particularly relevant is the fact that firms with considerable discretion over wage and price decisions may stimulate inflationary pressures even in a period of stagnation or recession and rising unemployment. This latter economic situation has prevailed in the American economy during recent decades and yet is just beginning to receive the attention of economists and policymakers.

The Role of Concentrated Economic Power in Promoting Inflation

As noted previously, dominant firms in concentrated industries (or large firms with economic power) have the ability to raise or maintain prices when demand is stagnant or declining and capacity is unused. The price and wage behavior in the steel industry contributed to the initial stagnation development in the 1950s. Between 1953 and 1959 pricing policies in the steel industry contributed heavily to the increase in the Wholesale Price Index. Finished steel prices rose by 36 percent during the period, while all wholesale prices rose an average of 9 percent. Wholesale prices, exclusive of all metals, rose only 1½ percent in the period.

Steel prices increased, despite substantial excess capacity in the industry. For example, although capacity utilization declined from 95 percent in 1953 to 71 percent during the 1954 recession, finished steel prices increased by 4 percent; also, when capacity utilization dropped from 85 percent in 1957 to 61 percent in the recession year of 1958, prices rose by 5 percent. This price behavior in a concentrated industry led Otto Eckstein and Gary Fromm to conclude that "The wage and price behavior of the steel industry represents an important instance of inflation caused to a substantial degree by the exercise of market power. This type of inflation cannot be controlled by policies aimed at restricting total demand."[12] The same pattern of pricing and capacity utilization was also apparent during the 1969–70 recession, although there was evidence of wage and price restraint in the steel industry during the period when capacity utilization rates were increasing in the 1960s and jawboning and guidelining were being utilized by the Democratic Presidents. Steel is but one of a number of microeconomic examples of price behavior in concentrated industries, indicating the need for industrial reorganization and effective antitrust policy.

Industrial, Financial, and Commercial Reorganization

As the word implies, this long-run microeconomic policy alternative is designed to focus attention on the major basic concentrated industries, with the objective of restoring a free-enterprise competitive market system to these areas and to the economy in general. The next chapter will treat some of the economic and legal aspects of this policy alternative in more detail, since an examination of the economic power problem leads inescapably to the need for this policy course to be applied on a comprehensive basis.

Effective Antitrust

The antitrust alternative contains a body of statutory and judicial law which has been developed over a period of about 85 years in the United States. This policy may be considered separate from the industrial reorganization alternative discussed above, yet it would appear that both are needed simultaneously. This observation is based upon the fact that the existing nature of the American economy (discussed in the previous chapters) basically emerged during the life of these statutes. Since the vigor of enforcement is so serendipitous and the nature of this policy alternative so tied to political power, standing alone it is subject to generally benign neglect. For example, the Antitrust Division of the Justice Department has an appropriation which will allow an extremely limited amount of litigation to be initiated, particularly in view of the comprehensive nature of the problem. In addition, the process is generally time-consuming and in some cases may take many years and substantial resources before an issue is resolved.

Perhaps the biggest boost the antitrust alternative has received stems from the growing interest of states, private firms, and individuals. For example, the State of New York initiated an antitrust action against seven major oil firms for price fixing during the so-called energy crisis in 1974. Equally important, private "trust busting" has become a major development in antitrust law, as the number of private antitrust actions increased from 422 cases in 1964 to 1,270 cases in 1974, a hefty increase indeed. Thus, while federal policy in this area is severely constrained by political and budgetary considerations, action at the private and state level is capable of adding a measure of potency to this policy alternative.

THE ROLE OF INDUSTRIAL ORGANIZATION MICROECONOMICS

The concentrated economic power and stagflation problems are particularly suited to microeconomic analysis since the major related developments in these areas are traditional areas of interest to students and others interested in industrial organization. Especially important are the economic developments which lead to increased levels of concentration, power, and firm size at both an aggregate and market level.

Since corporate mergers and acquisitions have played a great part in the concentration and growth process, considerable attention has been devoted to these economic events. The behavior of government regulators and the role of government in general are also important areas of interest. Thus, the existence and exercise of economic power are a special problem area in the economy where viable solutions and effective policy formation are an open field awaiting serious research, as well as legislative and practical attention. The next and final chapter contains a variety of public policy proposals aimed at restoring some semblance of price competition to the economy. The challenge persists, and needless to say, the opportunities for those interested in the problem are abundant.

NOTES

1 Another price index which is broader and utilized for some purposes is the GNP price deflator, a product of national income accounting.
2 The degree of concentration in an industry is measured by the percentage of a size variable (assets, sales, value of shipments, etc.) of a specific industry or

product accounted for by usually the top four or eight firms. Although these ratios or any other single statistic cannot fully describe the number and size distribution of firms in an industry, they are generally acknowledged to capture the essential feature of the distribution—namely, the combined market position of the largest firms. For this reason, they have come to be commonly used summary measurements of industry or market concentration.

3 Means' administered pricing proposition has been supported by three empirical studies. The initial one consisted of a statistical analysis of the relationship between concentration and price rigidity of 38 industries that met specific standards for comparability between price and concentration data. Of 12 industries with concentration ratios of less than 25 percent, eight registered price declines of over 30 percent between 1929 and 1932, and only one had a decrease of under 15 percent. In contrast, only one of the 14 industries with ratios of over 50 percent registered a decline of over 30 percent, while seven had decreases of less than 15 percent (see National Resources Committee, *The Structure of the American Economy,* 1939, Part 1, p. 143). The second study was a comparison of the price behavior of 180 identical products in two depressions, 1890–1897 and 1929–1933. For products which remained unconcentrated, prices were flexible in both downturns; for those which became concentrated during the interval, prices tended to change from flexible to rigid; and for those whose structure changed from concentrated to unconcentrated, the price behavior changed from rigid to flexible (see John M. Blair, "Economic Concentration and Depression Price Rigidity," *American Economic Review,* vol. 45, no. 2, pp. 566–597, May 1955). The third study examined price margins above direct costs and found that in the 1929–1931 period, margins per unit of output decreased less in concentrated industries than in those which were unconcentrated (see Howard N. Ross, *The Theory and Evidence of Price Flexibility,* doctoral dissertation, Columbia University, 1964).

4 For a discussion of the German experience, see Helmut Arndt, "Competition, Price and Wage Flexibility, and Inflation: The German Experience," *The Antitrust Bulletin,* vol. 17, no. 3, pp. 859–883, Fall 1972.

5 John M. Blair, *Economic Concentration,* New York: Harcourt Brace Jovanovich, 1972, chap. 17, pp. 438–66.

6 John M. Blair, "Market Power and Inflation: A Short-Run Target Return Model," *Journal of Economic Issues,* vol. 8, no. 2, pp. 453–478, June 1974. For conflicting opinions on the role of administered prices, see Gardiner C. Means, "The Administered-Price Thesis Reconfirmed," *American Economic Review,* vol. 62, no. 2, pp. 292–306, June 1972 and George J. Stigler and J. K. Kindall, *The Behavior of Industrial Prices,* New York: National Bureau of Economic Research, 1970.

7 Blair, "Market Power and Inflation," op. cit., p. 494.

8 For a more limited study of 90 wholesale Price Index Industry Sector Price Indexes for the November 1969–November 1970 period, see J. Fred Weston, Steven Fustgarten, and Nanci Grottke, "The Administered Price Thesis Denied: Note," *American Economic Review,* vol. 64, no. 1, pp. 232–234, March 1974.

9 Willy Sellekaerts and Richard Lesage, "A Reformulation and Empirical Verification of the Administered Prices Inflation Hypothesis: The Canadian Case," *The Southern Economic Journal,* vol. 39, no. 3, p. 356, January 1973.

10 A difference of opinion among some economists concerning the effectiveness of guidelining is evident; for a discussion, see G. Schultz and R. Alibu (eds.), *Guidelines, Informal Controls, and the Market Place,* Chicago: University of Chicago Press, 1966, especially the comments of Arthur M. Okun, Gardner Ackley, and John T. Dunlop.

11 It is possible that in some degrees of oligopoly there will be an increase in innovation and technological change; see, for example, Kalman J. Cohen and Richard M. Cyert, *Theory of the Firm: Resource Allocation in a Market Economy,* Englewood Cliffs, N.J.: Prentice-Hall, 1965, pp. 386–390.

12 O. Eckstein and G. Fromm, "Steel and the Postwar Inflation," *Study Paper No. 2,* Joint Economic Committee, November 6, 1959.

Chapter 16

A New Economic America

It should be obvious that the competitive free enterprise market system, long valued by Americans, is bent out of shape and in need of a massive overhaul if it is to function in the public interest. This chapter is devoted to a presentation and evaluation of various alternative proposals designed to revitalize economic America.

Numerous public policy prescriptions concerning concentration and merger problems have been advanced over the years since Senator Sherman introduced the original antitrust act in the latter years of the nineteenth century. Many of the proposals are interesting; for example, Morton Mintz and Jerry S. Cohen recently advocated that corporations be chartered on a national level rather than at the state level.[1] The purpose of this proposal, contained in their book, *America, Inc.: Who Owns and Operates the United States,* is to effectuate more federal control over the operations and policies of American business firms. Recent congressional hearings, filling 11 volumes and thousands of printed pages, prompted the introduction of legislation by Senator Philip A. Hart of Michigan during the summer of

1972 and subsequent sessions. In addition, the abuses revealed in the IT&T antitrust case (during the Senate Judiciary hearings on the nomination of Richard Kleindienst as Attorney General) prompted Senator John V. Tunney of California to introduce special legislation concerning antitrust consent decrees.

Additional legislation concerning both concentrated industries and merger activity has been proposed by a task force on antitrust policy, chaired by a law school dean. These various legislative proposals deserve careful consideration. Other original alternatives and additions are advanced in this chapter to round out a growing list of public policy proposals designed to renew and restore the vanishing free enterprise system in economic America. Each component of this policy mosaic is presented below.

THE INDUSTRIAL REORGANIZATION ACT

On July 24, 1972, Senator Philip A. Hart introduced the Industrial Reorganization Act on the floor of the United States Senate.[2] Senator Hart stated that "It seeks to bring closer to reality what this country has pretended to have for years: a competitive economy. . . . If it lives up to my expectations, it also could be a giant step toward eliminating some of the feeling that opportunities no longer exist for the individual and that the economic life of the nation will always be dominated by a few. We all recognize that too much power in too few hands is bad for social and political reasons, as well as for economic reasons." Hart further warned that "Unless competition is restored to the economy we are headed toward a society dominated by a few corporate giants with an army of government clerks as their listless watchdogs."

The act proposes to set up an Industrial Reorganization Commission and give it tough new monopoly-busting powers for its limited life of 15 years. The commission would give priority attention to seven industries:

1　Chemicals and drugs
2　Electronic computing and communication equipment
3　Electrical machinery and equipment
4　Energy
5　Iron and steel
6　Motor vehicles
7　Nonferrous metals

These seven industries account for nearly 40 percent of the total value created in United States manufacturing, and 140 of the top 200 corporations participate in these industries. Nearly two-thirds of the nation's industrial assets are held by these firms. Perhaps the biggest omission is the food industry, which appears to deserve special attention, along with the other consumer goods industries.

In addition to forming a commission with limited life (15 years), the Hart antitrust bill would bring a couple of important new aspects to antitrust enforcement: trustbusters would no longer have to rely on evidence that defendant firms *intended* to create monopolies to control prices or to exclude competitors; and the enforcement agencies would be geared to deal with the mechanics of dismantling monopolies.

Under the bill, a company or companies are presumed to have monopoly power if:

1 The average rate of return on net worth for any corporation exceeds 15 percent for 5 consecutive years of the 7 years preceding the complaint, or

2 If there has been no substantial price competition among two or more corporations in any product line for 3 consecutive years of the preceding 5, or

3 If any four corporations account for 50 percent or more of sales for a product line or industry in any year of the most recent 3 years.

Firms operating under any of the above conditions would be liable to the charge that they possess monopoly power unless they can justify their position. A firm could escape sanctions by showing that its unusually high profit levels were due to patent rights or its size was necessary for efficiency. Cases would be tried by an industrial reorganization court set up to handle nothing but cases brought by the commission, and decisions would be appealed directly to the Supreme Court.

Besides attacking corporate giantism, the bill reaches big labor by requiring the commission to study the effects on competition of collective bargaining practices in our major industries. The commission is directed to come back to Congress with appropriate legislative recommendations.

As for government, Hart believes that the market policing power of real competition will relieve the need for burgeoning regulatory bureaucracies. The Senator said that the bill is based on the "old-fashioned notion that honest competition is far more protective of the consumer interest than all the regulatory bureaucracies ever devised."

Relating inflation and unemployment to the lopsided economy, Senator Hart stated on the floor of the Senate that:

Concentrated industries not only display little price competition but tend to maintain or increase prices as demand falls—in order not to erode profits.

Thus, Government steps to halt inflation by cutting demand tends in these industries to backfire. Cuts in demand too frequently result in higher prices—and more layoffs—as the companies seek to make the target profits.

Mr. President, the situation has been all too familiar the past four years. Government used all the traditional tools in its arsenal to fight inflation, but inflation and high unemployment have flourished.

I suggest this is because we were applying medication designed for a competitive enterprise system when concentrated industries had wiped out much of the competition.

Competition must exist before fiscal and monetary policies can work effectively.[3]

THE ANTITRUST TASK FORCE RECOMMENDATIONS

The Concentrated Industries Act

There exists a proposal for legislation which was the result of a study made by a task force on antitrust policy appointed by President Johnson in December 1967 and which was submitted to him on July 5, 1968. The task force consisted of three practicing lawyers, three economists, five professors of law, and the Chairman, Phil C. Neal, dean of the Law School at the University of Chicago. Initially, the report was "secret" and gathered dust on the shelves of President Johnson's office. The report was not released to the public until the spring of 1969, when it became an issue in the government's attempt to secure a temporary injunction preventing the Northwest Industries–B. F. Goodrich merger in Federal District Court in Chicago.

The task force recommended the enactment of several statutes including the "Concentrated Industries Act."[4] Under this proposed statute, the Attorney General and the Federal Trade Commission would be directed to affirmatively search out all "oligopoly industries" in the United States, with the Attorney General to bring legal proceedings against all "oligopoly firms" in those industries. An industry is considered as oligopolistic if there are sales of $500 million or more and the four largest firms have held 70 percent or more of the market for a prescribed number of years. An oligopolistic firm is one having 15 percent or more of the market under scrutiny. The statutory objective is to "reduce the four-firm concentration ratio below 50% and the market shares of individual firms below 12%." Limitations on advertising expenditures and other such forms of supplementary relief would also be available.

The purpose of this proposed legislation would be to give enforcement authorities and the courts a clear mandate to use established techniques of divestiture to reduce concentration in industries where monopoly power is shared by a few large firms. The proposed statutory language provides no defenses except as to relief, although a firm could resist dissolution or divestiture if it could demonstrate affirmatively that such remedies "would result in substantial loss of economies of scale."

This proposed legislation is another alternative approach to deconcentration of industries and an attempt to restore some measure of competitiveness to the imbalanced economy. The objective could be implemented easily by the affected firms on a voluntary basis through spinning off divisions as separate corporate entities and distributing the stock to the existing shareholders whose property rights would be protected.

Provisions should be added to eliminate interlocking directorates and other ties which could undermine the spirit and intent of the law. The point is that the process is simple, and not complicated as some would argue in defense of the status quo. A few people, such as big business managers and/ or legislators, can effect a profound and necessary change in the American economy in an uncomplicated manner. Existing industrial giants could be trimmed down to a size consistent with efficiency and the desire to compete and innovate. Corporate overweight in the lopsided economy would be lopped off in short order and a trimmer competitive environment would emerge.

The Merger Act

The Task Force made a second recommendation aimed at preventing the use of merger to achieve concentration and economic power and which would supplement section 7 of the Clayton Act, the existing antimerger law. The primary impact of the new legislation would be on diversification, or conglomerate, mergers. The proposed legislation would prevent some possibly anticompetitive mergers which might have gone unchallenged before because of the difficulty of applying section 7 standards and thus would act as an effective supplement. This act would prevent large firms from acquiring leading firms in concentrated industries, forcing them to seek other outlets for expansion which would be more likely to increase competition and to decrease concentration.

The recommended statute would flatly prohibit any merger or acquisition by a large firm (a firm with $500 million in annual sales or $250 million in assets) of any "leading firm" (a firm with a market share greater than 10 percent in a market where four or fewer firms have 50 percent of the market and industry sales exceed $100 million). In the words of the proposal, "Since the [Merger] Act prevents future acquisitions, unlike the Concentration Act, which undoes existing concentration, a four-firm concentration ratio was picked which was at the lower end of the spectrum in which concentration leads to market performance departing from the competitive norm."

This proposed legislation has the positive effect of preventing large mergers which contribute to concentration, either within a broad industry or overall. As noted in Chapter 5, the principal cause of concentration and an important element in the growth of many firms is the corporate merger. A stronger law than that proposed by the task force would be preferable in curtailing the merger problem. Due to the extent of the economic mess and the imbalanced structure of the American economy, a moratorium on *all* large-firm merger activity (except in the failing-firm case) would be an alternative course, particularly if economic prosperity returns on a sustained basis in the years ahead.

Patent Legislation

The task force proposed that a patent licensed to one person should be made available to all other qualified applicants on equivalent terms. The patentee should not have the right to confine the use of the patent to a preferred group. The proposal does not fix or limit the royalty to be charged by the patentee, nor does it involve compulsory licensing. It merely requires that if the patentee chooses to license others rather than exploit the patent alone, licenses shall be made available on nondiscriminatory terms to as many competitors as may desire to use it.

Availability of Economic Data

In addition to the proposed legislation discussed above, a nonlegislative proposal made by the task force merits implementation and expansion in scope. The report proposes improvement in the quality and availability of economic and financial data relevant to the formulation of antitrust policy, the enforcement of the antitrust laws, and the operation of competitive markets. Specifically, it recommends the formation of a standing committee of representatives of the Census Bureau and other government agencies which gather or use economic information to consider "(1) improving the gathering and presentation of economic information within the statutory limits on disclosure of information on individuals; (2) new interpretations of existing laws or, eventually, new legislation to minimize restrictions on disclosure of types of information which are not highly sensitive from the point of view of individual firms but are of great value in the formulation of policy and the application of law; and (3) machinery for developing information on the competitive structure of relevant markets. . . ."

The special emphasis is on more refined definitions of "markets" and on profit figures (reported by corporate divisions and product lines) and other data having special "antitrust significance." Data of this type could also be profitably utilized by shareholders and the investment community in general. It should be remembered that one of the conditions for pure or perfectly competitive markets is substantial market information and knowledge. Thus, this proposal assumes quite a bit of importance to a program for a new economic America. The costs of implementation of such a proposal are quite small relative to the public benefits.

ANTITRUST PROCEDURES AND PENALTIES ACT

It is doubtful that antitrust (standing alone) will ever be effective in curbing concentration and merger activity. The record clearly indicates that *following* the passage of each major antitrust act there has been a substantial wave of merger activity accompanied by growing industry and market concentration. Perhaps prior to the centennial of antitrust in 1990 some new developments will eventually change the existing condition, such as improved legislation and vigorous enforcement; however, this is purely speculative.

Senator John V. Tunney introduced legislation in the fall of 1972 designed to improve a serious weakness in the antitrust laws as they relate to consent decrees. The recent disclosures in the IT&T-Hartford case are only an example of a long line of abuses. In a speech on the Senate floor, the Senator noted that increasing concentration of economic power carries with it an increasing concentration of political power: "Put simply, the bigger the company, the greater the leverage it has in Washington."

The frequency of consent decrees as an antitrust enforcement tool, their importance in particular cases, and the need for public confidence in consent decree procedures, the Senator believes, require specific standards and procedures "to assure that the decision to settle and the settlement itself are in fact in the public interest." Section 2 of the bill provided that any consent decree proposed by the government must be filed with the court and simultaneously published in the Federal Register at least 60 days prior to the effective date of the decree so that interested parties may have an opportunity to comment.

The government would also have to file a "public impact" statement containing (1) the nature and purpose of the proceeding, (2) a description of the practices giving rise to the alleged violation, (3) an explanation of the proposed judgment, including the relief to be obtained and the anticipated effects of that relief on competition, (4) the remedies available to potential private plaintiffs, (5) a description of available procedures for modification of the proposed judgment, and (6) a description and evaluation of alternatives to the proposed judgment and the anticipated effects on competition of such alternatives.

Tunney regarded the "public interest statement" requirement by this bill as analogous to the environmental impact statement presently required from governmental agencies by the National Environmental Protection

Act. He noted that regardless of the ability and skill of the government's attorneys, they are neither omniscient nor infallible, so that "the increasing expertise of so-called public interest advocates . . . and of defendants' competitors, employees or antitrust victims may well serve to provide additional data, analysis or alternatives which could improve the outcome."

Quoting Justice Brandeis' axiom that "sunlight is the best of disinfectants," Tunney further proposed that "lobbying" activities on behalf of any defendant in connection with the consent decree proceeding be disclosed by filing with the trial court any and all written or oral communications with the officers of the government dealing with the consent judgment. The shadow of Dita Beard and other IT&T lobbyists is apparent here.

Another part of the bill increases the penalties for criminal violations of the antitrust laws from the present $50,000 maximum to $100,000 for individuals and to $500,000 for corporations. This is one aspect of antitrust that has been long overdue if the laws are to have any economic deterrent value. The present fines are more like lunch money to the giant firm in the imbalanced economy. The request by Senator Tunney must be considered modest by modern standards. A logical extension would be to tie the penalty amounts to the Wholesale Price Index, providing for flexibility over time.

The final portion of the bill amended the Expediting Act to facilitate and improve procedures for appeals in antitrust cases and, particularly, to permit immediate Supreme Court review of cases involving "general public importance." Other provisions of the bill established a variety of discretionary procedural devices to assist the court in making a sound determination of what the public interest requires before approving any consent decree. Legislation of this type is a sensible addition to the antitrust arsenal.

Other Antitrust Enforcement Suggestions

Since corporate merger activity seldom follows a monotonic pattern, that is, there are periodic waves of activity with peaks and valleys which complicate the enforcement activities, then new policies and procedures are needed. One method of beefing up the caseload activities during increasing merger activity would be to "lease" out casework to private law firms on a bid basis.[5] This proposal has the advantage of preventing a bureaucracy and would bring fresh talent to the antitrust enforcement scene.

Careful analysis of the thrust of particular merger waves would also help in the selection of cases to be brought to court. For example, as pointed out previously, the main thrust of activity during the recent merger wave has been the *product-extension* type of merger rather than the conglomerate. The Mitchell-Kleindienst-McLaren justice department team spent a considerable amount of their limited resources during the 1969–1972 period on so-called test cases concerning conglomerate mergers.[6] A more prudent course would have been to concentrate on the *product-extension* merger types where substantial case law has been developed, i.e., the Procter & Gamble–Clorox case.

FISCAL POLICY AND THE IMBALANCED ECONOMY

In the course of debate over economic policy during the past several years some of the monetary economists have suggested that fiscal policy is relatively unimportant and has a negligible effect upon the economy. Superficial arguments of this type contribute little to the solution of economic problems. For example, the structure of taxes at the federal, state, and local levels has a discernible impact upon investment spending and other types of business, government, and consumer behavior.

The persistence of the imbalanced nature of the American economy can be traced in large part to fiscal policies which affect income and wealth. A prime example of this development is the dividend–retained earnings policies of business firms. The option of postponing the payment of income taxes and the provision of lower tax rates to high-income people through capital gains taxes have had a definite effect upon decision making. In a lopsided economy, this bias has directed the retention of large sums of money in the hands of a relatively few firms. The consequence is that the nature of the structure feeds upon itself and is actually encouraged by government fiscal policy. In short, the large firms which have the highest levels of wealth and income are perpetuated in their positions as much by fiscal policy as by market conditions. In the process, vast sums of potential tax dollars on current income are diverted from the public purse.

A serious side effect of the retained earnings situation is the retention of capital in the firm without that capital having been subjected to a market test. The large firm making profits has a continuous flow of capital to use for various purposes, and management avoids a direct price tag on that capital which the market should determine. Thus, fiscal policies can have a deadening effect upon market forces and artificially direct the flow of capital. The role of government is curious, since the government is directly promoting the retention and expansion of economic power on the one hand and supposedly checking power on the other hand through the antitrust laws. A policy that promotes the potential for abuse and then displays a benign neglect of abuse is a paradoxical paradigm.

A very simple solution is readily available to Congress for correcting this ominous dichotomy in policy—that is, eliminate the capital gains tax and require firms to pay out all earnings in the period when earned. An earnings distribution act would be an important element in developing a new economic America and in restoring some balance in the capital markets.

Fiscal policy can also be utilized in another important and rational manner to help restore a competitive, free enterprise economy. Currently, investment tax credits and accelerated depreciation for new plant and equipment are given to all firms, including those in the highly concentrated industries as well as the oligopolistic firms. In an imbalanced economy, this helps to perpetuate the existing inequities. A sensible and easily implemented alternative would be to limit these fiscal incentives to selected investments made by outside firms in concentrated industries and markets. In other words, the tax laws could be utilized on a temporary basis to encourage entry into existing concentrated markets by other firms.

A "free enterprise commission" could issue a priority list which would designate product, service, geographical, and other elements of markets so designated by a predetermined standard for eligibility for the tax credit. Congress could easily implement this plan as part of a tax package, and it could be identified as a "new entry investment tax credit" or a "concentrated industry investment incentive credit." The purpose should be clear: to use fiscal policy to promote free enterprise, rather than to blunt it as has been the case in the past.

The Imbalanced Economy and the Capital Assets Markets

Since most of the existing assets (including cash) are controlled by a handful of large firms, the market for capital assets (that is, business firms) is almost completely lopsided in the favor of these larger firms. For example, if a firm worth $500 million is up for sale, how many potential buyers are there for this firm? Consequently, those firms with the wealth are the ones in a position to purchase other large firms. Each new increment in lopsidedness further complicates the situation in the decidedly imperfect market.

Passage of a "Comprehensive Reorganization Act" or the proposed Concentrated Industries Act and Merger Act would help to correct this imbalance. The lopsided nature of the market for capital assets feeds upon itself and contributes to the problem, as has been noted in discussing the retained earnings situation. Thus, passage of an earnings distribution act would be a further step in balancing the economy and contributing to the improvement of a fundamental and crucial market.

Capital Redeployment and Procurement

Additional legislation which would be helpful in correcting another imbalance in the capital markets would be a "Capital Redeployment and Procurement Act." This act will be designed to stimulate the market for loans to small businesses by the banking community. The lopsided commercial banking structure naturally finds affinity with other lopsided business markets, to the detriment of small business firms. This is particularly true during periods of tight money and thus becomes a form of hidden subsidy to the larger firms.

Under this proposed act, commercial and savings banks would maintain a separate "Free Enterprise Investment Asset Account." This account would consist of loans up to $250,000 made to small businesses, and the total loaned to small firms would be expected to equal some percentage (such as 30 percent) of a bank's deposits. The purpose of this legislation is to improve the capital market for the smaller firms in the imbalanced economy. New entry would be facilitated, and many more new entrepreneurs would have the economic opportunity to control their own destinies and contribute to the economic component of the nation. Other financial institutions should also be included under the provisions of this act; for example, insurance companies and mutual funds would be required to hold debt or equity equal to a specific percentage of their total assets in firms with less than $10 million in asset size. This legislation would be an added stimulus to the development of a new economic America.

Public Policy and the Regulators of Banks and Holding Companies

Legitimate legislative concerns and mandates have been frustrated by the actions of the bank regulatory bodies, which were presumably created to protect the public interest. The persistent neglect of the public interest by these agencies must be recognized as a serious flaw in the system.[7] As a starting point, Congress should recognize the need to repeal the prohibition of the payment of interest on all demand deposits.

The pricing and quality of checking accounts (demand deposits) have not been regulated in the public interest except to prohibit the payment of interest on these accounts, which is rationalized on the grounds that payment would impair the *safety* of deposits. This prohibition is an outdated paradox which needs reexamination, since an institution (the FDIC) has been created to serve this function. Presumably, a competitive structure would provide for the "convenience and needs" of the public along with a measure of *price* competition. The empirical evidence cited previously demonstrates the importance of structure as it relates to pricing performance on the services most in demand. This neglect suggests either the creation of a new agency concerned solely with bank structure or a clear legislative mandate to existing agencies minimizing their discretion on matters relating to mergers and concentration in the financial markets. Abolition of the regulatory process with statutory mandates is another alternative.

Another area of public interest relates to monetary policy operations. This is presently handled by the Federal Reserve System. The magnitude of this task has increased considerably since the founding of the Federal Reserve over 60 years ago. For example, during the critical year of 1970, the Board of Governors faced a number of important policy decisions concerning monetary policy and other financial crises and held hearings on 31 bank merger cases and close to 150 multiple-bank holding company applications. The caseload has reached the point where decisions affecting bank structure are almost a daily occurrence. On top of this heavy schedule, Congress has specified that the Board of Governors has sole responsibility for the expansion activities of the one-bank holding companies. While the record suggests that the board has been slightly less permissive in its approval of bank mergers than the other banking agencies, the basic regulatory problem as it relates to structure is a long way from solution.

It is becoming apparent that the workload involved in the administration of the bank holding company laws is much too great to be vested in an agency whose primary and more important responsibility is the formulation and execution of monetary policy. Governor J. L. Robertson, former vice chairman of the Board of Governors of the Federal Reserve System, has long advocated that the bank supervisory functions of the various agencies of government be consolidated into a single Federal Banking Commission, leaving the Federal Reserve free to devote itself to its primary task. Governor Robertson does not contend that this proposal is the only answer. However, in his words, " . . . the task needs to be undertaken and carried through to completion, for the failure to reduce the work load of the Federal Reserve will result in its eventual demise."[8]

Since the justification of the regulation of banking is the protection and promotion of the public interest, why not permit the public affected by proposed bank mergers and consolidations to have a *direct* voice in these decisions? That is, permit the voters of the communities involved to directly register their approval or disapproval as part of the decision-making process. This would be valuable input to those responsible for important decisions related to local and state banking structure. For example, in a proposed bank merger in Mississippi, discussed previously, the county board of supervisors and the city council voted to express their disapproval of a proposed bank merger. In addition, about 3,000 local citizens, in a relatively small city, also signed a petition opposing the acquisition. In spite of this strong local opposition, the bank regulators in Washington approved the merger as being in the interests of the locality. Since much of banking activity is relatively localized, it would be logical and sensible to let the public express their views in a more formal manner through the voting process at the local level. Deconcentration and deregulation *together* should be the objective of public policy.

THE STATE AND LOCAL ALTERNATIVE OR SUPPLEMENT TO FEDERAL ACTIONS

Economic and political society can no longer rely on traditional approaches and ineffective remedies to handle the awesome and complicated economic problem. The federal government has failed in its responsibility to the individual citizen (and the business community at large) in its failure to curb combinations and the resulting concentration of many industries and markets. As noted previously, the price tag to the consumer and voter has been substantial. The costs as measured by excessive prices paid annually exceed that of all the other current major social problems. If this abrogation of responsibility at the federal level continues, then there should be action at the state and local levels of government if the system is to survive and be responsive. Ideally, state and local governments should be more involved in matters related to the structure of the economy, despite the massive nature of the problem.

Contrary to the conventional wisdom, there are important avenues of action available to state and local governments. This section will contain some suggestions for bringing about positive action in the areas of taxation, improving the "capital assets" market, and applying pressure at the federal level of government for responsible action.

Capital Assets Tax

Taxation can be used as a method of generating revenue and influencing the direction in which resources may be allocated. Since the loss of corporate headquarters can have an adverse effect upon a community and state, there should be some method of reparation available. Many states and communities devote considerable amounts of resources (both financial and human) to attract industry. Ideally, the industry would also headquarter in the local community, since it would be prone to have more interest in the locality and the quality of life in the area. The loss of a locally headquartered firm can be a serious negative development (as was displayed in the Nebraska and Wisconsin studies). Even if the production facilities remain in the community after a merger, there is an element of loss. The enactment of a state and/or local capital assets tax is one method of recovering some of the loss and may also serve as a partial deterrent to merger activity of the type prevailing in the recent major wave of business combinations.

In the state of Illinois, for example, if the transfer of capital assets was included in the general sales tax, a substantial amount of reparation would have been generated during the recent merger wave. If only the 91 large mergers (out of a total of 932) of Illinois firms acquired by out-of-state firms are examined, the amount of assets involved was close to $6 billion during the 1955–1968 period. The considerations paid are generally higher; thus a figure of $7.5 billion would have produced over $300 million in tax revenue to the state. If all mergers were taxed, the amount would obviously be considerably higher, with hundreds of millions of dollars added. Thus, the simple act of adding the sales of capital assets to the sales-tax base would produce a sizable "reparation fund" which could be used for general or specific purposes at the state and local levels of government. In other words, if mergers are not curtailed by other methods, the individual state could receive some compensation which could be used for a variety of local economic purposes.

Creation of a State Free Enterprise Commission

While any proposal related to taxes has both positive and negative aspects, the proposal discussed in this section is designed to make a distinctly positive contribution. This proposal calls for the creation of a state free enterprise commission, designed to protect the interests of the citizens (as well as other groups) in the state. The basic purpose of this agency would be to make the free enterprise system become more of a reality to the citizens of the state through a series of positive steps and programs.

Certainly one such program would be designed to aid in the elimination of some of the imperfections in the "capital assets" market. The merger data related to the size characteristics of the firms involved in national, as well as Illinois activity, clearly demonstrate that the buyers are generally large firms. The capital markets favor these large firms, which are also generating vast amounts of cash through their relatively larger cash flows. Thus, the number of buyers is limited to a relatively small group, causing the market imperfection discussed previously.

There are some steps which a proposed state free enterprise commission could take to curtail the above-mentioned dilemma. One step would be to set up a fund from money collected on the capital assets tax (mentioned above) to guarantee loans for interested local qualified purchasers. More important in this aspect of the problem would be a close working relationship with the state's commercial and investment bankers to find and encourage local ownership.[9] Information is vital in this area; thus firms should be required to give the commission a 90-day notice concerning any proposed or intended merger. The commission, with the help of bankers, could then attempt to use local resources to preserve local ownership and opportunity.

The problem would be more difficult with large, publicly held firms; however, it would not be impossible. Many state agencies can be called upon, such as the Securities Commission, Insurance Commission, Attorney General, and others. Much can be accomplished at the state and local levels with preconceived plans and direction. States do much to attract industry, while attempts to retain industry have had a relatively low priority, as the New York "merger magnet" has demonstrated in recent years. The reason for this paradox is that states and communities are generally not prepared to cope with these economic events in a systematic way.

In summary, the logical method of protecting the public interest concerning merger activity at the state and local levels is to impose a "capital assets" tax on transfers of this type as a method of reparation as well as raising revenue. In addition, the tax may serve as a possible deterrent to those events which make a generally negative contribution to the attainment of the various economic goals. The creation of economic machinery at the state and local level to add more perfection to the vastly imperfect market for capital assets would be a substantial contribution to the free enterprise system and the quality of life in many communities and states.

State Pressure on the Federal Government

The various regulatory and enforcement bureaucracies at the federal level have generally failed in their task of protecting the public from various economic abuses. The evidence is abundant to support this position, particularly in the area of merger activity.[10] Less than 1 percent of reported mergers have been challenged since the passage of the Clayton Act in 1914. Ironically, a major wave of mergers has developed *following* the passage of each so-called antimerger law: the Sherman Act (1890), the Clayton Act (1914), the Federal Trade Commission Act (1914), and the Celler-Kefauver Antimerger Amendment (1950).

During the calendar years 1966–1969, a period when there were 15,921 merger announcements recorded by W. T. Grimm & Co. of Chicago, the Antitrust Division of the United States Department of Justice had either tried or were at trial on a handful of cases under section 7 of the Clayton Act. This is an incredible development which has not received sufficient recognition.

Pressure from state and local groups directed toward Congress and the various regulatory agencies to actually promote a competitive, free enterprise system would be a constructive step in the right direction. The costs would be small relative to the possible benefits for citizens and communities.

Another avenue for state and local action which has a vast potential is the filing of class-action suits by the states' attorneys general concerning economic abuses. Anticompetitive mergers and other practices of concentrated industries can be attacked in this type of broad-scale grass-roots approach.[11]

THE ROLE OF PEOPLE IN A NEW ECONOMIC AMERICA

As noted previously, a relatively small group of Americans possess a vast amount of economic and political power. It is within the potential of this small group of people to restore the American economy to a new workable, competitive, free enterprise system. Among this group exists a handful of business people, members of Congress, senators, regulators, bankers, and others who are dedicated to restoring the system. If these leaders are joined by others among their peers, then economic America can be restored to a more sensible balance and rescued from its lopsided nature. The words of Robert C. Townsend are particularly appropriate as they relate to the imbalanced economy, as noted previously in the Preface:

> "It's getting late. The time to start is now. In the Consciousness Zero land of the corporate giants, competition where it counts is a myth, and what's left of free America is being eaten alive by a few hundred monster corporations while government agencies serve as chefs, waiters, and busboys."[12]

The pattern can be reversed; however, the challenge, both individually and collectively, is substantial. The nature and quality of the response of those with economic and political power in the decade ahead will do much to determine the future of economic America.

This amalgam of public policy suggestions has encompassed each level of government, since the task is comprehensive. Taken collectively, the policy suggestions are designed to alleviate the existing concentrated structure in all sectors of the economy, and, equally important, they treat the *process* by which the problem develops.

A CONCLUDING NOTE

The most powerful argument against the various proposals advanced above is that concentration of economic resources is no greater than that required by economies of scale. Some evidence has been presented to challenge this assumption, and the question of scale economies and diseconomies should be faced head-on and given priority. Existing data are of two general types. Joe S. Bain has focused on the theoretical minimum optimum plant scale "in particular industries, i.e., the smallest size at which a single plant can be built and still realize the lowest possible per unit costs (given the existing state of technology)."[13] William Comanor and T. A. Wilson assume (in the absence of better estimates) the "average" plant size actually found in an industry is a fair measure of the minimum "efficient" size.[14] Production, marketing, financial, and other aspects of economies of scale for firms and organizations also need consideration. Yale Brozen has argued against deconcentration and reorganization on the basis of his limited study examining profitability and concentration in the 1936–1940 period. Brozen concludes, "Persistent high concentration, where it is found, is a consequence of the economies of scale or the relative efficiency of specific managerial groups. Mandatory deconcentration would cause a loss of efficiency with no gain in the competitiveness of the economy."[15] The concentration question is obviously more complex than suggested by Brozen. Low or average profit rates in some concentrated sectors of the economy do not necessarily indicate that market power is absent. Firms may become lax in minimizing costs when the discipline of competition is weak.[16]

In discussing the relationship between structural reorganization, technology, and scale economies, David D. Martin has observed that "Deconcentration in the structure of control does not need to interfere with appropriate plant design. . . . Deconcentration of control of investment decisions seems more likely to yield continued technical change than bureaucratic, centralized control."[17] Martin also addressed the problem of curtailing the tendency toward bureaucracies in the existing structure:

> If society wishes to restructure the economy by moving toward more use of competitive markets, then the chief problem is not economies of scale but the identification of appropriate points within the economy at which to interpose markets with arms-length bargaining to replace bureaucratic administration. Particularly important is the question of vertical integration. Only by creating markets for inputs in which autonomous firms can buy on equal terms can we encourage autonomous decisions on investment and technical change.[18]

The evidence as it relates to the economic power question is extensive, and while there are periodic indications of conflicting positions, the weight of the evidence indicates the need for a new economic America. Concentration, however measured, is relatively high and appears to be growing in a wide variety of industries and markets. The problem persists as new economic collages are etched into the national profile. Progress toward solutions to the economic problem await recognition and action.[19] Instead of various lumps of concentrated power, America needs to reconstruct a nation that develops a massive mosaic built upon individual effort, opportunity, purpose, and preference. A new economic dialogue which addresses this task is in order and should challenge the nation's latent and abundant capacity for ingenuity and resourcefulness. The question is understandable and clear—economic power and public policy for whom in the new industrial order?

NOTES

1 Morton Mintz and Jerry S. Cohen, op. cit., pp. 357–377.

2 The actual drafting of the bill was under the direction of Howard E. O'Leary, Jr., chief counsel of the Senate Antitrust and Monopoly Subcommittee. The bill was introduced again in 1973 as S.1167. See Senate Subcommittee on Antitrust and Monopoly, *The Industrial Reorganization Act,* 93d Congress, 1st session, Washington, D.C., 1973.

3 From mimeographed remarks of Senator Philip A. Hart made on the floor of the U.S. Senate, July 24, 1972.

4 For details of this proposal, see "Concentrated Industries Act," *Antitrust Law and Economics Review,* vol. 2, no. 2, pp. 65–70, Winter 1968–69.

5 Lawyers are currently prohibited from bidding on legal work through the canons of professional ethics. A change in this philosophy would add a needed dimension to professional competition when price-fixing has been practiced for years.

6 See Stanley E. Boyle, "U.S., v. IT&T—Incompetence, Irrelevance and Confusion," *The Antitrust Bulletin,* vol. 19, no. 2, pp. 327–362, Summer 1974.

7 For an excellent discussion, see Almarin Phillips, "Regulatory Reform for the Deposit Financial Institutions—Retrospect and Prospects," *Journal of Financial and Quantitative Analysis,* vol. 9, no. 5, pp. 795–802, November 1974.

8 Letter from J. L. Robertson, dated December 14, 1972.

9 The various firms and individuals involved in the promotion of mergers could also make a contribution here. Instead of concentrating on the "easy" sale, more effort could be devoted to finding buyers with a vested interest in the community. Developing lists of potential buyers *in advance,* including present management employees, should also be considered and promoted.

10 See Samuel R. Reid, "Antitrust and the 'Merger Wave' Phenomenon: A Failure of Public Policy," *Antitrust Law and Economic Review,* vol. 3, no. 1, pp. 25–42, Fall 1969.

11 There is precedent for legal action of this type; i.e., the state attorneys general of most northeastern states filed suit in Federal Court in January 1975 to challenge the legality of the President's imposition of a tariff on imported petroleum.

12 Robert C. Townsend, *New York Times Book Review,* May 30, 1971.

13 Joe S. Bain, *Barriers to New Competition,* Cambridge, Mass.: Harvard University Press, 1956.

14 William S. Comanor and T. A. Wilson, "Advertising Market Structure and Performance," *Review of Economics and Statistics,* vol. 49, no. 4, pp. 428–429. Of limited usefulness is the "survival technique" used in identifying "optimal" scales of firm and plant, see George J. Stigler, "The Economies of Scale," *Journal of Law and Economics,* vol. 1, pp. 54–67, October 1958; T. R. Saving, "Estimation of Optimum Size of Plant by the Survivor Technique," *Quarterly Journal of Economics,* vol. 75, no. 4, pp. 569–607, November 1961; and Leonard W. Weiss, "The Survivor Technique and the Extent of Suboptimal Capacity," *Journal of Political Economy,* vol. 72, no. 3, pp. 246–261, June 1964.

15 Yale Brozen, "Concentration and Profits: Does Concentration Matter?" *The Antitrust Bulletin,* vol. 19, no. 2, p. 391, Summer 1974.

16 See Carl Kaysen, *U.S. vs. United Shoe Machinery Corporation,* Cambridge: Harvard University Press, 1956, pp. 114–116.

17 David D. Martin, "Beyond Capitalism: A Role for Markets?" *Journal of Economic Issues,* vol. 7, no. 4, p. 782, December 1974.

18 Ibid., pp. 782–783.

19 During the spring of 1975, Senator Hart (together with Senator Hugh Scott) introduced the Antitrust Improvements Act of 1975 (S.1284) designed to strengthen the existing antitrust laws in several areas. This legislation can be viewed as an initial step in what will have to be a economic and political marathon if comprehensive concentration is to be reversed.

Indexes

Name Index

Ackley, Gardner, 263*n*.
Adams, Walter, 147, 158*n*.
Alexander, Herbert E., 43
Alexander, Sidney S., 58*n*.
Alibu, R., 263*n*.
Anderson, Jack, 221
Ansoff, H. Igor, 104–106, 120*n*., 136*n*., 176*n*., 249*n*.
Arndt, Helmut, 262*n*.

Bain, Joe S., 7*n*., 58*n*., 280, 281*n*.
Balderston, C. C., 186, 204–205
Barr, J. W., 205
Basset, William R., 98*n*.
Baumol, William J., 52, 58*n*.
Baxter, W. F., 161*n*.
Beard, Dita, 271
Bell, Frederick W., 216–218, 226*n*., 227*n*.
Benston, George J., 217, 218, 227*n*.
Berle, Adolph A., 103, 120*n*.
Bierman, Harold, Jr., 99*n*.
Blair, John M., 7*n*., 13, 24*n*., 46–47, 58*n*., 80*n*., 253–254, 262*n*.
Blough, Roger, 256
Bobst, Elmer H., 156
Bock, Betty, 43*n*., 74, 81*n*.
Bodoff, Joan, 34, 44*n*.
Bork, Robert H., 161*n*.
Bowman, W. W., Jr., 161*n*.
Boyle, Stanley E., 44*n*., 112, 122*n*., 281*n*.
Brandeis, Louis, 271
Brimmer, A. F., 186, 204–205
Brozen, Yale, 48, 58*n*., 280, 282*n*.
Brue, Stanley L., 78, 81*n*., 237–238, 247, 248*n*., 249*n*.

Burck, Gilbert, 24*n*., 94, 99*n*.
Burns, Arthur R., 147, 186, 204–205
Bushnell, J. A., 8*n*.

Camp, W. B., 204–205
Caves, Richard E., 52, 59*n*., 174–175, 177*n*.
Celler, Emanuel, 200
Chiu, John S. Y., 52, 59*n*.
Clapham, Sir John, 234, 248*n*.
Clark, Ramsey, 229*n*.
Cleveland, Grover, 147
Coase, R. H., 161*n*.
Cobbs, John, 56, 60*n*.
Cocke, Erle, Jr., 205
Cohen, Jerry S., 41, 44*n*., 264, 281*n*.
Cohen, Kalman J., 110, 121*n*., 214*n*., 228*n*.
Collins, Norman R., 48, 58*n*.
Comanor, William, 280, 282*n*.
Cordtz, Dan, 158*n*.
Cox, Kenneth, 42, 44*n*.
Crampton, R. S., 161*n*.
Crum, William T., 58*n*.
Cyert, Richard M., 263*n*.

Daane, J. D., 186, 204–205
Dam, K. W., 161*n*.
Dewing, Arthur S., 102, 119*n*.
Dirksen, Everett, 143
Dunlop, John T., 263*n*.

Eastland, James, 24, 229*n*.
Eckstein, O., 260, 263*n*.
Edwards, Franklin R., 216, 226*n*.

285

Subject Index

Hartford Fire Insurance Co., 56, 243
Harvard University, 105
Headquarters, local firm, 276–278
Highway trust funds, 23
Holding companies:
  1920s, 180
  one-bank, 275
  (*See also* Bank holding companies)
      Act of 1935, 149
Horizontal merger, definition, 87
Horizontal mergers with vertical aspects,
  85
House Banking and Currency Committee,
  38, 160*n.*, 163, 176*n.*, 198
House Committee on Judiciary, 160*n.*, 200
House Committee on Standards of Official
  Conduct, 160*n.*
House Subcommittee on Domestic Finance,
  38

Illinois, 74–77, 225–226, 277
  Department of Business and Economic
    Development, 81*n.*, 99*n.*
  merger study, 88–90
Import quotas, 2, 46
  foreign crude oil, 130–131
Income taxes, 272–273
Independent Bankers Association, 199
Individual inventors, 50–52
Individual opportunity, 245
Industrial chiefs, average salary and bonus,
  53–55
Industrial organization, 1, 6, 9, 219, 250,
  261
  economists, 235
Industrial reorganization, 260
Industrial Reorganization Act, 23
Industrial Reorganization Commission,
  265–266
Industrial reorganization court, 266
Industrial structure, 11
Industry effect, 65
Inflation, structural, 255
Inflation problem, 251
Inside information, 38
Institutional investors, 38, 40, 41
Interlocking directorates:
  banks and insurance, 36–38
  banks and railroads, 163–164
  big business and banking, 36, 38
Internal growth, 63
  and productivity gains, 115
  pure, 109
International merger pattern, 4

Interstate Commerce Commission, 143–
  144, 164, 166, 244, 258
Interstate Commerce Commissioners, 54
Inventions and innovations, 18, 19, 50–52
  role of small firms, 51, 52
Investment banking, 180
Iron and steel, 265–266
Island Creek Coal Co., 136*n.*
ITT, 18, 53–56, 157, 243, 265
  effect upon economy, 56
  Hartford case, 270
  officers and directors, 54, 55
  stockholders, 18, 55

Japan, 27, 144
Jawboning, 255–256
Justice Department (*see* Department of
  Justice)

Kentucky, 143
Knight, E. C., case, 151
  decision, 147

Labor unions, 14
Large firm growth, role of conglomerates
  study, 74
Large firm size, 101
Large firms, share of profits, 29
Law enforcement:
  antitrust record, 145–153
  index, 153
  limited resources, 154
Law firms, 271–272
Lawyers:
  dilemma, 246–248
  do-it-yourself, 249*n.*
Legal environment, 2, 150, 157
Legal loopholes, trust device, 151
Lexington case, 199
Limited branching states, 36
Litton Industries, stockholders, 244
Lobbying, 22, 271
Local ownership and bankers, 277–278
Lockheed, 22, 55
Lone Star Steel, 85
LTV, 105

McLough Steel, 51
Macroeconomic impact, 116–119
Macroeconomic intrusions into economy,
  118–119